ON TIME

FINDING YOUR
PACE IN A WORLD
ADDICTED TO FAST

CATHERINE BLYTH

WILLIAM
COLLINS

William Collins
An imprint of HarperCollins*Publishers*
1 London Bridge Street
London SE1 9GF

WilliamCollinsBooks.com

First published in Great Britain by William Collins in 2017
This William Collins paperback edition published in 2017

1

A catalogue record for this book is
available from the British Library

ISBN 978-0-00-819000-2

'Primavera' by Robin Robertson, from *Swithering* © Robin Robertson 2006,
reproduced with permission of Pan Macmillan via PLSclear; 'This Is the First
Thing' from *The Complete Poems* by Philip Larkin, reproduced with
permission of Faber and Faber Ltd.

Printed and bound in Great Britain by
CPI Group (UK) Ltd, Croydon, CR0 4YY

MIX
Paper from
responsible sources

FSC
www.fsc.org   FSC˘ C007454

This book is produced from independently certified FSC paper
to ensure responsible forest management

For more information visit: www.harpercollins.co.uk/green

For Saskia and Rafael

'I would have written a shorter letter,
but I didn't have the time.'

Blaise Pascal, 4 December 1656

Contents

Part Three: How to Get it Back

Introduction

There is enough time

Hurry up.

Is this your catchphrase? It used to be mine. I lived like a criminal, always on the run, but perpetually running late. For the life I never got around to living, there was never enough time. Each day I climbed onto an accelerating treadmill, and each evening my to-do list grew longer, just like Pinocchio's nose. It was as if all my good intentions were lies whose only productive property was to create more of themselves.

Until I realised that there is enough time – if you stop trying to outrace the clock. This book explains how such a change is possible, even for a hurry slave like me. It is for anyone who longs to understand time better: what it is, where it goes and how to get it back.

Time is a dangerous subject to tackle. Once you begin exploring this thing that permeates everything, where to stop? But I had to take it on; I was too time-boggled not to. It was also increasingly clear to me that my problem, as personal and painful as it felt, was not mine alone.

Rising numbers of us rattle through our weeks, feeling like the inadequate servants of an insatiable mob of commitments. On the rare occasions that we leave work on time, we slink out, guilty as adulterers. Many friends, outwardly successful, appear trapped in a busy loneliness. Life passes in a blur of images glimpsed from their runaway train.

At first I imagined this was a generational issue. Now I see it is systemic. Our world is on fast-forward – bursting with miraculous new ways to be speedy, spontaneous, melting the boundaries of time and space. We are barnacled by gadgets that let us contact anyone, instantly, in any time zone, without stirring from our chair. Countless products promise to save us time. Yet time hunger is the defining challenge of our age. If we flounder, we feel as if we are failing personally, because living in conditions of extreme time pressure has come to seem normal. In fact, this situation is both odd and new.

How do we respond to the challenges? I know exhausted souls who nevertheless haul themselves out of bed at 5 a.m. to meditate, to calm themselves in preparation for the day's onslaught. One acquaintance calculated that since the week contains 168 hours, she can fit in the travel required for her job and sufficient face-time (her phrase) with her sons – provided she forgets about me-time, and her partner, and rations her sleep to four hours per night. Another working couple meet on Sunday nights to argue about how to cudgel in a minimum of one fun evening together the following week. I am not sure why they do not have fun on Sundays, although I am fairly certain it is not anything to do with religious scruples.

Stealing time, stretching the day, haggling over minutes for companionship. On paper it looks absurd. In life it feels wretched. And these are people at the luxury end of time poverty, able to afford meditation classes, travel, dates. But time poverty is not restricted to the well-heeled. The misconception that being time poor somehow makes you cash rich has arisen because only the wealthy are silly enough to brag about it, mistaking it for a mark of success.

The truth is that time poverty, like every other variety of poverty, is a form of powerlessness. And how easily, how devastatingly, we give our power away. This book invites you to think a little harder about why time has become so complicated, and how it could be simpler.

I have been researching time poverty for most of my life – probably since my father drove me into town for my first day at kindergarten. It was my first encounter with rush hour and I was the last to walk into a room full of strange little girls. All had tangle-free hair tied in shiny ribbons, but my hair was not long enough for ribbons. It turned out that these little strangers also knew each other; they had all attended the same nursery and been braceleting themselves into little girl gangs from the age of three. I was late not by ten minutes but by a year.

The lateness habit, this out-of-step feeling, lingered, becoming as familiar as an old friend. But it was corrosive. As a student (80 to 95 per cent of whom procrastinate, according to the American Psychological Association) I had a textbook case of what is classed perfectionist, tense-afraid procrastination. Fear of spending time on the wrong thing paralysed me. Thankfully the internet's tentacles had yet to reach me then, so I managed to graduate. I fought back, first becoming a workaholic, then learning to relax. Lateness gave way to last-chance-itis (the technical term for flying by the seat of your pants). As deadlines whooshed by I consoled myself with the Spanish proverb 'Tomorrow is often the busiest day of the week'.

Today I have no house room to spare for procrastination; the space is occupied by two charming time thieves, my daughter and my son. After their arrival life entered a reverse time zone. Like many new parents, we battled to meld competing schedules: for sleep, work, eating and the endlessly streaming coughs and colds. Amid this biological and logistical warfare, I often yearned, late at night, for a 48-hour day. Except this was pretty much the hell I was already living. There was the hoped-for day – the one that I rose each morning intending to enjoy – and there was the reality: buggered up by delay, disruption and incessant, insidious distraction.

Friends agreed that if there was one thing that might improve our quality of life it would be a time machine. But I had one of those already, vibrating in my pocket, and another on my desk. My husband had three. Did they help?

No, what I needed was two of me: one to accomplish everything that I tried to do, and another to parry the demands that routinely torpedoed my plans. Unfortunately I could not afford a clone or a wife. So I was stuck with busy.

Then I discovered the extent to which busy is a state of mind. It makes time our enemy by turning us into the servants of fast.

* * *

When I told people that I was writing about time, most assumed that my true subject was productivity – in other words, how to squeeze more juice from our bitter lemons. It is not. It is freedom.

Talk of free time is usually a gripe. As in, Where is it? And why does it go so fast? I try to answer both questions. But what interests me most is freeing time – the verb.

We treat time as a thing: to spend, save, waste, lose or kill. But time is not a commodity: it is a dimension of experience and in the final analysis, it is all we have – it is our only vehicle to be alive in. It is also a wonderfully adaptable instrument, like a compass, that humanity invented to organize itself. It can help us navigate this fast-forward world, if we appreciate how it works.

Book after book promises to salve our pains with time. Peel back their surface differences, however, and most are transfixed by the mantra of doing or getting more. Arguably, it is the compulsion to consume time, and then to produce evidence that it has been consumed, that causes many of our problems, not just in how it interferes with our motivation, but in how it makes us inattentive, passive and parsimonious.

This book offers neither a New Age manifesto nor a recipe for speeding up. Instead it sets out how our sense of time shapes our life, and how little it takes to improve its quality – or ruin it. It may help you to work time harder. But it is also a call to savour the time you have. How you spend your one-stop trip to earth is up to you. Still, many would benefit from more of that vital pastime, doing nothing. How much is lost if you never forget time? Like Friedrich Nietzsche, who repined, not long before he went mad: 'One thinks with a watch in one's hand even as one eats one's midday meal while reading the latest news of the stock market.'

I wanted answers to the big questions that productivity guides ignore. As captivating as the spangled wonders of atoms and stars are, great mysteries lie in the muddy foothills of everyday time. Why does it crawl when you ache for it to hurry? Why do we procrastinate when we can least afford it? Why is each hour of the day different? Holly Golightly really is not lying in *Breakfast at Tiffany's* when she protests, after a barman refuses to serve a third cocktail (it is not yet noon), 'But it's Sunday, Mr Bell. Clocks are slow on Sunday.' These complexities are fascinating, and also uncover practical tools that will let you spend less energy on managing time, the better to luxuriate in it.

Your brain is always playing games with time. Be aware of its tricks and you can reset the pace. Read on and you will learn plenty about your mind and body; how fast food and bright colours change your tempo; why deadlines can kill, but inserting the words 'if' and 'then' into a plan ups its odds of success; how autonomy takes the stress out of time pressure and cunning time thieves take your good intentions for a walk; which activities best suit particular hours of the day; how we turn into habit zombies; ways to speed up, or slow down, or become an early bird; why you sleep when you do; and how to harness momentum, by making time simpler.

Feel free to skip ahead to whichever chapter seems most relevant. I have tried to satisfy not only readers who like to curl up with a mind-expanding topic, but also those who read guerrilla-style, snatching what they need on the run.

Philip Larkin wrote:

This is the first thing
I have understood:
Time is the echo of an axe
Within a wood.

It seems that way, if you let it. All too easily we overlook the role that our attitude towards time plays in how life unfolds. But raise our awareness and with minute changes we can transform our outlook. And it is worth it.

In Dante's *Divine Comedy*, Virgil drags Dante up the mountain to Paradise, away from the terrible waiting room of Purgatory, as fast as he can: 'He who best discerns the worth of time is most distressed whenever time is lost.' Those who best discern time's worth are generally those who have brushed the crust of mortality – the survivors, the bereaved, those staring down the barrel of a terminal diagnosis. Like my parents' friend, Henrietta, who described the gift she had received, after safely emerging from a life-threatening illness. 'My husband and I became acutely aware how little time there is. There is no point deferring. When we wanted to do something, we just did it. It was the best time in our marriage.' Their joy lasted two years, until his sudden death. His final words to her were, 'That was a really lovely day.' I would like them to be mine.

Years of my life have been cramped by the inhibiting belief that I did not have enough time. Writing this book reminded me that we can all take greater pleasure from what we have. Why wait until its sands are low? 'In truth, there is enormous space in which to live our everyday lives,' wrote Buddhist thinker Pema Chödrön. It is never too late to seek this sense of abundance.

Now is the time of your life. What might happen if you spent your day only on what was necessary or delightful to take you where you want to go? Millions have been inspired by Marie Kondo's advice to tidy up, and to ditch possessions that do not serve a purpose or spark joy. How much more might we gain from decluttering time?

Imagine a day in which you accomplish everything that you intend, as well as coping with all the unanticipated demands, without getting thrown off track. A day in which you feel one step ahead, not constantly behind, trapped in a reactive cycle that seems to drag you backwards. A day of hours that feel satisfying, not cramped. A day in which the minutes for dull tasks dash by while hours for pleasure meander. A day that exploits the give in time's elastic, giving you more time off. A day of miracles?

Not a bit. Your definition of time rich might mean working more effectively, or elegantly doing less. Whatever your goal, if you cease to feel like time's slave then everything improves.

The mistake of rushing is to imagine that your time is not your own. The solution is to live in your own good time, at a pace that suits you. So quit chasing white rabbits. Stop stockpiling self-reproach. Set aside a few minutes, perhaps a few hours, to ignore the clock, and rediscover what time has always been, since the first hominid tracked the day's passage by the slant of his shadow in the sun: your servant.

THE TIME TEST

Here is a question. Give yourself three seconds to answer. Do not scratch your head, worrying about getting it wrong. There is no wrong answer. You want your first response, because the purpose of this experiment is to open a window into your mind.

> My birthday party is not happening on Saturday due to a scheduling clash with my midlife crisis. The party will go ahead, but has been moved forward by three days.
>
> What day will the party be held?

Did you answer Tuesday? Or Wednesday?

If the first, then you have what psychologists define as an ego-moving perspective on time. This means that you see time as a track that you run along. You are a forward-moving agent, racing towards your future.

If the second, your perspective is time-moving: you stand there, facing time's incoming tide.

These two ways of perceiving time are not simply spatial metaphors. They express divergent psychological dispositions. I always give the second answer and rather wish that I did not. But it is fine to regard time as a mighty force, so long as you do not feel like its victim. View it as the vehicle of your life and it is easier to drive to your chosen destination.

Part One

How Time Went Crazy

Includes: how time created consciousness; why Singapore is faster than New York; why delivery boys feared the noose; how wealth accelerates us but the costlier our hours, the poorer they feel; why we should listen to Steven Spielberg; the battle of the eyeballs; and what Socrates had in common with Thomas Edison.

1

Is the World Spinning Faster?

Why time feels less free

This is the mystery:

We have more hours at our disposal than any humans in history. Few of us toil for the six 12-hour shifts that constituted our grandfathers' working week. Many of us also enjoy flexible employment arrangements. According to current estimates, lucky citizens of the developed world may enjoy around 1,000 months on this planet. The average man's life expectancy is 80 and is increasing by six hours a day. Women's rate of improvement lags behind slightly at four hours per day, but given that their average lifespan is 83, they can afford to take it slower.

Better yet, what we can do with our time transcends anything yet seen on earth. Our present has been transformed by astonishing powers of telepresence. Own a smartphone and you can operate in multiple time zones, see, learn or buy pretty much anything, interact with almost anyone, whenever you wish, with a swipe of a finger, without leaving bed. Never have we been able to accomplish so much, so fast, with so little effort.

Yet despite these everyday miracles, many of us feel time poor. Why?

The short answer is that we are living in a new sort of time, and it is creating a new sort of us. Our instinctive response is to speed up, but we would gain far more from these glorious freedoms if we slowed down and concentrated.

This is not always welcome news. 'I am fed up with being told to be "in the moment",' said my friend, when she heard I was writing about time. 'Please do something about it.'

I feel her pain. I associate this advice with a certain kind of lifestyle guru – the wealthy, ex-film star kind, who has never ironed a shirt without a stylist or a camera crew to immortalize this act of humility. But although this phrase sounds like twaddle from certain lips, it is harder to dismiss if you recognize it as the echo of wisdom that reverberates across continents and centuries.

'What is past is left behind. The future is as yet unreached. Whatever quality is present you clearly see right there, right there,' said the Buddha, two and a half millennia ago. Philosopher Henry David Thoreau, who beat a solitary retreat to Walden Woods, Lincoln, Massachusetts, in 1845 to 'live deliberately' for two years, riffed on the same theme:

Time is but the stream I go a-fishing in. I drink at it; but while I drink I see the sandy bottom and detect how shallow it is. Its thin current slides away, but

eternity remains ... You must live in the present,
launch yourself on every wave, find your eternity in
each moment. Fools stand on their island of
opportunities and look toward another land. There is
no other land; there is no other life but this.

Anyone too busy to take off to a log cabin in search of
enlightenment might be annoyed by Thoreau's lovely words,
since they imply we may be missing out on the times of our
life. But that is a philosopher's job, to ask the nagging question, how to live well. And there are signs that it is increasingly urgent.

The architecture of time in our lives is being dismantled at
an astonishing rate, in an astonishing variety of ways.
Previously, days were paced by work schedules, TV schedules, meal times, home time – with breaks built in; moments
to rest, reflect, plan. These rhythms managed time for us.
Now these boundaries are crumbling. Linear time coexists
with flexitime, its disruptive pulse the irregular chirrup of
smartphones. It is a social and technological revolution, with
profound, personal consequences that we have been tardy to
recognize.

This is the situation: as the steady and sequential are
displaced by the instant and unpredictable, our time can be
freer than ever. The complication is that this brings pressures
and responsibilities. We need to manage time more actively
or else we can feel we are falling apart.

Using time effectively is not an innate gift. It is a skill,
though one sadly not taught in schools. We acquire it – some
of us better than others – through interaction and experience.

But nobody has inherited the cultural knowhow required for this new sort of time; our parents could not teach us, it is all too new. And managing time is itself a pressure that can make us feel we have less to spare.

You need not be Stephen Hawking to understand that time is a dimension. But, each waking moment, we also create our own sense of it. And when that sense alters, we behave differently too. Of course everybody's relationship with time is always changing – we are all getting older; however, today's changes are redefining the quality of experience. With small, practical steps, we can use it to improve our quality of life. Or alternatively, we can trip into the hurry trap.

Long ago, our ancestors depended on moving fast to survive. The fight-or-flight response was an emergency gear designed to speed them out of trouble. Today our tools and toys can do the fast for us. This is the great gift of our new sort of time, if we use it. We can custom fit our hours to suit us. If we really want, we can do what nine-to-fivers have always dreamt of and live like guitarist Keith Richards, Lazarus of the Rolling Stones, who for years slept twice a week – 'I've been conscious for at least three lifetimes,' he boasted – and, mystifyingly, grew old. (Note: the hazards of such a lifestyle include being crushed by a library, plummeting headlong from a palm tree and mistakenly snorting a line of your father's ashes.)

This chapter explores why, rather than seize the freedom to set our own pace, instead we are speeding up – and how this is a problem.

1. Why time sped up

The twentieth century was the age of acceleration. Obsession with speed summoned planes, trains, automobiles and rockets, culminating in the design of a mighty particle accelerator, the Large Hadron Collider, the construction of which began at Cern in 1998. Breaching human limits was of equal fascination.

Who does not want to go faster? In the 1950s a young neurologist decided to learn how. In particular, he wanted to find out why overdoing physical activity leaves us breathless. It was widely held that as muscles burn energy, lactate alters the blood's acidity, increasing the nerve impulses to the brain – in effect saying 'Breathe harder! Oxygen required!' But he suspected something more: that when we push ourselves beyond a certain point our lungs cannot deliver enough oxygen, stopping us in our tracks. Sampling arterial blood could confirm his theory; however, opening an artery mid-workout was not safe. Instead he took the indirect route, recruiting a team of athletes, a treadmill and a stopwatch.

Each runner sprinted to exhaustion. After giving them a period to recover the neurologist called them back, strapping on facemasks that delivered oxygen in concentrations of 33 per cent, 66 per cent and 100 per cent (20 per cent is a normal concentration in air). Those who received 66 per cent saw a drastic improvement in their performance. Most went twice the previous distance. One finally quit out of boredom, another to catch a train. The hypothesis was correct. Stamina was a matter of both resources and willpower.

A few years later, distinguished exercise expert Professor Tim Noakes interviewed the neurologist. What was the most important limiting factor in exhaustion? The young man did not hesitate. 'Of course, it is the brain, which determines how hard the exercise systems can be pushed.'

His answer is to be trusted. He too was an athlete. His name was Roger Bannister, and he well understood the mind's power to overmaster time.

On the morning of 6 May 1954 Bannister was due to attempt to run the mile in under four minutes, which would make him the first man to do so. But he awoke to blustery winds, and these would add one second to each lap. His best practice time for a lap to date was 59 seconds, so triumph would require him to run faster than his sunny day's best. He did not want to try, dreading failure, having already been vilified by the press for previous disappointing races.

He travelled alone on the train from London to Oxford, brooding on his dilemma. Apparently by chance, although surely by design, his coach, Franz Stampfl, was in the same carriage. Stampfl pointed out that Bannister's rivals were due to race in the coming weeks. 'Remember,' he said, 'if there is only a half-good chance … If you pass it up today, you may never forgive yourself for the rest of your life. You will feel pain, but what is it? It's just pain.'

Bannister arrived at the Iffley race track determined to run for his life. Later that day, three hundred yards from the finish, his pace lagged, his body exhausted.

There was a moment of mixed excitement when my mind took over. It raced well ahead of my body and drew me compellingly forward. There was no pain, only a great unity of movement and aim. Time seemed to stand still, or did not exist. The only reality was the next two hundred yards of track under my feet. The tape meant finality, even extinction perhaps …

With five yards to go, the finishing line seemed almost to recede. Those last few seconds seemed an eternity. The faint line of the finishing tape stood ahead as a haven of peace after the struggle. The arms of the world were waiting to receive me only if I reached the tape without slackening my speed. If I faltered now, there would be no arms to hold me and the world would seem a cold, forbidding place. I leapt at the tape like a man taking his last desperate spring to save himself.

In 3 minutes 59.4 seconds, Bannister had changed history. But he would be prouder of his later achievements, becoming a leading authority on the autonomic system – the hidden clock that controls the most vital beats in your life and mine, our heart and breathing rate.

The lessons of Bannister's early breathing experiments are transferrable. We can increase our pace, mental or physical, given the right resources. But our mind is in charge. Unless it has the means to remain in control, speed wears us out, fast. Yet we can test the limits, and even feel, as he did in Iffley, that time no longer exists. Controlling time makes us powerful if we take choices.

So what do you want to do today?

Perhaps this seems a frivolous question. Perhaps you are fully occupied by what you need to do. Before you answer, it is worth reflecting that your ability to ask it is a privilege unique to our species.

'We all have our time machines, don't we,' wrote H.G. Wells in *The Time Machine*. 'Those that take us back are memories ... And those that carry us forward, are dreams.'

Being aware that one day we must die is the cruellest term of the human condition. But to compensate, we also have the capacity to appreciate that since this is a one-way ticket, why not embrace the adventure?

Our powers of mental time travel make this possible. They endow us with the riches of culture and knowledge, not to mention aeroplanes that (in theory) run on time, as well as computers, virtual worlds and machines to roam outer space. And how wondrous it is to be able to walk outside after a hard day and – if you are lucky, if the night sky is not cloudy or gelded orange by city lights – turn your eyes heavenward, as I just did, spot a white smudge hovering above the shoulder of Pegasus, and appreciate that there is Andromeda, our nearest major galaxy, one trillion stars and 2.5 million light years away – a vision that began travelling to earth around the time that your immediate ancestor, *Homo habilis*, 'handy man', first picked up a tool, 2.3 million years before a mind like yours or mine existed.

And here we are. Here is your hospitable consciousness, meeting mine, leaping through time, long after I flung these words into a laptop, late one summer's day. It is impressive, given that we started out as apes and, rather longer before that, as stardust.

Time travel – the ability to understand and organize our actions – is a commonplace marvel. It matters because each conscious instant of our life presents a decision: where to allocate our time and attention. Consciousness enables this, not only by performing the feat of simulating our outside environment inside our head, but also furnishing us with an inner reality. Our every moment is infused by previous moments, anticipated moments – giving life depth and perspective, and us our sense of self.

Grace of these riches, our mind's eye, as if wearing magical spectacles with lenses fashioned from a clairvoyant's crystal ball, is able to serve as a questing prosthesis for our other five senses: it supercharges the insights they glean from the world around us to let us see beyond where we are into the possible future, supplementing it with information drawn from memory and knowledge to plot a wise and (it is to be hoped) safe course through space and time.

The desire to peer around life's corners is surely the evolutionary mechanism that summoned consciousness. Certainly, it distinguishes humanity from other animals, freeing us to control our path. These faculties enable you to remember birthdays, plan a surprise for somebody you love, cook a meal without burning down the house, force yourself to study for exams, judge exactly how long it is safe to loiter in Starbucks before running to catch that plane, know you will never like liquorice, watch *Dirty Dancing*, sing along and have the time of your life. Time is the foundation of your sense of self. Your sixth sense.

Strangely, although everyone agrees that time is scarce and precious, it is remarkable how readily we give it away. Statistics suggest that whilst we wonder where the time goes, in truth we have plenty to spare. In 2013 the US Bureau of Labor Statistics' Time Use Survey found that on average men aged 15 and over had 5.9 daily hours of leisure. Women had 5.2 hours, and employed workers an average of 4.5 hours – a sizeable chunk of the waking day.

This does not tally with how busy we feel. Are we deluded?

What these numbers do not reveal is the form this leisure comes in: whether those free minutes are scattered through the day or available in useful blocks. Time leaks from us in many ways, after all. Count them, however, and you may feel queasy.

In 2014, Ofcom found UK adults spent 8 hours 41 minutes a day on media devices, 20 minutes longer than they spent asleep. Of this tally, four hours went on TV – the same for children. (On average, Britons donate nine irreplaceable years to box-goggling.) Across the Atlantic, in 2014 the average US citizen watched six hours of TV per day, spent an hour on a computer, another on a smartphone, and almost three listening to radio. Tot them up. It sounds a lot like leisure.

Yet other information suggests that the pace of life is accelerating. The rate at which we walk is a good indicator. In 1999 sociologist Robert Levine led a study of cities and towns across thirty-one countries and found that urbanites march significantly faster than their less wealthy country cousins. London, one of the world's richest cities, topped the speed list. A decade later, similar research concluded that the average tempo had risen 10 per cent. Far Eastern cities accelerated the most, with Singapore (up 30 per cent) becoming the new global leader.

Why are we hurrying up? Researchers concluded that several factors increase a country's pace of life: economic growth, large cities, rising incomes, accurate, plentiful clocks, an individualistic culture and a cool climate. (Asian tiger economies sped up with the spread of air conditioning.) Imagine those lonely hordes, their collars upturned as blistering wind chases them into their skyscrapers to put in another twelve-hour stint.

The picture these statistics paint is confusing: of fast-moving, exhausted individuals, who spend half their existence slumped in armchairs while imagining they are hurtling about at full throttle. This contradictory image begins to add up when you consider the engines behind economic growth: flexible hours (of employment and consumption) and hyperfast communications.

If the steam engine fired the industrial revolution, the driver behind wealth in recent decades has been semiconductors. As they got cheaper and faster, so did computers, enabling us to do more, faster, without moving an inch. The possibilities are endless. What is less obvious is that acceleration has psychological, physiological and practical side effects which are increasing time pressures, with complicated consequences.

Speed has long been both the goal and the index of human progress. The history of civilization hops and skips in innovative leaps that let us do more in less time: from the invention of the wheel, to bank notes that let us transmit funds without trundling about caskets of gold, to machines for washing clothes. Swift communication unleashed scientific discoveries in the sixteenth and seventeenth centuries via epistolary relationships between the likes of Galileo and Kepler, thus hastening the Enlightenment. In the same way, great cities are superconductors of knowledge, gathering together like-minded people – as in California's Silicon Valley, where dreams of the future led to where we are now, with the boundaries of space and time defeated, and more or less every idea under the sun available more or less instantly, Wi-Fi server permitting.

It is worth pausing to consider how extraordinary today's fast is. When the Royal Mail relaunched in 1662 after the restoration of Britain's monarchy, a letter dispatched in London would reach a continental city between three and twenty-five days later. Postmen travelled on foot at a regulated seven miles per hour between March and September, five miles per hour in the winter months. (Horses were not used, since they lacked staying power, while 'footmen can go where horses cannot'.) Priority was given to letters of state, carried in a separate bag known as the 'packet'. If the packet went astray, an official letter was easy to recognize by the forbidding motto on its exterior: 'Haste, Post, haste for thy life'. In case the postboy was illiterate, it was accompanied by a grim sketch: a gallows with a corpse hanging in a noose. Arguably today's fast should also carry a health warning.

Undeniably speed enlarges minds and fortunes. It is an article of faith among management consultants, citing a popular study, that a product that runs 50 per cent over budget will be more profitable than one that strolls in six months late. Fast technology conjures myriad new businesses, some great, some questionable – such as high-frequency stock trading, in which tech-savvy individuals exploit differing lengths in computer cable between exchanges to skim lucrative sales data milliseconds ahead of the pack, thus creaming off millions. We are a long way from this complaint, made to the Royal Mail in the seventeenth century, about a conniving merchant who 'has had most singular advantages, having had his letters many hours before a general dispatch could be made to all the merchants'.

But the advantages of acceleration and unfettered access via digital media bring new time pressures. Businesses routinely purloin customers' time, cheekily passing this off as being for our convenience. Is it liberating to have a dehumanizing supermarket experience, swiping produce at the automated till, or to act as data inputters, filling in forms to order something online, then lose ten hours indoors awaiting the delivery, or to go to the shop and wait ages for a runner to disembowel your item from the store? Each unpaid minute we work for the retailers, freeing them to employ fewer of us.

Worse burdens fall on employees. Lengthening working days reach into the home, as companies swallow the creed that staff should be on standby on their portals of perpetual availability, as if each were a branch of the emergency services. Only France has sought to protect employees' right to disconnect. It is easy to see why we may imagine we are always working – even if we are enjoying those fabled leisure hours that the statisticians claim we have, watching television with half an eye on office emails rather than actually doing anything with them. Then again, is time really free if, like a dog, you are attached to a leash that may at any point be yanked, dragging you back to the cares of the office?

Constantly larding our minds with pending tasks is time theft. It may be self-inflicted, but not entirely, if – given the pressure to hold on to jobs today – monitoring work from dawn until midnight is part of your workplace culture. What it is not is efficient.

The most notable weakness of our superfast world is ourselves: we cannot seem to apply the brakes. A study of 1,500 Dutch people revealed that those who constantly rush feel as if time is also going faster, and this perception encourages them to rush yet more. Humans are wired to mirror the world around us, setting our pace in tune with our environment, a phenomenon known as entrainment. This is why we bustle in a busy city like London but wander in Wyoming. Unfortunately bustling has side effects. Not least that it becomes addictive.

Ambrose Bierce's *Devil's Dictionary* defines hurry as 'the dispatch of bunglers'. Although everybody knows this intuitively – doing things at speed requires skill – speed encourages us to overreach ourselves. The more we can do, simultaneously, at the touch of a computer button, the greater the temptation to overdo it. Multitaskers often imagine that they are faster and more efficient, working harder and longer than they are in reality, because busy, distracted hours feel fuller – when in fact they complete tasks 30 per cent more slowly. Really they are servants of fast – trying to match the fluid possibilities of technology. Worse, tackle eighteen tasks at once and the probability that one will go wrong is far higher than doing them sequentially. Screw up and it is the difference between breaking down on a sedate B road and crashing on a motorway. More is the pity, because a smooth tempo is best for mind, body and productivity. In effect, in our alacrity to make the most of our superfast tools we render ourselves deficient.

There is no sign that we are ready to wean ourselves off speed: on the contrary, we celebrate it. In 2015 Nike, the iconic sports brand, refreshed their legendary anti-procrastination slogan, 'Just Do It', with a campaign that urged us to 'find your fast'. That same year boxes of Tampax were jazzed up by cartoon women on the run, their hair flying, their flailing hands clutching bags and phones. Advertisers select images either to flatter or scare us into buying a product. But the multitasking tampon lady does both. Like a doctor dashing about the emergency room, saving lives, this testament to heroic female dynamism also appears ripe for a heart attack.

Sure enough, statistics also reveal that the citizens of faster countries show higher rates of smoking, coronary-related death *and* of greater subjective wellbeing. In other words, we imagine that we are happier pursuing a lifestyle that actively harms us. And what makes it deadly? Stress of a particularly pernicious variety: the unpredictable, uncontrollable stress we get when life's beat is erratic. The type that we overdose on if interruption, hurry and time pressure are our daily diet.

The side effects of busyness help to answer a puzzle that has long preoccupied economists: why, after incomes reach a certain level, does a rise in a country's wealth have no power to lift its population's happiness?

The usual explanation is that we exist on a hedonic treadmill. In other words, wealth and the stuff we buy with it makes us happier in the short term, but soon we adjust. Even lottery winners, after the initial ecstasy, revert within months to their former level of contentment. What we are beginning to realize is that hedonic adaptation often occurs because we are poor at investing our surplus time and money in pastimes or objects that enhance our wellbeing or manufacture enduring daily happiness.

According to Epicurus, the ancient Greek philosopher famously associated with pleasure (although his life was pretty ascetic), 'Not what we have, but what we enjoy, constitutes our abundance.' Could you disagree? But speed and wealth interfere with our capacity to delight in our abundance. Yes,

happiness = having choice over how to spend time

and also

wealth = having more choice over how to spend time

But unfortunately

wealth = more complicated choices over how to spend time

No account of happiness is complete unless time is factored in.

Weirdly, acceleration seldom liberates extra hours: more often it creates extra work. 2011's *European Social Survey*, studying twenty-three countries, found that people had the least leisure not in the richest places but in those where economic expansion was most rapid. (The pace of development was measured by internet use and car ownership – not, coincidentally, things that make us speedy.) Employers' demands intensified when salaries rose, driving up the pace. But workers' choices changed too. The more they could earn, the less time they spent on other activities.

Self-consciousness about time depletes our ability to relax and relish it. Fascinatingly, if you trick someone into feeling richer, studies find that instantly he also feels more time-pressed. Just remind somebody what they earn in an hour and relaxing to music becomes harder for them. Why? An hour feels less disposable the more we are paid for it, increasing the pressure to squeeze out every penny – even if in theory you can better afford to slack off.

No wonder that when time pressure intensifies, we often make rum choices. In a 2008 survey, 57 per cent of respondents who identified themselves as busy cut back on hobbies, 30 per cent on family time, but only 6 per cent on work. Perhaps in an era of credit crunch, then at its nadir, these priorities were understandable. Equally, it is possible that those questioned preferred to see less of their family. In order to thrive, love needs space, yet in an age of Velcro unions and widespread divorce, investing time in love instead of a career can feel risky, and deafening cries for me time suggest that our priorities are less collegiate. Fostering love is even harder if we are distracted and the continuum of relationships is interrupted, whether by business trips or our chirruping smartphone.

When we design our lives, it is easy to underestimate the importance of unhurried time – even those of us who should know better. Such as behavioural psychologist David Halpern, who confessed he is a commuter. 'We'd probably have been happier in a smaller place with more time at home.' In his defence, he argued that such trade-offs are common: 'We buy expensive presents for our kids that they rarely play with, when they – and we – would probably be happier if we had spent the money and the time on doing something with them.'

Opting to go home instead of earning overtime – even if it means missing those you love – *is* difficult. Love is shown by what we provide, is it not – and if we do not put in the hours, what will it mean for our promotion prospects?

Of all the curiosities of time in our speedy world most striking is that our horizons seem increasingly short-termist. Our huge 1,000-month lifespan gives us a greater stake in the future, yet fewer save for old age than in past generations, and external mechanisms, such as government initiatives to compel us to invest in pensions, are weak or vanishing. 'Affluence breeds impatience, and impatience undermines wellbeing,' remarked economist Avner Offer.

In business too, grab and go is the order of the day. 'Silicon Valley venture capital firms are starting to seek fantastically short life-cycles for the companies they finance: eighteen months, they hope, from launch to public stock offering. Competition in cycle times has transformed segment after segment of the economy,' wrote James Gleick in *Faster*, noting that the turnaround in car manufacturing from design to delivery, traditionally five years, was down to eighteen months by 1997. Everyone wants a fast buck – and they want it faster. Can it be that as a whole we are reluctant to look ahead – to imagine the planet, the climate or the hands that steer the tiller of our global future?

'There is no quality in human nature, which causes more fatal errors in our conduct, than that which leads us to prefer whatever is present to the distant and remote,' wrote philosopher David Hume in *A Treatise of Human Nature* (1738–40). Neglecting the joys of the present is no wiser. We need both. But if we are losing sight of the future, it could be because our present is so drenched. It has never been harder to live in the moment, never mind see beyond it.

2. The great time heist

'If you only do the easy and useless jobs, you'll never have to worry about the important ones which are so difficult. You just won't have the time,' wrote architect Norman Juster in 1961. Sadly humanity's artistry at dreaming up new essentials on which to spend money is exceeded only by our ingenuity at confecting fresh tosh on which to waste time.

In the decades since Juster made his joke, the industry of easy and useless grew exponentially. As it did, his joke turned into a prediction. Free time is increasingly a thing of the past.

I have nothing against wasting time. It is a joy, a right and a duty, and an aid to creativity. This is why we have so many plum terms for it: bimbling, dallying, dawdling, dillydallying, dissipating, frittering, idling, lazing, loitering, lollygagging, mooching, moseying, pootling, pottering, slacking, squandering, tarrying, tootling. I am grateful to the nameless men and women who bumbled away their hours conjuring these delicious words. 'Forget your cares,' they seem to say. 'Savour us.'

If there is poetry in distraction it is because diverting people is an art, and poets are prodigality's special envoys. In his 106th sonnet, William Shakespeare summed up literature as 'the chronicle of wasted time'. Luckily he had enough of a work ethic to write down his musings; he was, above all, a businessman, and made his fortune by writing plays distracting enough to entice Londoners to sail the Thames for the stinking stews of Southwark, not to be waylaid by dancing bears, taverns or brothels, but to spend time, and cash, in his theatre.

Business has always sought to capture attention. But arguably, attention grabbing is today's leading enterprise. We were promised the age of information, but stand back and it looks closer to the age of inattention. Although information may appear to be free (provided you have Wi-Fi), in reality it is a greedy, tireless consumer of an infinitely valuable resource: attention. That is, your time.

The greatest stunt that digital media pulls off is to persuade us it saves time, whilst encouraging us to overstuff it. Many theoretically time-sparing tools are time thieves in practice – each smartphone a portable shopping mall, the kind where somebody is always tugging your sleeve to spritz you with perfume. Things were bad enough with the invention of television, since the advent of which we sleep on average two fewer hours per night (not forgetting the average nine years Britons devote to that pastime). Heaven knows what the cumulative lifelong impact of Facebook and Tinder will be. But a 2011 study calculated that in a typical company of over a thousand employees, the cost of time diverted by digital distractions amounted to more than $10 million a year.

Love it or hate it, virtual reality threads experience so completely, it is our new sixth sense – and it is filling the space formerly occupied by the original one, our conscious, reflecting self.

To give an idea of how nimbly the great time heist is proceeding, when in 1999 the Kaiser Family Foundation surveyed over 2,000 eight- to eighteen-year-olds, it found that young adults were using media for 6 hours 20 minutes a day. The report's authors concluded they were close to 'saturation'. A 2004 survey seemed to confirm this, with media use up only two minutes per day. Yet five years later it had leapt to 7 hours 40 minutes – or if multiple devices were separated, to 10 hours 45 minutes a day (for leisure alone, and excluding work or study). Doubtless these figures under-estimate current norms, since they were recorded before Snapchat hoovered up what was left of teenagers' social lives. As commentator Tom Chatfield has observed, this is not saturation: it is integration. 'Time away from digital media is … no longer our default state.'

Saying no to technology is fast becoming the greatest time pressure in our lives. With constant access to shopping, newsfeeds and social networks, how not to overdose? Even if you log on with a specific purpose, how not to get waylaid by the ever-expanding brain buffet on offer? How to choose what to buy, who to trust? Do you rely on habit, Google, or diligently research all your options, gorging yourself daft on the boggling banquet of choice? And for each thing you choose to do with your time there is far more to refuse – magnifying scope for regrets.

In a situation without precedent in history, time alone with our own thoughts, time fully present within the moment or exclusively with another person, is something we must actively cultivate. Top-flight attention thief, the film director Steven Spielberg, hardly a technophobe, lamented this, calling technology potentially the 'biggest party-pooper of our lives ... [it] interrupts our ability to have a thought or a daydream, to imagine something wonderful because we're too busy bridging the walk from the cafeteria back to the office on the cell phone.' Essentially, we are participating in an unfolding experiment in a new way to be. There is no opt-out for anybody participating in the economy or a social life. If every second is colonized, the notion of free time is itself a misnomer.

Why did Apple mastermind Steve Jobs ban his offspring from using Apple's iPad? I suspect, like Spielberg, he feared the death of daydreams. I do. It is impossible to imagine today's teen spending hours lying on a bed, watching shadows tickle the ceiling, grubbing up thoughts, as I once did, not unless a mindfulness app explains how.

Our technologies are full of useful potential. But only if used as tools. What Jobs will have known, and is increasingly widely understood, is that digital media are addictive. Pierre Laurent, formerly of Microsoft and Intel, who also forbade his children computers or smartphones until the age of twelve, explained why one glance into the wormhole of Facebook can easily turn into a lost afternoon:

Media products are designed to keep people's attention. In the late 1990s, when I was working at Intel and my first child was born, we had what was called the 'war of the eyeballs'. People don't want you to wander and start playing with another product, so it has a hooking effect ... And there's a risk to attention. It's not scientifically proven yet, but there's an idea that attention is like a muscle that we build. It's about being able to tune out all the distraction and focus on one thing. When you engage with these devices, you don't build that capacity. It's computer-aided attention; you're not learning to do it.

What Laurent is suggesting is that not only are media products designed to have a hypnotic appeal, but their strength might weaken our apparatus for concentrating. For evidence to support this theory, how about the 2015 report by the Organization for Economic Co-operation and Development, *Students, Computers and Learning*? It concluded that 'most countries that invested heavily in education related IT equipment' witnessed no appreciable improvement in student attainment over ten years. OECD education director Andreas Schleicher added: 'Students who use tablets and computers very often tend to do worse than those who use them moderately.' Moderate use requires self-restraint – but this is not something digital media encourages. If you never feel the slave of a smartphone, congratulations; however, it may only be a matter of time.

Theoretically our horizons are broader, our intellectual reach enhanced by computers' memory, pace and data, yet our engagement is often shallow, compressed. We cram thoughts into ever slighter packets of time and space (140 characters or less). Our powers of concentration are also depleted if our time is monopolized by what writer Linda Stone described as 'continuous partial attention', grazing multiple media instead of zoning in and focusing – the old and still optimal way to get things done.

Snapchat demonstrates how slyly digital media evoke compelling time pressures. Users exchange messages that self-destruct in seconds, eradicating potentially embarrassing backlogs. This should make time feel freer (unlike email silt, which haunts our inbox). But Snapchat does not offer the deeper social satisfactions of face-to-face contact: it scratches the social itch rather than satisfying it. Each time a message vanishes it creates a void – and the compulsion to fill it.

No gadget or app yet – not even by Apple – has added a millisecond to our day. Arguably, technology shortens it, since our distracting toys rip gigantic holes in the space-time continuum because our brain cannot compute frictionless, virtual time; we evolved to grasp it through memorable experience. The stimuli delivered by this technology locks us into dopamine loops, often triggering fight-or-flight stress responses, even as our bodies are perfectly still – stranding us on a toxic neurochemical plateau, unable to escape it in the way we are designed to (by fighting or fleeing). Meanwhile the hours that are hoovered up by gadgets must be taken from something else – such as daydreams.

I did not sign up to a life divided between a load of junk hours and a few good ones, but this is exactly the deal we risk striking if life becomes a spectator sport. Who will lie on their deathbed fondly remembering their Facebook posts, unnecessary work meetings, or zingers on Twitter? Life gains perspective from experiences – first-hand ones that you can share.

Spend too much time online and you become less yourself. Social media addict Andrew Sullivan grew so unsettled that he could not read a book:

> In the last year of my blogging life, my health began to give out. Four bronchial infections in 12 months had become progressively harder to kick. Vacations, such as they were, had become mere opportunities for sleep. My dreams were filled with the snippets of code I used each day to update the site. My friendships had atrophied as my time away from the web dwindled. My doctor, dispensing one more course of antibiotics, finally laid it on the line: 'Did you really survive HIV to die of the web?'

He went off on a retreat to relearn how to live in the moment. One day he noticed something beautiful – then was beside himself when he realized that he had no phone to share it with his followers.

The quality of your time – how fast, fun or deadly it feels – depends on the quality of your attention. Our attention is us. It is no coincidence that yoga, meditation, mindfulness apps, and – what must be the definition of voluntary tedium – colouring books for adults, are boom industries amid all these time pressures. Some claim that such trends reflect a thirst for spirituality in a godless world. In fact, what unites them is that they all help us to focus our minds. We turn to these tools to nurture our capacity to pay attention. And well we might. Otherwise someone else will snatch it.

A great battle for our attention rages. Each time you surf the net or saunter into an online store, you participate in tacit tests designed to sniff out smarter ways to detain you in these wonderlands, so they can convert what were once experiences and opinions into crunchable data. Google routinely runs parallel experiments to see which web pages intercept the most pairs of eyes, which shade of blue holds the greatest goggle-appeal. Alas, the trillions of insights aggregated by algorithms from the information we generously donate when we go online exceed the ingenuity of a billion distracting Shakespeares.

Eyeball grabbing is not always subtle. Witness the shouty, freakshow journalism that empurples once-stately broadsheet newspapers, desperate to monetize flighty readers with clickbait (the more people click on an article, the higher the advertising rates). Witness the soap opera storylines: psychopaths, aeroplane crashes and baby theft are standard fare in hitherto staid fictional villages. Witness computer games like Candy Crush, devised to render you a fairground duck, ready to be hooked. In this context, the allure of slow-moving Nordic television serials might appear out of kilter. It is not that thrillers gain gravitas when mumbled in Danish, but that viewers have to read the subtitles or they lose the thread. How delightful and rare to concentrate wholly on one thing, without a gadget.

Think of those intriguing, big-bottomed celebrities or grumpy cats whose mountain of renown is founded on a pea of proficiency – primarily their talent at diverting vast numbers of us from what we should be doing, perhaps for ten seconds, but fast – and long enough for advertisers to pay top dollar to hire eye-space on their YouTube channel. Now ask this: who benefits most from our increasingly waylayable attention? When you consider that advertising is the chief force driving the internet's development today, the implications are scary. Who wants to end up feeling like a bystander in other, more scintillating, fat-bottomed lives?

'Several "generations" of children have grown up expecting parents and care takers to be only half-there,' observed sociologist Sherry Turkle. A dangerous message to send anyone, let alone a child. Paying attention is not just polite and loving but a skill and, like sensible time use, we need to cultivate it. Rare is the soul who likes hearing 'I'm bored' or feels relaxed watching children climb trees, yet both such experiences are pathways on the scramble to maturity. The quiescent children we see in cars or cafés, their ears stopped by headphones, their eyes fused to tablets and DVDs, are glazed into silence by technological dummies. They look happy, as do adults ogling smartphones. But whatever our age, let hypnotic media syphon off opportunities to conduct conversation, to notice and engage, and wellbeing suffers. Why do we need to silence children anyway? Are they not interesting – or at least, not quite as interesting as emails?

Being online teaches us to be impatient, to want more and more – right now! That is why computers have spinning daisies: to show us that something is really happening, that the screen has not frozen – to soothe us when we are forced to wait three seconds for data to upload. But we are too ready to imagine that we are not responsible for our impatience – as if rush were some impersonal force, a malignant god whom we must helplessly follow.

'I do not have time for this' is the message that we send the world, and the people we profess to love, when bustling about in myopic fugs of busyness. There is a recognized phenomenon of 'time entitlement', in which people imagine time moves more slowly because they consider wherever they are or whatever is going on around them to be unworthy of their attention. It suggests an explanation for why we need our time to be so full – and to proclaim as much, burrowing into busyness as if to make ourselves feel more important. Rather like paranoia, all this time-stuffing resembles a self-cure for insignificance. We are one of six billion, after all, so we cannot hope to lay a fingerprint on posterity.

We may have less time to play with in future. Quantified working policies prevail in many companies, with employees' actions monitored and timed throughout their working day. In 2005, the Ford Motor Company permitted workers a total of forty-eight minutes per shift to go to the bathroom. By 2014, Chicago's WaterSaver Faucet company felt six minutes a day would suffice for ablutions (presumably saving water). It appeared refreshing in 2016 when Aetna, a US insurer, paid staff a $25 bonus for every twenty nights they managed to sleep seven hours or more rather than stay up late on their gadgets. But how telling that such incentives are necessary.

Manipulating our time, nudging it in a remunerative direction, is where the money will be; it always has been. Already we have Google spectacles to steer us to the nearest coffee shop. Next AI will infiltrate our clothing. When self-driving cars rumble along our streets, it seems inevitable that certain routes and information will be preferred, leading the traveller to certain stores and rest-stops, past certain billboards, which will sponsor the technology provider for the privilege.

'Quality time' is the phrase parents and lovers murmur when trying to justify how little they spend with us. It always sounds like a crap excuse. But we desperately need to think about the quality of our time. The greatest beneficiaries of our new sort of time recognize this. Microsoft's Bill and Melinda Gates are masterly time managers, scheduling meetings to discuss their children's progress, treating each strand of their lives as a project to be nurtured. Carving out space to let their interests blossom – and to have a date – is their religion.

Custom-fitting time to suit you is a noble goal, but also rather high-maintenance. Personally, I would prefer the rhythm of my life to do the time management, leaving more for me. As Paul Dolan writes in *Happiness by Design*, 'It's worth thinking about how you could *find* more time without having to *plan* more time.'

For some, busy will always be a boast. No problem – unless the resulting tradeoffs do not stand up to scrutiny. Fixate on being on it, all the time, in the tense present, and we feel we have no time. Because the Achilles heel of lightning-speed living is us: we cannot keep up with it. Tragically this does not stop us trying.

As boundaries dissolve, distraction breeds distraction, and pressures seem to intensify. It is easy to believe time itself is beyond our control. Or to overpack our days, leaving no slack time, space or pause for thought. This overwhelms us. No wonder procrastination is also rising. If it seems crazy, consider this: what better way to assert that you will do things in your own good time? Now that our relationship with time is dysfunctional, it seems only logical that our timekeeping should go awry too.

The result?

Never enough done. Never enough time.

We need time in all its dimensions in order to live fully and well. Daydreams. Plans for the future. Spontaneity. Time for reveries about nothing. And the ability to think things through, then carry them out in linear, organized stages, not chaotic flexitime.

I will defend unto death your right to fritter away your time, but having it stolen is another matter. Throw it away and we are complicit. Control is the heart of the matter: it is what makes us feel that we are living by our own priorities, or constantly racing to catch up. That way lies the hurry trap.

Fast incites us to speed up, but changing our response changes the situation. The range of choices available to us may be daunting, but slow down and you can exercise them. No need to turn your back on the wonders of this fast-forward world. Transformation is available at the point where you encounter it, the bit that you are in charge of. You.

To survive in a world without limits is simple. Set your own.

BUSY

When I am in a flap – texting, talking, eating, fixing meetings to discuss meetings I did not attend – I often think of the fly in Aesop's fable, the one who sat on the wheel of a chariot crying, 'What a lot of dust I raise!'

'How are you?' friends ask.

'Busy.' I may smile, but basically it is a non-answer, just one boastful notch up from 'Fine'. Like a stock cube, the word condenses life's banquet into a deadly four-letter word. This makes it ideal for shutting down unwelcome lines of conversation. Curiously, although everybody understands that busy is dull, it is our proudest alibi for whatever we do all day. Lars Svendsen, author of *A Philosophy of Boredom*, suspected that a lot of busy is a time-filling tactic – one that enlarges the vacuum it aims to fill:

> The most hyperactive of us are precisely those who have the lowest boredom thresholds. We have an almost complete lack of downtime, scurrying from one activity to the next because we cannot face tackling time that is 'empty'. Paradoxically enough, this bulging time is often frighteningly empty when viewed in retrospect.

In the short term, busy makes us feel important, the buzz of even bogus tasks generating a seductive sensation of efficacy, like static fuzzing a TV. But while engaged in our frenzied show of bustle, what are we omitting to do? It is a question posed by two very different men, both of whom transformed civilization in their way.

43

The first was Socrates, a lapsed stonemason with a face like a punched potato, who is said to have cautioned, 'Beware the barrenness of a busy life.' By all accounts he lived out this philosophy, downing his tools to become a free-range teacher. He roamed Athens with a retinue of wealthy students, collaring citizens with sly questions that made them feel silly, expertly getting up the noses of the elite while leaving his wife to bring up their three sons, whom he ignored. Until 399 BC, when he was put on trial as a public menace. The guilty verdict brought a choice: exile or execution. Typically, he argued that leaving Athens was not worth the bother and downed a cup of hemlock. A noble death, wept the flower of Athenian youth, perhaps forgetting Socrates' family, left with neither wealth nor a noble name to protect them.

Socrates became the wellspring of Western thought without writing a word (he left that to students such as Plato). It is tempting to take his warning against busyness for the counsel of the original dude. But he was too subtle a thinker to underwrite a slacker manifesto. Why else would his warning have been echoed twenty-four centuries later by the most industrious man in history?

'Being busy does not always mean real work,' said Thomas Edison. 'There must be forethought, system, planning, intelligence, and honest purpose. Seeming to do is not doing.' Edison was an arch doer. The indefatigable wizard of Menlo Park's inventions, including the phonograph and film camera, secured 1,093 patents in the US alone and sired several major industries. 'I have got so much to do and life is so short,' he told a friend. 'I am going to hustle.' Edison had a simple scam for packing it all in: pickpocket time. On average he worked eighteen maniacal hours a day (up to sixty on the trot for truly intractable puzzles), snatching a few hours' sleep a night and taking restorative daytime catnaps in one of the cots that dotted his workstations. By the age of forty-seven he estimated his true age was eighty-two, since 'working only eight hours a day would have taken till that time'.

You may shudder to measure your life's output in Edison years, and no healthcare provider would recommend it. Fittingly, it is thanks to him that everybody's day stretches beyond its natural limit, courtesy of the light bulb.

I doubt whether Socrates' and Edison's definitions of a time-rich life would have had much in common. However, both recognized a timeless danger: if you mistake frothing from task to task for meaningful activity in its own right, you will fizz about like a pill in a glass of water, expending vast amounts of energy on increasingly invisible returns. It is also a licence for rudeness and thoughtlessness, for avoiding events we do not want to attend, relieving us from the responsibility of interrogating our choices. Not my fault: I'm just too busy! Margaret Visser, a historian of everyday life, wrote:

> 'No time' is used as an excuse and also as a spur: it both goads and constrains us, as a concept such as 'honour' did for the ancient Greeks. Abstract, quantitative, and amoral, unarguable, exerting pressure on each person as an individual, the feeling that we have no time escapes explanation and censure by claiming to be a condition created entirely out of our good fortune. We have 'no time' apparently because modern life offers so many pleasures, so many choices, that we cannot resist trying enough of them to 'use up' all the time we have been allotted.

In reality busy is a hollow word, a descriptive term for effort; it reveals nothing about whether that effort is productive, purposeful or a waste of disorganized time. Next time I feel busy, I will ask myself, what for?

Part Two

What is Time and Where Does it Go?

Includes: why time was a god, then a gift, then a bully; how your view of time shapes your life; what is the point of a femtosecond; the joy of cattle time; what happens when you lose time sense; why seconds slow down in sinking ships; how to think faster – although time-poor thinking makes us stupid; why distractions are addictive; why Roman philosophers hated hanging around; and what Hilary Mantel and *Hamlet* gained from procrastination.

2

How Time Gives
Us the World

Why we invented it, how it reinvents us

Sometimes I wish that nobody had invented clocks. Then my days would not be chopped into miserly minutes. I would have all the time in the world.

It is a sweet fantasy. But I need not hunt far to find it. This is the land of time that our toddler inhabits, and what a merry place it looks. How he howls if we urge him to hurry while he is studying a marathon of ants on a pavement, or try to scoop him up before he has patted the last jag of jigsaw into place. Often we ignore him; we have to bowl him off to nursery on time, into his bath on time. But how he blossoms on weekends when the day ebbs and flows with the hunger, curiosity and vitality that set the beat of his clock.

'Just stop for a minute and you'll realize you're happy just being,' advised psychologist James Hillman. 'It's the pursuit that screws up happiness. If we drop the pursuit it's right here.' If this is bliss, my son has it. Ask when something happened and he answers, 'Yesterday.' Ask when something is going to happen and he smiles, 'Today?' then gets back to what he was doing. The only clocks he respects are dandelions, because his present consists of whatever present thing grips him.

Children remind us that obeying time does not come naturally. When my son rears in protest as we try to saddle him with our schedule, I worry that he is learning to see time as his enemy. Because clocks are not going anywhere, and thank goodness for that. This chapter explores why we invented time and how it reinvents us. To a surprising degree our life is shaped by something often hidden from us: the version of time that we carry around inside our head. There are persuasive arguments for seeing time as your friend.

1. How time changed the world

Time is confusing. It is invisible, unbiddable; we cannot touch, taste, see or smell it, although you would have to travel a long way – as far as the Pirahã tribe in the Amazon rainforest – to find anyone above the age of ten with their wits intact who might deny that it exists.

The Pirahã are not just foxed by time. They also have no concept of numbers. Show them five soya beans and two soya beans and they cannot count the difference. Time blindness is an extension of their number blindness. This is because what we are talking about, when we talk about time, is something by which to count life. Its many puzzles have bewitched astrophysicists and befuddled philosophers, but set aside the black holes and the sophistry and you could do worse than this explanation given in 1762 by Henry Home, an industrious farmer-judge, who served as mentor to Adam Smith and David Hume and as the midwife to Scotland's Enlightenment: 'A child perceives an interval, and that interval it learns to call time.'

The complication is that from a user's point of view, time is actually two separate things: it is the dimension in which we exist, and an organizational device like a compass. The compass's job is to help us to navigate the dimension: to orientate ourselves in space, to measure the duration of events, to co-ordinate actions, and to plot our next steps. Day to day, however, we tend to think of time as something else entirely: a resource, divided into days, hours, minutes, seconds – the stuff that we never have enough of.

If you can bring yourself to forget its dismaying habit of marching on, then time grows easier to admire. This utterly ingenious intellectual technology lets us impose order on the rolling hurry of succession that is existence, by subdividing experience into three categories – past, present and future. It is also elastic, spanning infinitesimally tiny intervals such as attoseconds (a quintillionth or billionth of a billionth of a second) and epic photonic journeys across space called light years (5,878,625,373,184 miles). Its applications are numberless.

Try to imagine life without atomic clocks.

take a ten-second pause: really picture that thought

Did you envisage a world without smartphones, satellites or the internet? Almost certainly there were no nuclear submarines. It would be a slower place by far.

This little thought experiment illustrates an odd thing that happens when we find new ways to measure time: we transform what we can do with it. It is what cosmologist Gerald Whitrow was getting at when he spoke of 'the invention of time'. Clocks were not simple witnesses to humanity's story but accelerants. Each technological leap in timekeeping sprang a change.

The earliest evidence that humanity looked to the sky in search of answers about time is a painting on the wall of a cave in Lascaux, France, dating to 15,000 BC. Twenty-nine black dots undulate like hoofprints beneath a stippled brown horse; they are thought to represent the cycle of the moon, making this the oldest surviving calendar. Venerable obelisks still serve as shadow clocks in Egypt, a function some have performed since 3500 BC, but the circle of megaliths at Stonehenge is Britain's oldest clock. Built around 3100 BC, its design ensured that their arches would frame sunset on 21 December, the northern winter solstice, and sunrise on 21 June, the high point of the northern summer. And those ancient worshippers had reason to celebrate it. Once our hunter-gatherer ancestors understood the meanderings of the moon, the sun and the seasons, they were armed with the co-ordinates that would enable them to stop living from hand to mouth and begin farming the land. As agriculture developed, communities grew until eventually there was not only enough surplus food but also enough time to spare people to foster new skills and interests. Society developed.

Seasonal rhythms were central to life, as is reflected in the ceremonies of organized religion. Look past the burnt offerings and the vestments and you will find that the pulse behind the stories and traditions is agriculture's calendar and the urge to control time, with festivals contrived to coax heaven into supplying timely sun and rain. Émile Durkheim, the forefather of sociology, identified this coercive property: 'A calendar expresses the rhythm of the collective activities, while at the same time its function is to assure their regularities.' If festivals paced time's passage, with every culture offering sacrifices to encourage the New Year to be a kind one, the day's staging posts were events: meal times, work times, sleep times, sun up, sun down, lengthening shadows and bells, just as the muezzin's call to prayer sets the beat of a traditional Islamic day. Briefer intervals could be measured – a trained stargazer in ancient Babylon could tell time to within a quarter of an hour – but clocks were unnecessary. At such a gentle pace, who needs minutes?

Horology, the art and science of measuring time, soon fascinated rulers, because whoever controlled time could control people. Dates and hours supplied tools for synchronizing actions, whether to wage wars or to co-ordinate workers. It is no accident that the greater the number of clocks in an environment, the swifter people will go, as sociologist Robert Levine discovered when investigating the pace of life around the world. No wonder every major civilization invested heavily in the study of time, often hoping to prise open a window onto the future. Chinese and Babylonian astronomers (who were also priests) used their observations to predict not only astral phenomena but events on earth – a covert means of telling kings what to do.

A stroll through the history of clocks is like turning the pages of a flicker book of civilization's greatest hits. Each occasion the timekeeper is reborn it is in a form that both mirrors and distorts its age. Shadow, sand, water, incense and candle clocks came early, but to trade event time for bossy, precise, hour-and-minute time, mechanical means were necessary.

The first automated timepieces appeared in European monasteries in the thirteenth century; named after the Latin *clocca*, 'bell', these faceless, armless clocks struck the hour as religious houses always had. Otherwise they were the preserve of the wealthy. To encounter a clock was to learn that here lived somebody to be reckoned with, as did Elizabeth I's visitors at Whitehall Palace, where they were greeted by a needlework map of Britain, a sundial shaped like a monkey and a wind-up clock of an 'Ethiop riding upon a rhinocerous'.

Clocks also supplied passports to power. In 1601, Jesuit missionary Matteo Ricci presented the Wanli emperor with a chiming clock, hoping to gain admission to China's capital city. This device, so pettable compared to the huge water-clock towers that then thumbed the kingdom, inspired what would become an imperial passion for collecting clocks.

As navigation dissolved the oceans' frontiers, a series of shipwrecks led Britain's government to offer a prize to whoever found a means of tracking longitude. John Harrison, a carpenter from Yorkshire, devoted forty-three years to create a timepiece with sea legs steady enough to keep time, week after week, in heat, cold and tropical humidity on an ever-bobbing ship – saving lives, accelerating commerce, defeating the limits of space. Next, industrialization brought factory clocks and managers brandishing pocket watches, leading to the birth of a science called efficiency.

After engineers parcelled up the land in railways, the need to co-ordinate timetables led London Time to be decreed the whole country's in 1880 – the first national standard time in the world. Towns no longer had their own time, and the loss of these gentler rhythms was mourned by Thomas Hardy in *Tess of the D'Urbervilles*: 'Tess … started on her way up the dark and crooked lane or street not made for hasty progress; a street laid out before inches of land had value, and when one-handed clocks sufficiently subdivided the day.'

Once wristwatches became wardrobe staples, people were cuffed to time's rule – an intrusion that was not always welcomed. In the 1950s Anirini, a Greek island, was so dull that clocks proved unnecessary, reported one traveller, describing how the suspected homicide of a husband, sent plunging down a well, was forgivingly ascribed to tedium. Locals bridled at neither the murderess nor the investigating police; however, the fat Yugoslav timepiece on an itinerant fisherman's wrist horrified them.

As time technology grew nimbler, so did temporal thinking. It could be on a galactic scale; Albert Einstein theorized that billion-year-old collisions between black holes would be detected in waves of energy that continue to ripple across the universe, a prediction finally confirmed in 2016. Einstein also claimed correctly that time slows if you move fast enough (accelerating clocks grow heavier). Put an atomic clock, which keeps time by means of caesium electrons, losing one second in thirty million years, on a GPS satellite, which orbits earth at 18,000 mph, and sure enough, it loses 38 microseconds a day, requiring special electronics to recalculate its positioning. Thanks to such awesome precision, we can build targeted missiles and little gadgets capable of traversing chasms of space, landing on speeding comets and burying their noses in faraway planets' secrets.

Computers and digital faces replaced the soothing flow of revolving arms with numbers, giving time a staccato beat – an apt prelude to the disruptions ahead, when smartphones would become our favourite means of telling time. Yet to some amazement, the watch is not dead. Luxury sales soar. The Rolex, Hublot or diving watch, equally true on the seabed or atop Everest, sits like a jewel on its owner's wrist – perhaps, if he is a man, his only jewel. It is there less to indicate that its wearer is manacled to a schedule (even if this is how he is able to afford it) than to imply enduring success – the same message issued by Elizabeth I's rhinoceros clock in Whitehall. Canny manufacturers market these beauties as heirlooms-in-waiting: a signal of your grip on time. This is in marked contrast to today's other horological success story, Apple's smartwatch, which does not passively purvey temporal information. No, it is a nagging device, buzzing like a wasp to alert its owner to an appointment or to that dire emergency, the arrival of another email – rupturing the user's attention while ostensibly micromanaging her time.

We have travelled far from event time, which patterned our forefathers' days according to the occasions that mattered, to a strange new, non-event time, which continually interrupts our flow. The smartwatch reminds me of that disquieting truth: whoever controls time also controls people.

Does this version of time work for you? Or does it make you its slave?

2. Our fictional units of time

In 1914, as the world geared up for the Great War, an inquisitive seven-year-old began dissecting her new favourite toy, an alarm clock. She wanted to see this peculiar thing, time. Seven alarm clocks died grisly deaths before her mother cottoned on to what was happening and gave her one device on which to experiment.

Grace Brewster Murray Hopper never found what she was looking for. Instead she became a mathematician, joining the US Navy in the next world war to help devise a computer. When hostilities ended in 1945, the Navy said that at thirty-eight she was too old to join the regular force, so off she went to devise the first programming language using solely English words, flooring sceptics who imagined computers could only do arithmetic. The Navy soon took her back.

Rear Admiral Hopper was reluctantly demobbed at seventy-nine, two decades after the regular date. By then she was known as Amazing Grace, having popularized the term 'debugging' after fishing a dead moth from a computer's innards. But she is best remembered for her post-retirement lectures. One day, fed up with being asked why satellite signals were so slow, she chopped a telephone cable into 11.8-inch lengths. This, she explained, doling them out to her audience, is the distance light travels in a nanosecond (a billionth of a second). Yes, even lightning speed takes time.

Hopper stretched the limits of her era, ignoring rules and feminine expectations in order to prolong her career, as well as to turn computers into fatally word-friendly devices. Yet even one as resourceful as she could not locate time either within or outside an alarm clock, for the reason that time does not exist. Our units for measuring it – millennia, centuries, years, months, weeks, days, hours, minutes – are also fictional. A nanosecond seems solid enough when you flop it about in a length of copper cable, but is no less arbitrary a way to measure our progress through the fourth dimension of existence than the gold stars on the badge of a McDonald's trainee, marking his rise from novice to expert burger flipper. The crucial feature of seconds and years is their regular arrival (unlike McDonald's stars).

All units of measurement are belief systems created to organize facts. Universality bestows a veneer of objectivity, yet these units are no less subjective than the yard, which was introduced by Henry I, ruthless fourth son of William the Conqueror, who outmanoeuvred his brothers, standardized measures and restored England's coinage. His yardstick? The distance from his thumb to his nose. Similarly, calendars are the legacies of quarrels between astronomers, theologians and monarchs. Although most of us follow the solar year (identified by sixteenth-century Polish astronomer Nicolaus Copernicus as approximately 365 days, 5 hours, 48 minutes and 45 seconds), the Christian, Islamic and Chinese religious festivals stick with lunar months, just like our oldest calendar in the Lascaux cave.

In AD 398 St Augustine of Hippo queried the validity of such celestial yardsticks:

> I heard from a learned man that the motions of the
> sun, moon, and stars constituted time, and I assented
> not. Why should not rather the motions of all bodies
> be time? What if the lights of heaven should cease, and
> a potter's wheel run round, would there be no time by
> which we might measure those revolutions?

And it turns out that not even the sky is reliable. As life accelerates, the planet's solar orbit is slowing by fractions of a second each year. Blame gales in our mountains, which cause the earth to jiggle on its axis, and the friction of tides, which drag the earth's rotation by 2.3 metres per second, per day, every hundred years (an effect partially masked by a glacial rebound, since the last Ice Age, of land once trapped beneath continental ice sheets, which speeds earth's rotation by 0.6 metres per second per day). This slowdown maddens the engineers who nurse the atomic clocks on which our communications and defence systems depend. After all, if these fall out of synch with the planet, a missile or satellite will veer off course.

One nanosecond. One foot. If a misdirected drone were whizzing at you, you would care a lot about missing nanoseconds. But in general, such measures mean little to you and me, since our senses cannot compute such minuscule intervals. Time only gains purpose as a tool that we can use.

What is the point of femtoseconds (a quadrillionth, or millionth of a billionth, of a second)? It sounds a nonsense word, perhaps a satirical comment upon the emasculation of time, slivered into such absurdities. But although Concorde could not have travelled an atom's breadth in such a minute interval, scientists, aided by femtoseconds, can track, instant by instant, what transpires at the atomic level during phase transition, that mystifying moment when a liquid becomes solid and free-range particles suddenly lock into a lattice, like dancers at a military dance. Our tiniest temporal unit yet is Planck time (the time it takes light to travel 4×10^{-35} metres) – mind-boggling, yet necessary, since it permits quantum physicists to comprehend the force that keeps life turning: gravity.

3. The comforts of time – or, why we love linear

You too are a clock. The beat of your life is the tempo of events – occasions whose rhythm dictates how relaxed or stressed you feel. A life borne on a steady routine can be titanically productive, as the philosopher Immanuel Kant demonstrated, his schedule so unwavering that amused citizens of Königsberg are said to have set their clocks by his afternoon stroll.

We invented time from a need for predictability. In his 1781 *Critique of Pure Reason*, Kant observed that time is 'at the foundation of all our intuitions'. Without it, how could we make sense of the world, distil lessons from experience, decide what to do when, or guess how long it will take? Time's numbers and dates impose a reassuring form on vast existential uncertainties such as duration, decay and amorphous feelings like our sense of inevitability, empowering us to co-operate and compete as no other animal can.

Anything that gives time definition and direction is a blessing if you are an upright ape whose life's work is, essentially, to survive an unpredictable environment and convince yourself that fleeting existence has a purpose. Recalling yesterday, dreaming about tomorrow: these mental co-ordinates extend a miraculous thread on which to peg our lives, allowing us to weave irretrievable sensory data into something more substantial: a tale of who we are and where we are going. Time's script gives us history, identity, accumulating meanings, reasons to stay alive.

If time is foundational to our being, physicality defines how we conceive it. Concepts of time and space are interchangeable in indigenous languages, such as the Karen's of Thailand. Soon is '*d'yi ba*' – 'not far away'. Sunset might be 'three kilometres away' (if that is how far you could walk in the time it would take for it to arrive). Similarly, we think of time as an independent, often impatient being – time 'races ahead' or we are 'behind' it. These metaphors are pale shadows of beliefs in time as independent divinities, like Kairos or Chronos. But the main reason that we see time as a moving spirit and life as a journey is that we are upright apes, striding on two legs, facing ahead. If a spider, jellyfish or side-shifting crab spoke of time, doubtless its vocabulary would be different.

No doubt it is also because we are upright apes, who like to move on, race, climb, get ahead, that many of us feel contented only if we are metaphorically getting on – in a career or romance, or ascending a social ladder. Our craving for a sense of destination in life's journey (once we called it heaven) is preferable to the depressing alternative: to see life in purely physical terms, as a wizened decline unto the zero of death. How much better to mark life's milestones with accumulating numbers, from your first birthday to your hundredth, evoking achievement, progress: a story from a lifetime.

Today, though, linear time has a challenger: our superfast, flexible hyperdigital telepresent. As a result, holding onto a sense of life as progressive – or simply getting through our plans from start to end – can be a trial. Operate on too many channels simultaneously and attention frays. This is dislocating. Time can resemble less a comforting anchor than a harrying tormentor. How much better to feel led by event time – placing your actions at the centre of a life that unfolds in meaningful chapters?

For Ethiopia's Konso, the hour from 5 p.m. to 6 p.m. is *kakalseema* ('when the cattle return'). The word is so sumptuous, you could stretch out on it and swoon. By contrast, an appointment at 17.30 has an icy ring. It embodies the difference between a life organized by numbers and according to personal experience.

Few of us are tugged along by the rhythms of livestock, crops or the sea's moon-bound tides. But we continue to weigh our days by events: what happens and what we make happen. If, come evening, we cannot account for ourselves – if the day passed in a forgettable rush – we can feel at best frustrated, at worst panicky. In the same way that studies find we are far better at fathoming how long it will take to reach a destination using landmarks than numbers, so time gathers meaning for us from landmark occasions. Not just from big celebrations, but all the moments when our experiences are distinct enough to fashion into stories we can tell one another; then, life makes sense.

Multiple clocks have a hand in shaping our lifetime: social clocks, physical clocks. Many are cyclical, from the fiscal year to the twenty-eight-day menstrual cycle or the twenty-four-hour rollercoaster of the testosterone cycle. Not forgetting our metronomic heartbeat, and ageing – all too visible in growing children, the shrinking old, and any mirror (failing eyesight is a kindness of age).

There are so many versions of time to choose from, yet if I try to picture it, I see a ruler, subdivided into units. Here I stand in the middle, the past behind me, the future before. This feels entirely authentic, yet it is a product of my scientific culture. The philosophical Roman statesman Seneca, writing in AD 65, a less geometric age, saw a lifetime instead in 'large circles enclosing smaller' – banded by childhood, youth and maturity, like tree rings.

It is only when I try to think how I *feel* about time that the importance of event time surfaces. Because cyclical time is what grips my heart. From mild indignation when a birthday rolls around, to the March thrill of strolling along streets lined by magnolia trees, their boughs shivering with ballerina blooms ready to dance in the spring, to my pangs walking into Holland Park to find my favourite horse chestnut already an orgy of gold, autumn's first ravishment before setting about the oak next door. These events come sooner each year, until soon – too soon – there will be less time before than behind me. They remind me that all I love is temporary; life is not cyclical, and winter's frost is already upon me – inconvenient truths no hair dye can refute. Yet still it moves me to know (grace of Robin Robertson's poem 'Primavera') that Britain's spring walks 'north over flat ground at two miles an hour'.

Events may be as inevitable as the flush of autumn, or as unguessable as a black swan. But they are a benign organizing principle for life. Build days around occasions that matter to you, and time's march will root you.

4. Your view of time, your quality of life

One gusty evening in February 1969 a student sat in her college room, writing, when she heard the seven-twenty bell, summoning her to dinner. She was mid-paragraph in an essay due the next morning, yet the bell was hard to ignore. Until a few weeks earlier Karen Armstrong had been a novice, and to a nun, time is 'the voice of God, calling each one of us to a fresh encounter'. Each hallowed moment, 'no matter how trivial or menial the task', was a sacrament commanding obedience.

> At the first sound of the convent bell announcing the next meal or a period of meditation in the chapel, we had to lay down our work immediately ... It had become second nature to me to jump to attention whenever the bell tolled, because it really was tolling for me. If I obeyed the rule of punctuality, I kept telling myself, one day I would develop an interior attitude of waiting permanently on God, perpetually conscious of his loving presence.

But it had never happened. Heartbroken, faith lost, she left the convent's rule. Nothing seemed sacred. So, this night, unwilling to cast off her train of thought, she carried on writing then strolled over to the college dining hall, into the stunning roar of four hundred young people and tutors eating supper. After years at the convent, where conversation was a vice strictly rationed, she was shocked – but more so by what followed: 'Instead of bowing briefly to the Principal in mute apology for my lateness, as college etiquette demanded, I found to my horror that I had knelt down and kissed the floor.'

This peculiar episode resonates not simply because it shows how hard it is to shed the habit of God. Those dominated by time are often disconcerted to discover that views and rules relating to it vary enormously.

Ask an Australian aboriginal when she won the lottery or lost her mother and she might say very recently – even if these events occurred years ago. This would not be untrue because, to her, time is not purely linear; it also moves in circles, radiating outwards from her at the circle's centre. As a result, the more important an event is, the closer in time it feels. This elegant image is true of us all at a psychological level. Like magnets, significant events bend our perception of time. Our memories feel closer to the surface, or vivid, 'like yesterday', if they mean something to us.

We apprehend the future in the same way. A major occasion – be it an exam or a wedding – always, research finds, seems closer than its calendar date, looming delightfully or menacingly. This not only distorts our perspective but influences our actions.

What we tend not to notice is how, as a by-product of our experiences and expectations, we precipitate an attitude towards time itself – as if it were a force with a distinct personality. We see ourselves as always late, running to stand still, chasing after inexhaustible time. Or time is a lunatic whirligig; thrilling, fun, but a mite repetitious. Even if this view reflects reality, its feedback effect, like a prism, refracts the facts in another direction.

You might argue that our attitude towards time shifts from moment to moment – shit happens, we feel shit, then a shaft of pleasure shifts our barometer. True. But research finds that if you scrape away momentary differences, people tend to have a stubborn viewpoint that, like a compass, can set their life's direction. Our minds habitually use single events to predict how we will behave in the future; psychologists call it 'bundling expectations'. Let a mood crystallize into a belief – see time as divinity, friend or foe – and our behaviour shifts, determining whether we attack life or wait for it to happen. Expectations become self-fulfilling prophecies due to consistency bias (the term for our tendency to act in accordance with our self-image).

This is useful to know. Great swathes of your day may be hired out, subservient to others' whims, and you may have a limited say in what you do. But you can control your attitude. Budge the mood, expect better, and outcomes can improve.

It is worth a try. Persistent, nagging time stress, however trivial, becomes a chronic condition. Simply being exposed to multitudes of things happening at once percolates a state of constant expectation that is cognate with anxiety. This is the tax we pay for all those incomplete tasks, unsent or unread emails, grating Facebook posts, pieces of paper on our desk, meetings whose action points we have yet to enact, if they hum in our minds. This is why we write them down. Cognitive dumping outsources stress; an improvement, until to-do lists become the bully. Catalyze this stress into a permanently embattled perspective towards time and the minor magnifies: everything seems urgent, overwhelming; impatience becomes our default mode, and rush unavoidable.

What would a positive attitude towards time look like? I like this view, from Edmund Burke's *Reflections on the Revolution in France*, a model of eloquent rage written in horror at the tumbrels, guillotines and desecrated churches across the Channel: 'Society is a contract between the past, the present and those yet unborn.' Despite the legalistic language, for me it summons an interlocking chain of hands, reaching from the graves of the past to the cradles of tomorrow: the bond of trust required, as Burke saw it, to seal the deal that society offered – that is, to support all human interests. Current psychological research takes a similar view of what might be the healthiest attitude an individual can hold towards time. It has a catchy name: the balanced time perspective. It was invented by Philip Zimbardo.

Zimbardo is best known for the Stanford Prison experiment, a notorious 1971 study in which adults played prisoners and guards in a fake prison. Things got dark, fast. Guards grew sadistic, prisoners depressed and passive. Zimbardo killed the experiment in consternation after three days as it teetered into abuse and the man playing the role of prison governor – Zimbardo himself – fell in with it.

What this proved, if proof were necessary, is that much behaviour is a function not of innate character but of habitat: we follow the rules of our environment. Uncomfortable information after the genocidal complicity that marked Hitler's Third Reich.

Since then, Zimbardo has sought to understand how to steer character for the better. His research, based on reams of studies, finds that a perky temporal outlook will produce a perky, productive human being.

Want to test your attitude? Consider the following questions.

1. What are your strongest memories and how would you describe your view of the past?
2. What are you doing this weekend and why?
3. What does the future hold and what matters most?

A balanced perspective is marked by a warm sense of the past (happy memories, fondness of traditions) zest for the present, and positive plans. All of which sounds like a very long description of optimism. But consistent evidence lends weight to the theory. Future-orientated countries and individuals enjoy greater success (if slightly less hedonism) than present-orientated ones. Effective people tend to feel positive about both past and future. Those with precise, full memories are also better at making plans. The message is plain: the more connected you feel to yesterday and tomorrow – the greater your sense of life as a connection between past and future, the dead and the unborn – then the clearer your focus on time and your life potential.

Ingenious methods exist to measure the breadth of our temporal horizon. Individuals with good impulse control – those who override temptations and cleave to long-term goals – evince warm feelings for their future self when their brains are scanned, regarding that imaginary being as they might a friend. By contrast, self-destructively impulsive people, unable to see far beyond their present, can feel as little for their future self as they would for a stranger.

Of equal interest in our view of time is the role played by our sense of agency. There is the goal-setting approach, seen among individuals who chart their life course; then there is the fatalist, who are closer to corks bobbing on time's current, whither fate takes them – an outlook, Zimbardo notes, found in certain religions, as well as in pessimists, suicides and terrorists. Any one of us can feel either way, our perspective fluctuating by the hour, the season, our circumstances. In times of suffering, well may you believe in cruel fate or feel that time is the enemy. 'Of all things past, the sorrow only stays,' wrote Sir Walter Ralegh from his cell in the Tower of London, awaiting his summons to the axeman. Past successes, like the introduction of the potato and the courtly fashion for smoking, had proven an inadequate amulet against Elizabeth I's disappointment in him.

Autobiographical memories are scripts that we use to tell ourselves who we are, what we like and how to get it. If the memories that you carry around like pebbles in your pocket fund self-limiting behaviour, you can bevel their sharper edges. Successful interventions conducted by Zimbardo and others with sufferers of post-traumatic stress and mental illness prove that a more enabling outlook on time can be cultivated. If that sounds close to brainwashing, consider how unreliable memory is, always editing. Perhaps our brain's greatest gift is that it lets us forget so much that is dull or hurtful, instead spotlighting the peak experiences – the novelties, highs and lows – and giving them far more memory space than quotidian routine. This can mislead us into thinking that we had a wonderful trip or saw an incredible film because it ended well or there was one eye-wateringly hilarious incident, even – perhaps especially – if most of it was utterly unmemorable.

Years of therapy are not necessary to shift your angle on the future or past. A research team at the University of Miami asked three hundred students to recall an incident when someone had hurt them. One-third were then invited to spend a few minutes describing the event in detail, dwelling on their anger and subsequent misfortunes. Another third were also asked to describe the event, but in this instance to explore the good that had flowed from it (what they had learned or gained in strength and wisdom). The rest simply described their plans for the next day. Afterwards all three hundred completed a questionnaire setting out how they regarded the person who had upset them. Not surprisingly, the second group were far more forgiving, less likely to want to avoid the person concerned.

Spend a few minutes considering the profits drawn from a bad experience and you convert its value. Would your future look different if this kind of thinking became a habit?

Directions for a time-rich outlook

Past positive

The capacity to look warmly to the past is a psychological bridging loan, funding confidence for tomorrow. Although, as a financial adviser is obliged to remind you, past performance cannot guarantee future success, think more about the past and at the very least you will find your memory enriched – a good idea, since people with detailed recall have greater facility at drawing up detailed plans. To improve your powers of recollection, make a game of remembering happy things from different phases of your life. Could you also prioritize family or local traditions? If melancholy memories surface, dig a useful lesson from them. (Being bullied was my education in compassion, for instance.)

Present balance

Some pleasures render us passive recipients or consumers, others make us powerful and purposeful. Try to privilege experiences that help you to feel the author of your life's story, connected with the world. Zone in on what you are doing as you do it and moments are instantly livelier. Could you be more interested in people, or pick more absorbing tasks?

Future positive

It begins in the expectation: that time can deliver what you crave. But the slightest nudge in a hopeful direction lifts the mood. For this reason, always arm yourself with something to look forward to, be it a holiday or an emergency biscuit. You might seek to develop a clearer vision of who and where you want to be. To this end, work on your prospective imagination. Perhaps try a different point of view for size; reading a novel or memoir is a collaborative exercise in evocation. And start daydreaming about credible pathways towards your future: specific goals, detailed plans. Then set a date to begin.

MENTAL TIME TRAVEL

Time holds us captive to paradoxes. We imagine that life is heading in one direction, yet the instant we enter the present, off time scutters into the past. Our minds grope for the future, yet our hopes are forged on the anvil of yesterday. In his closing words, *The Great Gatsby*'s narrator mourns the stale dream for which his friend lost his life: 'So we beat on, boats against the current, borne back ceaselessly into the past.'

Nothing can reverse time's direction of travel. In his embarrassed memoir of serving as a German soldier in the Second World War, Günter Grass reflects on the gravitational pull of our past: 'After is always before. What we call the present, this fleeting nownownow, is constantly overshadowed by a past now in such a way that the escape route known as the future can be marched to only in lead-soled shoes.' By contrast, in 1940, German-Jewish philosopher Walter Benjamin, writing shortly before he swallowed a handful of morphine pills in preference to expulsion from Spain into Nazi hands, saw history as an angel blasted into the future, for ever looking back:

> His face is turned toward the past. Where we perceive a chain
> of events, he sees one single catastrophe which keeps piling
> wreckage upon wreckage and hurls it in front of his feet …
> The storm irresistibly propels him into the future to which his
> back is turned, while the pile of debris before him grows
> skyward. This storm is what we call progress.

Yet we can dart through time's rubble to find solace and answers, as Machiavelli did in 1513, after the Medici tortured and then exiled him to his farm, to revive in the company of ghosts.

> When evening has come, I return to my house and go into my study. At the door I take off my clothes of the day, covered with mud and mire, and I put on my regal and courtly garments; and decently reclothed, I enter the ancient courts of ancient men, where, received by them lovingly, I feed on the food that alone is mine and that I was born for. There I am not ashamed to speak with them and to ask them the reason for their actions; and they in their humanity reply to me. And for the space of four hours I feel no boredom, I forget every pain, I do not fear poverty, death does not frighten me.

The licence of mental time travel – adventures with other minds, ways of being and thinking – lets us surpass ourselves. This was demonstrated amply by Michel de Montaigne, a sweet-tempered landowner, so-so city mayor and middling winemaker, who thwarted his native idleness to invent a new artform. His *Essays*, published in 1580 and still in print, offered wisdom truffled indiscriminately from fields, friends and the larder of antiquity. This came naturally: he was a man out of his time, something of a living fossil, like the coelacanth (a fish rediscovered sixty-six million years after it was supposed to have been extinct) – stuffed to the gills with classical learning because his eccentric father decreed that he should only hear, think and speak in Latin from the age of three. (Neatly closing the door on the possibility of an intimate relationship with his testy mother, not to mention his father, who spoke no Latin at all.)

Montaigne grew into an adult fascinated with but detached from life, acutely conscious that his world was no less bizarre or ephemeral than that of the ancient Romans he knew so intimately. Not surprisingly, he became adept at gambits of mental time travel, reporting gleefully how once he used them to relieve a fresh-minted widow's grief by tiptoeing conversational manoeuvres – 'gently deflecting our talk and diverting it bit by bit to subjects nearby, then a little more remote'. To ward off depression at his impending death he summoned memories of youth to 'sidestep and avert my gaze from this stormy and cloudy sky that I have in front of me'.

Artful mental manoeuvres can change the future. Great Britain's Hollie Webb was twenty-five years old and one of her team's youngest players when she approached the goal to take the deciding penalty in the 2016 Olympics' women's hockey final. A single strike to win Britain's first gold in this event, or lose it. Few actions lasting under a second have such weight upon them. Webb looked, swiped … smack! Smack again as the ball rang off the back of the goal. 'I watched it go into the net and then I can't remember anything else since then. We practise them so many times and I just tried to imagine I was training at Bisham Abbey. I knew what I was going to do against their keeper, so I just stared her in the eye.'

Betraying no fear, giving away no clue as to where she would aim, was important, but more so was that Webb reduced the time's pressure, conceiving of the shot as simply the latest in a sweaty queue of such moments. Telling herself she was doing something ordinary allowed her to be extraordinary.

If mental time travel offers a refuge from the present, it can also draw life from the past. David Alliance left school in Tehran at thirteen to toil in the Grand Bazaar, then landed in Manchester in 1950 with £14 and a dream of starting a business. He was to create the largest textile company in the West. As age dimmed him, he developed a technique to reinvigorate himself that might have been whispered by Montaigne's ghost:

> When I was exhausted after a long day of doing business, I would close my eyes and become a little boy again in Kashan: the sun beat down on the courtyard of our family house and the ground was too hot for my bare feet. I could smell the dry desert air and feel the warmth of the sun, a sensation so real that sometimes it brought sweat to my brow. My father and sisters were there, and there was love and laughter and security. When I opened my eyes, I would find myself back in an office in Manchester, but refreshed and full of energy, ready to get on with the task at hand. I did this even in board meetings and no one in the room ever guessed the journey I had just been on, or understood how I could recover my energies so rapidly … sometimes, when I cannot sleep, I take a virtual walk through the bazaar, past my father's office and on through the cool alleyways, remembering happy times there. And then I'm relaxed again.

Time travel took him to a better place. It could do the same for you.

3

Slaves to the Beat

Why time changes speed and so do we

One day Jane,* a high-flying professional in prime middle age, had a catastrophic stroke. In time she recovered enough to leave hospital, pretty much the image of her former self, if slightly shabbier, given to minor personal neglect, but still bright, knowledgeable, her powers of concentration formidable. Yet something was absent.

'I am like an astronaut, lost in space,' she said, describing her eerie, untethered sensation.

Ask her how long she had been in a room and the answer was firm. 'Five minutes. Always five minutes, no matter what,' said Joe Mole, a psychologist who began working with her.

Eventually doctors pinpointed what was missing. The brain haemorrhage had destroyed Jane's capacity to estimate duration. As a result, her temporal compass was broken. She had no idea how long to cook a meal, how long she had been

---

* Not her real name.

77

talking, when to stop – little details, seemingly, but with life-changing consequences. Making plans became difficult. Socializing was difficult. Memories were jumbled, refusing to line up in order. Formerly one of those impossible people who surge ahead doing three things at a time impeccably, now she was riven by anxiety.

Jane's plight demonstrates how thoroughly our sense of time pervades life, grounding us in reality, keeping us safe. While we are awake our brains constantly estimate duration and pace, winnowing the onrush of sensory experience into sequential events. This orientation system directs our motor reflexes to put what part of our body where, when, at what speed, what to dodge, where to head next. Without it we could not walk, never mind cross a road.

'I think people are surprised when they find out that there is no mini clock in your head,' Mole told me. 'Time sense is an interaction between memory, attention and pacemakers.'

In other words, your feeling for time is a by-product of consciousness. It is easy to undervalue because it largely goes unnoticed, yet it is dazzling in its intricacy, constructed in a collaboration between many parts of your brain. As yet, nobody is sure which part does what. So people afflicted with Jane's condition, known as dyschronometria, can have a range of symptoms, depending on the nature of their brain injury; some lose sense of pace, some of duration, others cannot tap a beat without unravelling. This makes diagnosis elusive. Very many perplexed individuals must hobble on with similarly untethered feelings, the cause and nature of their problems unrecognized. It must be desperately lonely.

Losing traction with her context robbed Jane of time's steadying anchor. In exchange she was beset by uncertainty – a curse, since we can only make reliable assessments of anything if we have the means to calculate what is probable. To give yourself an idea of what she was dealing with, summon that purgatorial sense you have when you are unsure how long a journey will last – then imagine feeling that way about everything. Her trauma was deepened by being bereaved of her old self, whom she could recall but never recapture.

Dyschronometria has no cure. Instead Jane developed coping mechanisms: setting alarms to prompt her when to start or stop activities, creating checklists to advise how long things should take. She trained herself to seek time cues – to glance in the oven to check if food was bubbling or burnt; to observe people's faces for signs of boredom, to stop herself rambling on. But each tactic required vigilance. Fatigue became her constant companion – not ideal for anyone, never mind an anxious one recovering from a stroke.

Jane's predicament is a reminder that time sense is our mind's creation. The quality of our attention determines our quality and pace of life.

I hope that you, like me, can take a fairly sure-footed sense of time for granted. Dyschronometria is light years from normal experience. Yet we glimpse its disorientating shadow whenever we become detached from time's anchor. Outsource your sense of time – to a PA or a smartphone that chivvies you from pillar to post – and without that prop you can feel lost. Pack too much in, erode the spaces for noticing, thinking, let rush or distraction abbreviate your attention, and you are a skid from being out of control – as the escalating numbers of road accidents attributed to snacking or texting testify.

Pay attention to how we experience time, and the mysteries multiply. Why does a bad experience, or childhood, last so long, yet happiness and old age speed past? Is it possible to reverse that perception – to accelerate dull hours or to extend happy moments? Ask these questions and you begin to realize that our time sense is often out of control – because somebody else is manipulating it. This chapter explores why time changes speed, and how to set your pace.

1. Why time flies (when you are having fun but also when you are not)

In 1890 the philosopher William James captured the fugitive nature of the present: it is 'a saddle-back, with a certain breadth of its own on which we sit perched, and from which we look in two directions into time'. If consciousness is the horse we ride from our past into our future, our mood usually determines how fast – or bumpy – the ride feels.

Everybody experiences fast hours and marathon minutes – from the five-hour monologue while you vainly sieve your boss's Christmas party chitchat in hope of detecting a shaft of wit, to the five-second eternity as the radiographer scrutinizes a shadow on your pancreas, to the three-minute evening vaporized playing Grand Theft Auto. These time warps occur because in time perception, as in life, attention rules. Split it, dilute it and we feel, remember and accomplish less.

Time's pace shifts gear because *something has shifted in how we pay attention*. Little has changed since St Augustine's quill nailed the point, sixteen centuries ago, when he characterized time as the measuring by the soul of its expectation, its attention and its memory. (Swap the word 'soul' for 'brain'.)

When estimating the passage of time, your brain snatches temporal markers wherever it can, often from your environment. Just as we see a breeze in skittering leaves, so time is visible through motion, alteration; anything that produces contrast. By analogy, you may know from your speedometer that your car is hurtling along at ninety miles per hour (not that I ever do), but you only *feel* your velocity when you hit a bump or see trees at the roadside, whizzing backwards.

Any change in your environment, even a subtle one, such as music changing pitch, will make time seem slower. But once you are familiar with that music, the novelty wears off and it seems faster, because your brain is less engaged. What this means is that the more processes are whirring inside your head, the slower time (relatively) seems. Albert Einstein, discoverer of spacetime, explained this best: 'An hour sitting with a pretty girl on a park bench passes like a minute, but a minute sitting on a hot stove seems like an hour. That's relativity.'

Our emotions slow and speed up time as nothing else can because this is their job. Sense pain, danger, opportunity or pleasure, and this releases neurochemicals – which we recognize as shades of emotions – to alter our brain's vigilance.

Film director Alfred Hitchcock understood this well – hence all those eye-hooking blonde stars. Pace was his speciality. Remember how slowly the dagger moves in *Psycho*, milking anticipation, maximizing suspense? Eek! Eek! *EEEK!* It is a masterclass in suspense, demonstrating three points. First, fear slows time. Second, scary music makes it even slower. Third, slow time is itself scary. The longer he kept audiences waiting, the louder they screamed.

Emotions' time-warping effects range widely. Robert Burton glossed them in his *Anatomy of Melancholy* (1621):

> When I go musing all alone,
> Thinking of divers things
> When I build castles in the air,
> Void of sorrow and void of fear ...
> Methinks the time runs very fleet ...
>
> When I lie waking all alone,
> Recounting what I have ill done,
> My thoughts on me then tyrannise ...
> Methinks the time moves very slow.

Time quickens during moments of joy, yet that halcyon memory seems long in retrospect. This paradox occurs because different types of emotions lay down different types of memory. When happy, our dopamine-bathed mind is an errant butterfly, flitting about, taking in peripheral details. For this reason, my ten-minute wedding day – a lunch-plus-getaway car affair – streaked by for me, but afterwards trailed a confetti of precise memories. (By contrast, it was all epic to my father, who can cost it per minute.) Likewise, an hour crawls when you are adding sums or minding a baby, but leaves few memories: all our effort is concentrated on preventing errors, dangers, indeed anything memorable from happening. Hence parents agree that although the days are long, the early years are short, and accountants rarely discuss bookkeeping.

Under intense emotion we can enter a time warp. In 1960, Nelson Mandela, a leader of South Africa's banned African National Congress, became a fugitive. But the longest moments of his two-year ordeal took place in under a minute at a set of traffic lights. In the next car sat a colonel of the local Security Branch. 'He never looked my way, but even so the seconds I spent waiting for the light to change seemed like hours.'

Why did time slow? Because Mandela's brain was running so fast. He had entered fight mode, a state of high sensory and physical alert – every muscle primed to act, awash with noradrenaline – that fired extra neurons across his brain. Sensory data flooded in. This cognitive acceleration – literally faster perceptions – afforded him extra thinking time, per second, to decide how to respond. The only trouble was that he was paralysed, incapable of doing anything. His only safe response was to sit and wait in agony as his mind raced. This sort of situation is deeply stressful – the *ne plus ultra* of Hitchcockian suspense, and only enjoyable to spectators. But in emergencies where you can act, extra thinking time is a boon, as Captain David Hart Dyke discovered in the Falklands, when his ship, HMS *Coventry*, sank under enemy fire:

> I was aware of a flash, and tremendous heat, and the crackling of the radar set in front of my face as it began to disintegrate. There was smoke everywhere, complete devastation. It seems like an age but your brain does funny things with time and you just concentrate on getting out. I could feel nothing. No pain, nothing.

In his novel predicament, Captain Hart Dyke's brain delved into underused storage areas, seeking clues as to what to do, accelerating its cognitive action, slowing down time. He felt no pain from his burns, because pain, like time sense, is a sensation – one that his brain was too busy to create.

Without contrast, our sense of time melts, as psychoanalyst Stephen Grosz found when treating a silent man: 'After sitting with patients for thousands and thousands of hours, I'd developed an internal clock for fifty minutes. But with Anthony my clock broke. Now, a whole session could go by in what felt like minutes, or just the opposite.' Time vanished because there was nothing to remember it by. It is tempting to conclude that, although he was too polite to say so, he was numbingly bored.

In desperate situations – if movement or change are unattainable – frozen time presents an existential crisis. During what would be a twenty-seven-year jail term, Nelson Mandela recognized that his chief antagonist was time: 'Each day like the one before; each week like the one before it, so that the months and years blend into each other.' To him, solitary confinement was the 'most forbidding' aspect of incarceration: 'There was no end and no beginning.' So spare a care for hostages around the world, their lives contracted to a fog of dread, unable even to hope for an end, unsure where the exit might lead.

2. Can you trick your brain quicker?

Imagine that you are on a train. It has been a long day. A lengthier journey stretches ahead of you, but it will terminate at the end of the line. So relax. Plug in those headphones, close your eyes ...

You wake with a start. Something is wrong. It's your favourite song. Or is it? It's so fast. You fiddle with your iPod. No, that's working fine. Gradually the music reverts to its usual speed.

If this happened to me I would blame an iGremlin, then forget it. But it happened to Professor Sophie Scott, who is a neuroscientist. After a moment to gather her wits, she realized what had happened. The music was not too fast. Her brain was too slow.

To understand what happened, think of your brain as a fleshy computer, powered by electricity and neurochemical fizz. In sleep its pulse slackens: the deeper our slumber, the statelier the pace. As can be seen in a sleep laboratory in the fattening brainwaves that unroll across an electroencephalogram (EEG) as somebody slides into unconsciousness.

When Scott was barely awake, her brainwaves were still at sleepy running speed – not the pace they operated at when she usually listened to music – so the song appeared relatively fast. 'Normally our brain takes time cues from our surroundings. But in sleep it disengages from external stimuli, tuning into its own rhythms,' explained Scott. In other words, your brain keeps time by monitoring its own processes. The more cognitive processes go on, the slower time feels.

Nobody fully understands the mechanisms of our mind's metronome. But Norbert Wiener, a mathematician famed for inventing cybernetics as well as for riding his unicycle around the corridors of MIT, speculated that the brain's alpha rhythm (evident when we are awake but relaxed) sets the bass tempo – a master clock to co-ordinate our sensory perceptions, just as computers' clocks serve to synchronize the signals between their myriad components (hence the Y2K paranoia, before 1999 became 2000, for fear that confused clocks would throw computers into turmoil).

The important point to take from Scott's discombobulation is that when time appears faster or slower – whether in tedium or an emergency – there is one cause: the changes in electrical flow in our heads, moderated by neurochemicals (which speak to you and me in more poetic terms, such as fear, boredom or love).

If increasing the rate at which your brain manufactures perceptions helps you to think faster, this suggests enticing possibilities. Maybe you could put yourself in a dangerous or novel situation. (This might be one for adrenaline junkies.) But there are other means. An intriguing experiment exposed subjects to a series of fast clicking sounds. Afterwards, their computational skills and memory improved: their brain-waves had synchronized to the fast beat.

You might take this for an invitation to listen to techno to help you power through work. Alas, music absorbs cognitive capacity, limiting space for thought. So if it gets you in the mood – as it did novelist Edna O'Brien, who once enjoyed writing in the company of J.S. Bach – this may bring diminishing returns unless, once the mood is set, you press mute. (O'Brien subsequently renounced Bach for silence.)

Why time speeds with age

How grossly unfair that while time seems slow to impatient little children, it bolts as you get older, just when you are ready to slam on the brakes. What explains this design fault?

1. **Relativity.** Our time sense is framed by the extent of our lifetime, so twenty-four hours is a smaller fraction of life to adults than it is to children. Yet our diminishing days grow commensurately more precious. In 1517 Michelangelo de Merisi wrote in fury from a quarry to the Vatican after they tried to chisel his fee for a sculpture: 'Because I'm old I don't feel like losing so much time to save the pope two or three hundred ducats on this marble.' He had just turned forty-two, but life expectancy was shorter then.

2. **Our biological clock slows.** Therefore hours seem faster. In laboratory tests, children are better than the elderly at guessing an interval's duration. Since time estimation depends on recalling sequences, small persons with springy, ungristly brains have the advantage.

3. **We lay down fewer intense memories.** If we settle into routines, are in less of a hurry to get somewhere, and do fewer new things, life just is not as gripping as our dramatic early years, when choices have a longer afterlife.

These explanations suggest a number of remedies:

- Look after your brain: eat well, sleep, drink water, be happy, go out, soak up sun, exercise. And yes – neuroscanners prove it – meditation stems the decline of cognition, increasing the brain's blood flow.
- Resist the glide into autopilot: seek fresh experiences, make choices that matter, form memories worth sharing. You are not dead yet.

3. Slaves to the beat: how mood and pace are manipulated

On 25 March 2010 a mother clasped her tiny newborn. He had been born at twenty-six weeks' gestation, along with his twin sister. While she wailed in her incubator, he was unresponsive. After twenty frantic minutes doctors abandoned efforts to resuscitate him. His mother begged to hold him in her arms.

After five minutes he twitched – reflex movements, the doctors assured her. Two hours later, he opened his eyes.

The revival in a Sydney hospital of Jamie Ogg, a boy who went on to enjoy perfect health, is an instance of kangaroo care. Leading neonatal experts encourage all parents to clasp their newborns skin to skin. This bonding has profoundly practical effects.

We are all slaves to the beat, natural-born pace mimics from our first embrace, when our newborn heart and lungs regulate their rhythm in duet with our mother's, if we have the fortune to be close enough to hear. How exactly we find this rhythmic sympathy remains unclear, but the drumbeat's generator is the pacemaker. Your sinoatrial node, a nugget of ten thousand cells, creates electricity to make your heart muscle clench around three billion times over a lifetime – a miraculously reliable clock. Isolate a sinoatrial cell, put it in a Petri dish and its voltage continues to rise and fall.

When it comes to your preferred tempo, and what makes you want to dance, your body's architecture is responsible. The taller you are, the slower your ideal rhythm – in the same way that leggy people take fewer strides to cover a distance. But your pace is also an incredibly sensitive barometer of many things: your age, diet, health, emotions, breathing rate. All being well in your body, then your most influential tempo cues come from your environment.

Try walking through Manhattan at rush hour. No matter whether you are in a hurry or not, it takes real will to resist falling in with the scampering beat – and not just because if you go any more slowly you might be knocked over. This synchronization is called entrainment. We do it because we are social animals, programmed to copy each other. We smile when smiled at, fold our arms if a companion does; and if the

pace slackens, so do we. Given the advantages to our ancestors, who roamed in groups, this urge to align pace surely
evolved by natural selection. Moving in harmony made for
good hunting when men banded together to slay beasts
larger than themselves. Keeping up with the pace also aided
the survival of the fastest: lag at the back of the pack and a
predator was far likelier to pick you off.

I cannot count the reasons why tempo matters in this
non-hunter-gathering era, but top of my list would be that it
sets the tone for body, heart and mind. Derived from Latin
tempus (time), tempo stole into the English language in the
seventeenth century as a fencing term, then skipped into
music to denote the cut and dash of a melody. When Mozart
inscribed '*allegro con spirito*' ('quickly with spirit') on his
sonata in D major, it was not a serving suggestion; this tempo
imparted the vital soul of the piece.

Pace, mood and action are so interwoven that when music
is slow, we dance slowly, and vice versa. Music's power to
move us was shown during a mass experiment conducted
during a Scottish half-marathon. When fast music played
over the speakers it picked up the contestants' feet; down
tempo slowed the pace. Music amplifies feelings, but it can
also alter them. In another study, happy, upbeat songs were
played to happy students and sad, slow music to sad students,
plus happy songs to sad students, and the reverse. Afterwards
most participants said their mood shifted in line with the
music – an effect at its strongest if their mood at the outset
had been the opposite of the song's.

These congruence effects, as they are called, transcend
music. Our tempo is an expression of our emotional state;

for instance, we walk slowly when we are gloomy. But this is a two-way relationship. Adopt a new tempo, a different melody, and we can reset our mood.

If ever you wonder why top executives rise early to punish the pavements in $200 trainers instead of catching up on sleep or time with loved ones, it is not just in the interests of looking younger than the junior colleagues who are snapping at their heels. It is because running for running's sake (as opposed to fleeing for your life) makes us feel like winners. A forward-driving tempo is a great mindhack.

Run, raising your pulse, and time seems relatively slow – but also more capacious. The magic happens as you settle into a rhythm, and oxygen and brain chemicals set to work: you feel both calmer and smarter. Self-medicating with these uplifting neurotransmitters – endorphins, dopamine, serotonin – is the only acceptable addiction in blue-chip companies and polite society, and is healthier than anti-depressants too.

The music playing in your ears helps this mental mellowing along. Intriguingly, the myth that you can increase an embryo's intelligence by playing Mozart to your bump originated in a study that had nothing to do with pregnancy. A group of adults who listened to his music performed better at solving puzzles afterwards, their IQs rising temporarily. This ignited the intoxicating notion that Wolfgang Amadeus's genius might be contagious through the medium of his melodies. Sadly, subsequent research clarified that the real stimulant was narcotic: his music made listeners happy, firing their brains with dopamine. So if you wish to improve your intellectual performance but prefer heavy metal, you ought to seek out Ozzy instead (perhaps sparing your embryo the pleasure). And remember: when you want to do the cognitive heavy lifting, turn the music off.

Like all mind-altering substances, a strong tempo should be handled with care. It really can make you stronger. Music psychologist Victoria Williamson describes how it acts as a 'synchronization partner'. Think of it as another encouraging person, exercising next to you. Aided in this way you can prolong a treadmill-based workout by 15 per cent, or hold weights longer. But it may also be deployed to drive you where you wish not to go. Next time you notice your toes tapping to an irresistible beat, you might reflect on the fate of the terrified soldiers throughout history, who were herded into battle to the insistent thrum of a regimental drum. Then consider the landscapes of sound you walk through daily and how many aim to manipulate you.

Generations of market researchers have dried out their eyeballs observing the effect of music on consumers. Accelerated beats are prized because they drive shoppers onto hedonic treadmills – a mood in which we instinctively bolster our dopamine by seeking, trying and buying new things. This is why up-tempo numbers usher shoppers down supermarket aisles, raising their spend per minute. Fast music fills burger restaurants, and empties them quicker too, by encouraging customers to stuff their faces apace – fattening turnover and profits and consumers along with it. In fashion stores, especially at the low-cost, high-volume end of the business, we often browse to zippy dance and pop: these aim to boost impulse spending by evoking an upbeat outlook – to persuade us that we need three new outfits, for that social life we will enjoy when we find the time.

But there can be less to fast than meets the eye. For instance, a study in a mid-range Texan restaurant found that down-tempo music led patrons to linger longer – even if they had to queue for a table in a busy period. What is more, once at the table they drank more than if fast music played – a better outcome for the restaurant, because although fast music increases customer turnover, the mark-up on beverages is higher than that on food. A similarly nuanced effect applied in supermarkets. Shoppers serenaded with tranquil music saunter down the aisles and their spend per head goes up. To achieve the desired results, slow can be better for us all.

So beware the music poured into your defenceless ears in shops, restaurants and lifts, or when you are trapped on an automated telephone system. I, for one, briefly detested pop during a summer job working in a packing factory, where Radio 1 blared loud, long and unignorably. If this backing track made anyone happier, they were good at hiding it. Yet our hands obediently fiddled away, interring indeterminate metal objects in sticky cellophane cocoons for the Ministry of Defence until our fingers lost their prints.

4. The power of setting your tempo

Perhaps life's demands press so hard that you feel trapped by rush. Perhaps the pace seems morbidly slow, as numbing as depression. If you do, please remember Jane, drifting through life, feeling like an astronaut stranded in outer space. You can still feel the pressures of time. That means you can change gear, however little control you appear to have.

Walter Sisulu, held on Robben Island with Nelson Mandela, described how his hero converted his predicament into a chance to lead. Most days, the inmates marched to a quarry to shatter white stones under a blinding sun:

> The prison authorities would rush us ... *Hardloop*!
> That means run. One day Nelson said: 'Comrades let's
> be slower than ever.' ... the steps we were taking
> would make it impossible ever to reach the quarry
> where we were going to. They were compelled to
> negotiate.

From then on, Mandela set his own tempo. His lawyer recalled:

> He was brought to the consulting room by no less
> than eight warders, two in front, two on each side and
> two at the back ... in shorts and without socks ...
> unlike any other prisoner I have ever seen, he was
> setting the pace at which this group was coming
> towards the consulting room. Then with all gravitas
> he said, 'You know, George, this place really has made
> me forget my manners. I haven't introduced you to my
> guard of honour.'

Any shift in pace is mind-altering. Scriptwriter Daniel Klein described how his mindset, acuity and engagement sharpened during a philosophical retreat on a mountainous Greek island, where the paths twisted up and down and the sole means of transportation were feet and donkeys. 'In only a matter of a few calendar days here, my internal clock adopts this tempo, and along with that comes a slowed-down appreciation of just about everything – of what I hear and see around me and of the feeling of the movements of my body.'

I had a similar experience during the greatest culture shock of my life. It hit not when I was travelling through India but at home in London, after I bid goodbye to the nine-to-five and entered the land of the Day People. These individuals, unseen when I worked in an office, seemed alien in many ways. The first thing I noticed was how slowly they moved. Some had a bouncing gait, whether or not they wore earphones or wafted marijuana fumes. They had other odd habits too, such as smiling as they waited in queues. How long, I wondered, and dreaded, until I shed the spell of urgency that sped non-Day People to work?

Eventually I realized that many Day People worked – freelance, like me; their day simply ran to a different beat. Gradually mine, too, began to do so as I experimented with my schedule, and began noticing that different hours of the day suited different things. At a gentler tempo, oddly, work went quicker. What I had discovered – so obvious, it seems now – is that your pace decides not only how fast you act but also how you think. Often slow and smooth are swifter.

Speed cheats

To slow down time, try:

- **Fear** Give a forty-minute/four-year speech, in a PowerPoint black spot, to an audience whom you have just learnt do not speak English. Try this only once.
- **Tedium, depression** (insufficient dopamine) 'I was told that ten more days must pass for the drug to clear my system,' wrote William Styron in *Darkness Visible* (an ironic reference to another literary challenge: that happiness writes white). 'Ten days to someone stretched on such a torture rack is like ten centuries.'
- **Worry** A self-gnawing, thought-accelerating activity, but an intellectual cul-de-sac, well caught in a Chinese expression that describes insomnia as 'feasting on maggots'.
- **Stare at clocks** Pay time attention and it seems too slow – if you want it to go fast. (However, if you are late or under a deadline, it seems too fast.)
- **Arrogance** Time entitlement is a recognized condition. Those suffering it experience time as running more slowly in tasks they consider demeaning, believing it a waste of their superior life. This outlook helps to explain the contrastingly outstanding work ethic of entrepreneurs who learnt to graft in a deprived childhood – Charles Dickens, for example, whose experiences as a boy in a blacking factory gave us *David Copperfield*.

- **Pause** To form a memory, hit the brakes. Notice where you are.
- **Stimulation** A filled interval feels longer than silence because it triggers extra brain activity.
- **Listen to slow music**
- **Unfamiliarity** The brain works harder in unfamiliar situations, seeking clues. Journeys on unknown roads seem to last eons, with no familiar landmarks to anchor expectations or progress. Hence those fretful back-seat chirrups: 'Are we nearly there yet?'

To accelerate time:

- **Do many things, simultaneously, and badly** Time will seem fast, although you will be slow.
- **Be happy** Later you can revel in the memories.
- **Be late** The panic will make the clock speed up – unless you are one of those relaxed types who tend to stroll rather than run late.
- **Be busy** You need not even be busy yourself: just find a bustling place.
- **Drink coffee** As Hungarian mathematician Alfréd Rényi wrote, 'A mathematician is a device for turning coffee into theorems.' He could have been talking about his collaborator and fellow caffeine addict Paul Erdős, who wrote 1,500 mathematical papers in his lifetime (his nearest rival produced 823).
- **See red** Not only do we feel warmer in red rooms, but time appears faster, and our reaction times decrease. Many fast-food restaurants favour this colour in their

branded livery because it makes us eat faster too. It also encourages us to think faster. Presumably this is why Sir Isaac Newton's London home boasted only crimson furniture (a mohair bed, matching bed-curtains, hangings and settee). The flipside of red is that it shortens our fuse (Newton was a notorious grump). On location making his first colour film, *The Red Desert*, Michelangelo Antonioni noticed that after he painted a factory canteen red, the real workers using it grew agitated. Fights broke out. As soon as the shoot finished it was repainted pastel green, so 'the workers' eyes could have a rest'. Calm resumed.

- **Make your days a daisy chain of habits** You need never notice a thing.
- **Listen to fast music**
- **Enthusiasm** Engage with what you are doing and time speeds up.
- **Go online** What do you remember afterwards?
- **Familiarity**
- **Deadlines** Is it that time already?

WHAT NOW? A FLEETING BIOGRAPHY
OF THE PRESENT

'Out of your whole life give but one moment!' Robert Browning begs his lover in the impassioned poem 'Now'. A modest enough request, until he specifies the terms and conditions. His beloved should condense all 'thought and feeling and soul and sense' into a single eternal instant, in order to assure him that for 'this tick of our lifetime's one moment you love me!'

The complexity Browning describes is an accurate rendering of all that must merge into this strange moment we call now. Of the many tricks played by the human mind, its slyest ruse is our seemingly seamless stream of consciousness.

We imagine that we hear, see, taste and touch simultaneously. But our sensory data processing systems run at slightly different speeds, each relaying information to the frontal lobe at a different rate. The frontal lobe is your brain's CEO, responsible for command, control and forecasting. Synthesizing sensory information is the initial task; then it must decide what to do next, be it to swat a fly or bite into a burger.

Despite these impressive neurological acrobatics, nobody notices disorientating time lags in this moment that we call now. Neuroscientists are still debating how the brain confects this smooth-flowing illusion. Probably it takes sensory snapshot after snapshot, little slices of time, splicing them together like frames in a movie reel. Each frame spans a tenth to a fifth of a second – the time it takes a burst of electricity to travel a circuit of brain cells. Events occurring within this timeframe seem to happen simultaneously;

anything slower appears consecutive, anything faster and our senses cannot discern it sequentially. We see smeared spokes instead of a spinning wheel, a blur, not the hummingbird's wings, and the flying bullet is invisible.

Sequence is itself a mystery. Pry into the brain's secrets on an EEG and it is clear that even the perception of an intention – say, to scratch your nose – is only registered consciously milliseconds after your motor neurons have issued their command. You think you are making the decision after you have instructed your finger to go ahead and scratch.

What does this mean? That consciousness is created after the event. In other words, your sense of now is always historic. Technically it is impossible to be fully in the moment.

Fortunately the duration of this moment that you and I call now is a mite more generous than the tens of milliseconds electrical signals take to circuit brain cells. Neuroscientist Ernst Pöppel defined now as the 'window of the subjective present' – meaning the period of time that you can bob along in a full state of awareness about what is going on in and around you, before the present moment leaves your short-term memory to be filed into the past – or forgotten. Extensive experimental studies suggest that this window – your right now of being alive – is open for three seconds.

Three seconds sounds a meagre platform from which to savour the miracle of existence. On the other hand, it is how long astrophysicists estimate it took the universe to go from unfathomable nothingness to the Big Bang and then to the first manifestation of matter.

An astounding array of human actions fit into three-second blocks. For instance, the hugs of gold medallists in 2008's summer Olympics, celebrating victory with their loved ones, almost always took this long. A study of three far-flung indigenous tribes – the Himba of northern Namibia, the Yanomami of the Amazon, and the Trobriander, who dwell on coral atolls off New Guinea – compared a huge variety of 1,542 action units of two different types: working processes and hand-to-body movements (pounding grain, say). Of these, 93 per cent took two to three seconds. On the other hand, find a surface and try to tap a beat with intervals of four or more seconds, and it is not sustainable.

Three seconds is roughly how long it takes to recite a line of our finest poems, from William Shakespeare's 'Shall I compare thee to a summer's day?' to W.H. Auden's masterpiece of grief: 'Stop all the clocks, cut off the telephone'. Iambic pentameter, the ten-beat, three-second soul of English verse ('te-tum-te-tum-te-tum-te-tum-te-tum'), is popular because it echoes the rhythms of life: the drumbeat of the heart, and the three seconds for which we can comfortably speak. Even in silence, at rest, we breathe once every three to four seconds.

Oxygen is the food of life. How perfect that your respiratory cycle should frame your experience, moment by moment. This now, which your brain furiously fashions between each hug, each burst of song, is the gift of your conscious present.

4

It's Not Working

How overload, digital distractions,
productivity myths and time-poor
thinking addict us to hurry

Time out. What do these words mean to you? A listings
magazine (until Google killed it)? An ineffective sanction for
a brat your granny would have smacked? Your answer will
depend upon your age. But for most, time out is an unsettling
euphemism. You hear it from the man whose relationship is
over but is not ready to accept it, or the burnout whose
bashed-up bicycle of a career has tumbled into a ravine, but
who prefers to call it a sabbatical.

The truth is that we all need time out, yet many fear to
take it. This is a pity. The developed world enjoys unprece-
dented comfort; anyone old enough to recall the 1930s
chuckles to hear people with free medical care, dentistry and
television gripe about poverty. But our zest for life is flagging.
In 2013 the UK Office for National Statistics revealed that
depression and anxiety affect one in five adults. Half the
respondents to a 2014 YouGov poll reported that they were

more anxious than they used to be, saying anxiety had stopped them from doing what they wanted in life. Perhaps this is because life is not quite turning out as advertised.

At my school, teachers predicted a leisurely twenty-first century. Drudgery would be taken care of by kindly butler robots not unlike *Star Wars*' C3PO, as unmanned assembly lines spewed consumer goods. Meanwhile happy adult us would do inspiring things in service industries, when not on four-day weekends.

As it turns out, technology and globalization are rewriting the script for what work can be, but the tale is one of widening inequality. Society is increasingly divided between the time rich but resource poor, and the time-poor work rich, who are also, all too often, resource poor. This chapter explores how pressures and digital distractions feed a time-poor mentality that makes us rush – and why everything then gets worse.

1. Overloaded: the myth of more from less

On 25 December 2015, in a company dormitory of Dentsu, Japan's largest advertising agency, Matsuri Takahashi took her life. It was the twenty-four-year-old trainee's eighth month in employment. That December alone she had logged a hundred hours' overtime, despite having already complained of being 'mentally and physically shattered'. The coroner classed her fate not as suicide but as *karoshi* – 'death from overwork'.

Takahashi's story seized public attention; not because it was unique, but as an especially tragic emblem of a growing trend. In 2016 the government estimated that *karoshi* claimed two thousand lives to suicide each year, excluding workers suffering strokes, heart attacks and other stress-related illness. Twelve months after Takahashi's death, Dentsu's president Tadashi Ishii stood down as prosecutors began investigating the company for criminal abuses.

This young woman's despair resonates beyond her predicament, beyond Japan. It is echoed in the death of British teacher Laurian Bold, who leapt to her death from a viaduct after temporary promotion brought an overwhelming workload, with demands made on her at home even after she signed off sick. To some it seemed a mockery of such concerns when Goldman Sachs, the investment bank, announced in June 2015 that interns' workday would be capped at seventeen hours (leaving by midnight, not arriving before 7 a.m.) – but possibly not to the 2,600 youngsters girding themselves to join the bank that summer. This announcement followed the discovery of Moritz Erhardt, twenty-one, collapsed in a shower after working seventy-two hours straight at Bank of America Merrill Lynch. His death was attributed to seizures triggered by exhaustion.

These cases are unusual, canaries from the coalface of extreme work. But culturally driven busyness is rife in all countries and sectors of society, at all pay grades, and it is doing our heads in. There are multiple causes. The grab-and-go imperatives of investors who are seeking fast returns drive down the benefits of employment. As a result of this productivity push our human capital is being downgraded, harming our productivity as individuals. More is asked of workers for less. As pensions vanish, zero-hours contracts multiply, requiring that their signatories be available to work without the guarantee of so much as a dime – a one-way loyalty that embodies the short-termist direction of the economy. Perhaps the thinking is that seeing as there are plenty of grunts, why not squeeze us? If so, how blinkered; businesses consist of human actions, so the fleeter and better aimed those actions, the more productive – as opposed to tired, panicked and inefficient.

Flexitime, oft vaunted as liberation, is frequently one-sided. Tina works part-time at a daycare nursery, but is routinely – with a few hours' notice – asked to stay late, throwing her daughters' childcare into disarray: 'Last week I had to stay until nine, however long it took, to do a deep clean – not the cleaners, they have to pay them. They won't pay me. I'm forced to take it as time off in lieu. Only, when I asked they said I can't book it until everybody else has taken their year's holiday.'

Tina never retrieved her time or any extra wages. A similar story emerged from clothing company ASOS, where warehouse employees received little warning before hours were added to their shifts – the time being compulsorily logged into a 'flex bank', to be paid months in the future, if at all.

Disdain for zero-hours practices is widespread. But nobody considers it scandalous if a senior employee's contract demands 365-day flexibility, hours to be worked 'according to the business's needs'. Such a clause is the price of success. The more we are paid, the more employers expect, and faster – with the return on their investment displayed in long visible hours or emails answered at midnight, in whatever time zone a client may be.

Performance should be assessed by judgement – a product of rest and reflection – but this is hard to measure. Instead managers fixate on time, and micromanaging it. After all, demonstrable commitment, bowed before the holy laptop, is easy to measure. Homicidal working hours are justified in the interests of productivity – a claim undercut by the fact that sprawling days deplete our focus, creating a sensation of slack that can sap momentum. For instance, student doctors see more patients on nine-hour shifts than on twelve-hour ones. Whereas pressure on the NHS saw errors, such as operating on the wrong body part, more than double between 2013–14 and 2015–16. So when the UK government threatens to sack GPs unless they offer a daily twelve-hour service, we may face a different kind of health crisis, due to those depleted human resources.

Technology heightens pressures – not least the prospect that it will replace us. In 2016 Mark Carney, Governor of the Bank of England, claimed that fifteen million UK jobs will be ceded to automation (and around 57 per cent of jobs across the OECD, according to research by Citi and Oxford University). Already, thanks to supposedly time-saving devices, 28 per cent of an average worker's week is absorbed by email. And it often feels like more, because these devices disrupt our flow, locking us into reactive cycles: we respond too fast, trying to wring sense from others' hasty verbiage, instead of doing something that resembles solid work.

Tellingly, according to a 2014 poll one third of British employees do not use all their holiday entitlement. Another survey in 2015 found that three in ten logged into work email on holiday. Four in ten regretted taking holidays, so great was the pile-up that met their return. The market leader in work–home bleed is the United States, the world's leading economy. Research in 2013 revealed that 81 per cent of workers monitored office email at weekends, more than half doing so after 11 p.m. any day; 59 per cent checked in while on vacation. Although an average US employee receives just two weeks' paid leave plus nine national holidays – well below the average in Europe – one in four felt guilty taking their full allocation in 2014.

Work creep is greatest among millennials, too young to remember the days before we were so accessible. Guilt about taking holidays is at 40 per cent among younger employees, compared to 18 per cent of baby boomers. In the UK, twenty-five- to thirty-four-year-olds are likeliest to contact the office while on holiday. Evidently the kids of the swinging 1960s did not pass on the gene for tuning out to their children.

If the members of the wired-up generation feel the greatest pressure to be available, they also need to work the most, with no expectation of plump baby boomer pensions if ever they retire. Feeling haunted by incomplete tasks thickens the miasma of unpredictability and uncertainty, of constantly running to catch up: the essence of anxiety. Uncertainty is, by definition, unmanageable; attempting to micromanage it away only makes it worse. Then switching off gets harder. And we wonder why anxiety is highest among the young?

There is, however, another possibility: that we cling to our jobs not out of anxiety but because we love work more than previous generations. Want to consider it?

Maybe not. Yet a strong love of work is eminently desirable. It makes me laugh that 'Great job!' – an expression I never heard once in my childhood – is now a reflex term of parental praise. Stand in a city park and you will be amazed to learn what a job consists of: flinging wet sand, sitting on a swing, dropping a lolly stick into a bin. This phrase, though wonderfully encouraging, smacks of indoctrination. After all, if today work is tough, parents can guess how it will be by 2050, when postmen are extinct and the treetops buzz with delivery drones. Tomorrow's jobseekers shall need reservoirs of eagerness, skill, willpower and concentration. Perhaps this is why we boast of our long working days. Time poverty is the only form of impotence we are proud of, trapped as we are on our accelerating treadmills, blind to the diminishing returns.

Hurry is lonely. Long working days are lonely. Emotions hit harder, flare faster, if we are alone (a little-known fact that helps to explain the rancid mob voice so often heard online). But humanity evolved in groups. We need other people to moderate our feelings, to laugh with us and hug away our sorrows. Sadly, stress severs us from those who could relieve it: like a friend's husband, whose preoccupation with a business deal made her fear for his mind. When the deal was at last completed, he resurfaced. His reward was to lose his job.

Worrying about time disorganizes and rushes us. Relentless time pressure causes chronic stress. Overdose and we can believe, like Matsuri Takahashi, that we will never feel better.

A medical qualification is unnecessary to predict the penalties of overload. What is less obvious is how stress and distractions both grow addictive, sending us scurrying into the self-defeating hurry trap.

How digital distractions addict us to rush

Blame our restless ancestors for your distractibility. They migrated across the globe, managing to pass on their DNA by being alert, sensation-seeking survivors. The slightest change in their habitat represented a potential threat, food or pleasure, so their brains were highly responsive to any novelty. Thanks to them, you have been bequeathed a neurochemical rewards system that is rigged to addict you to distractions.

Distractibility has upsides. It lets you sift the data streaming via your senses and monitor many things at once: you can follow conversation in a bar; smell the toast burning; hear the rumbling tidal wave, and, with any luck, your brain's knowledge base will deliver the instruction to drop everything and scram. But the downside is that when you encounter something new – even the quiver of a muted smartphone – your attention will be hijacked.

Hear the ping notification for a text and your brain secretes dopamine, the happiness neurotransmitter: an alert to novelty. This feels good: you want to read that text. But your brain readily habituates to it and your dopamine receptors soon clamour for another shot, for a newer novelty, a higher dose, faster and faster! Welcome to your dopamine loop. Stuck in it, you will tend to grab any resource, food or data as if it were your last.

Often when you text or email you are also hunched, unconsciously holding your breath or breathing shallowly.

This creates an oxygen shortfall, sending your body into the stress response of fight-or-flight mode. In this state, you again tend to grab at any resource, food or data as if it were your last …

It is bad if you are running for your life. It is worse if you are inert, stranded on a neurochemical plateau, bathed in stress with no physical means to burn it off.

The collision of hooking technology with your hookable primate brain explains why you can lie in bed for hours massaging a square of glass, forgetting the person beside you, and why secondary renderings of other people's lives on Twitter, Snapchat or Instagram can compel you more than your own.

Next time you see someone itching to check their smartphone, realize that you are witnessing an addict in need of a fix. Intelligence is no protection against this vice. A Cambridge University professor told me that rising numbers of fidgety-fingered undergraduates seek dispensations to sit tests in unpressured, non-exam conditions, in deference to the trauma of being cut off from their social support systems for whole hours at a time. In South Korea, proudly the world's most hooked-up country, transfixed online gamers, deaf to their body's hunger and thirst cues, so lose their time sense that they collapse at their consoles.

The distraction epidemic is a sickness, yet like victims of a neurochemical Stockholm syndrome, we adore that which imprisons us. We become besotted by the instant, craving each ping of our smartphone and its delicious jolt of self-importance, reassuring us that we are on it and in demand. Hey presto: we are addicted to the buzz of bogus busyness! Until we notice that we are running late, and we panic.

....

2. In flight mode, going nowhere: how time poverty makes us stupid

The staggeringly consistent correlation between a city's size and its citizens' pace is a marvel of social science. No matter what continent or culture, the larger a place, the faster its citizens scuttle. It seems less surprising when you consider how the brain gauges time from environmental cues, adjusting our pace accordingly. If a lot is going on around us, this sensory blizzard creates an impression that time itself is rushing by, swishing and stomping and tooting its horn in an agitation of cars, trousers and feet.

What is a person to do facing such a monster but hurry up?

When time is short, the sage response is to use time judiciously. Unfortunately time pressure seldom makes good judges of us. All salesmen know time pressure is the whip to a daft decision: 'Hurry up, while stocks last …' We buy and do silly things if rushed, because a scarcity mentality overtakes us. It happens if anything is in short supply, studies have found. Whether you suffer poverty or a lack of confidence or time, the stress associated with that limited resource renders you impulsive, less able either to act in your long-term interests or to live in the mirthful moment. Yes, scarcity makes us stupid.

The impact of today's busyness is similar to what happens when we gorge on fast food – the stuff that heaps on calories yet leaves us wanting more. Just as fast food is obesogenic, acceleration is rushogenic. Trick yourself into feeling time poor and instinctively you crave more time, rushing, chasing, and in the process losing something vital. Like *Alice in Wonderland*'s watch-fixated white rabbit, derided by its creator Lewis Carroll: 'His whole air [should] suggest a total inability to say "Boo" to a goose.'

In rush, as in fear, your sense of time also changes. At an extreme, you enter fight-or-flight mode. This leads to cognitive tunnelling – in other words, your attention zooms in on what is before you and whatever looks helpful. This is ideal in an emergency, if, like Captain Hart Dyke in the last chapter, you need to escape a burning ship. But if time stress becomes your daily normal, everything may begin to resemble an emergency – changing you and your outlook on time. You might become panicky, over-hasty, like emergency room doctors who inadvertently miss steps on diagnostic checklists. You might even feel less yourself; tunnels are lonely places.

Let hurry contract your mental horizon to the immediate interests of the present and your moral bandwidth narrows too. In 1973 psychological researchers set out to discover what personality traits would predict kindness. Inspired by the New Testament parable in which a priest and a Levite hasten past a sick man, but a Samaritan stops to help, they recruited some trainee priests at Princeton's seminary to be guinea pigs. Test subjects completed a questionnaire about their religious outlook, then were sent to another building to write a speech: either about seminary jobs or the Samaritan parable. Some were told they were running late, others that they had a few minutes but should head over. Then came the real test. In an alley between the buildings, a man slumped, moaning and coughing.

Researchers predicted that planting 'helping thoughts' in subjects' minds (according to the theme of their prospective speech) would make no difference to the seminarians' response. But having plenty of time, or having a spiritual outlook based on a search for meaning (as revealed by the questionnaire), would incline them to stop for the sick man. The results amazed them.

As expected, the seminarians who were late walked on by. Some even climbed over the coughing body, so anxious were they to write their Good Samaritan speech! By contrast, those not in a hurry stopped to help. But, shockingly, their spiritual compass altered their conduct not a jot. Whether training for the priesthood out of spirituality or ambition, time pressure alone determined their kindness or indifference.

These lapsed Samaritans explain the statistic that the inhabitants of fast-paced cities are the least likely to be helpful. You can see why; moving through such an environment is an obstacle race. It also suggests a mischievous answer to a great mystery: why do the rich get richer? Answer: because the more money you have, the more value you place on each hour, the more time-pressed you feel – and therefore, the less generous. Such selfishness grows wealth.

Sadly time poverty, too, breeds more of itself. No matter if you are mistaken – if you only *feel* busy because you are disorganized or fritter time on addictive dross, or imagine you are always working solely because you compulsively check your office email. If you believe that you are time poor, then across this narrowed mental horizon will gallop the two horsemen of self-sabotage, impulsiveness and anxiety. This will make you abundantly less capable of rejoicing in the present, or acting in your future interests. Disabling panic will do it. Habits of deferral often come of being over-whelmed. See a hundred emails in your inbox and you may well scan them fast, hazing your mind in worries, promising to deal with them later.

Graver time theft comes if unpredictable, uncontrollable stress leads to heart problems. Not coincidentally, the citizens of fast-paced countries have elevated levels of coronary disease. But this may not be the worst that could happen.

Brain scans reveal that sustained stress impairs the neurological area devoted to goal-focused decisions and actions. Meanwhile, it enhances the part of the brain in charge of forming habits. Feel swamped and we release neurochemicals that incline us to rash, addictive behaviour: dopamine, epinephrine, noradrenaline.

'Thus, the part of the brain that enables creative problem solving becomes less available the more we need it,' wrote behavioural psychologist Walter Mischel, an expert in self-control. He devised the legendary 'marshmallow test'. In it, four-year-old children sat alone in a room at a table with a sweet on it. If they could wait ten minutes without eating the sweet they were promised two. Interestingly, those best able to resist went on in future years to perform better academically and become emotionally balanced adults.

Self-restraint, the capacity to take a long view, is invaluable, but is difficult to exercise when you rush, for the same reason that when you hurry, time appears to fly: you lack presence of mind. A sense of time, such a serviceable by-product of consciousness, is only created if the brain has space to do so. Without space, any form of control is difficult.

Spend a morning simultaneously attempting to email your boss, cook, wipe, brush and dress, all the while preventing a five-year-old from Lego-skating to a cranial fracture, and at the same time listening to the news and cajoling a small, unaccountable being with negotiating skills drawn from the Robert Mugabe playbook into socks that she deems the wrong shade of blue, and you will need to pace yourself with external sources of information: the ping of an egg timer, the crash of a half-empty cereal bowl, or somebody yelling 'We are late. Again!' Because it is suddenly a quarter past eight and you are still in pyjamas. And still you will wonder, where did the time go? Because a stressed brain, even a calm one, flounders if it tries to hold more than a few thoughts concurrently.

How often do you ask yourself to do too much? Work on multiple projects, or try to cook, talk, pin a thought on the wing *and* remember what your boss said that was so important? Every day? This is the cognitive equivalent of clapping your hands while cartwheeling, or masturbating while placing a stock deal – and potentially as hazardous. Perhaps you are prone to what attention deficit hyperactivity disorder (ADHD) expert Edward Hallowell calls 'screen sucking', to multitasking and idea hopping. Or what time-management guru Carson Tate dubbed 'popcorn' brain: forgetting tasks, only to remember them when you cannot act. These are all signs of overstretch.

Effectiveness and common sense, like time sense, require mind space. Despite this, multitasking is taken to be the benchmark of efficiency. The proverb goes: 'Want a job done? Give it to a busy person.' We fail to appreciate how sizeable an ask this is.

Considerable cognitive energy and time is required to lasso a train of thought and put it back on track. 'Switching from one task to another is effortful, especially under time pressure,' wrote Nobel laureate Daniel Kahneman in *Thinking, Fast and Slow.* 'Any task that requires you to keep several ideas in mind at the same time has the same hurried character.' To sustain a train of thought is harder at high velocity:

> Accelerating beyond my strolling speed completely
> changes the experience of walking ... [bringing] about
> a sharp deterioration in my ability to think coherently.
> As I speed up, my attention is drawn with increasing
> frequency to the experience of walking and to the
> deliberate maintenance of the faster pace.

What does this mean for wired-up workers lumbered with unpredictable, complicated workloads? In particular, for those whose projects require linear steps, but who are buffeted by wayward, interruptive work patterns?

Professor Gloria Mark, an expert in digital distraction, estimated that the average employee only concentrates for three minutes before something tugs their mental thread. Multitaskers commit double the errors, taking 30 per cent longer to accomplish tasks tackled in parallel, than if focusing on single tasks, sequentially. Yet they imagine that they are working even longer than that, because distracted time feels fuller. This is the ultimate example of getting less from more – and it is deeply demoralizing. Worse, when morale is low, we are even more distractible, and it costs. A 2005 study by productivity researchers Basex estimated that distractions and recovery time ate 28 per cent of a knowledge worker's day (an amount equivalent to twenty-eight billion working hours in the US alone – and this in an era before distractions such as unnecessary emails were redefined as work, long before Facebook and Snapchat). But check emails or social media at work, as many do, and 60 per cent of us will clean forget what we were doing before.

This is how, day by day, work seems harder and slower, and then we try to compensate by rushing, only to get stuck on an accelerating treadmill.

3. Pandemonium and other attacks on the will

We say we want to escape the noise. What we mean is that we feel overwhelmed. Noise is our preferred metaphor for today's busy because speed and sound have identical effects: both excite us and both exert cognitive pressure.

In *Paradise Lost* John Milton invented the word 'pandemonium' (from Greek *pan* – all – and *daimon*) to refer to a place of demons. As a blind poet, he had a peerless insight into the torments of superfluous sound. Torturers understand this well too; this is why they melt minds with thrash metal, which handily leaves no bruises. Oddly, office designers and managers seem impervious to such facts.

The fashion for open-plan design is the great time-bin of our time. Staff crammed around scrums of desks are urged to welcome synergies, to be inspired. This is a partial truth. Ambient noise in a café, for instance, can stimulate interesting ideas – which is useful for a creative phase or task. (If too far from a brewhouse, you could avail yourself of synthetic mental wallpaper at https://coffitivity.com.) White noise machines can also prevent our brains from locking onto distractions – and that is good for filtering traffic noise if your bedroom faces the road. But when we need to focus attention, hubbub is the enemy. According to Professor Dylan Jones, soft background sound reduces concentration by 20 per cent. Constant noise weakens our ability to pay attention full stop.

The threat of working in a distracting environment is that your voluntary attention (the ability to direct your thoughts by will) is disabled when your involuntary attention is constantly baited. To understand why, think of willpower as a time-sensitive muscle. It withers as the day goes by, and with it so does your concentration span, even your tolerance. Anything that requires you to exercise willpower – whether you are continually refocusing your attention after being interrupted, or trying to ignore your hungry stomach – drains your self-control. For such reasons, when researchers from Ben-Gurion University documented the decisions of eight Israeli parole-board judges over a ten-month period they found a consistent pattern. At the start of the day, two-thirds of applications were granted. This number plunged to nearly zero by the first of the day's food breaks. Afterwards approvals rose close to the initial rate, then began sinking once more until the next snack. It is an eerie echo of the way we register an intention – say, to scratch our leg – only *after* our brain has issued the instruction to our finger. In the matter of grave, life-changing decisions, conducted by people who are supposedly experts in judgement, it appears that reasoned arguments are often *post-hoc rationalizations* – what precedes them, shaping our opinions, is our emotional, animal state.

So willpower, like attention, like generosity, decays faster the more you pressurize or exert it – whether by resisting interruptions or maintaining your temper when you are feeling hungry. As it weakens, you grow more distractible and irritable. Now add another stressor to the mix: you are late. Next stop, panic. Then fast will not seem fast enough. If ever you find yourself heckling the car in front when it takes four seconds to move off at a green light, you know what I am talking about.

Daunting challenges lie ahead of us. As the landscape of time evolves, as distractions thicken and grow more efficient at co-opting our attention, will we become less generous human beings, more agitated, more instant-thirsty, more prone to rage?

Hurry makes anxious short-termists of the holiest of us. Pray it does not make you stupid.

Why willpower is weak and how to build it

Psychologists explain why willpower weakens over time using the concept of ego-depletion. It is a grim expression: I picture a loudmouth boasting at a party, his head puffed like a balloon, slowly leaking hot air. What it means is that when we are doing something difficult, our conscious self (the ego) must enforce it. Having spent willpower on one challenge (such as refusing a biscuit), we then have less resistance for the next (such as carrying on working), because our tested ego cries out for a reward.

So take care which battles of will you pick. If you stifle a craving to watch *CSI*, automatically it will be harder to say no to the offered cigarette or to spend another hour crunching numbers. For such reasons, large supermarkets often locate cakes, confectionery and ice cream at the labyrinth's end. Having exerted self-control at the start – buying virtuous vegetables, bypassing refrigerated desserts – by the end, as the yummy aromas of baking waft around us, we are ready to tank up on fat and sugar.

Overstress your willpower and your self-confidence suffers, because however mighty your self-control, a lapse will seem more significant. As pioneering psychologist Alexander Bain concluded in *The Emotions and the Will* (1859), 'every gain on the wrong side undoes the effect of many conquests on the right'. This is why, if an alcoholic does not drink for a hundred days, he is pleased, but one slip from the wagon is a catastrophe, and the excuse for a binge.

Distractions present a constant attack on willpower and, with it, character. This makes sense of a now frequent news story: the parent amazed by their suddenly delightful child, after a smartphone has been confiscated. Tomorrow's children, immured by tablet screens, will need help to grow their will if they are to have staying power.

Willpower is only as strong as the ego. To enhance yours:

1. **Be kind to yourself.** In studies, children given specific, descriptive praise persist longer at tasks than those who do not. Bad behaviour improves.
2. **Simplify life.** Limit the demands made on you.
3. **Build your capacity to concentrate.** But do it gently.
4. **Eat, sleep, be merry.** Distractions have less power over us if we are comfortable.
5. **Budget how you spend it.** See willpower as a limited currency and less time will bleed away on fatuity, like keeping your temper because you are so damned stressed.

WORK-LIFE BALANCE

Work-life balance. Are these words designed to make us feel inadequate?

Am I not already like a circus plate spinner, on a pogo stick, in a gale, with jelly being flung at me, as I bend and twist trying to juggle the conflicting wants, needs and schedules of this, my wonderful life? (Which I *love*, because mothers do not moan, lest somebody take our children into care or remind us how lucky we are to have them, *and at our age*.)

Work-life balance is a cliché uttered as a self-evident truth, but it is just a metaphor, and not an old one. Its origins are instructive. Coined in the late 1970s in the United Kingdom, it debuted in print in a paper entitled *New Ways to Work and the Working Mothers Association in the United Kingdom*. The issue under discussion was mothers going out to work.

Whether or not the authors realized it, the implication was that such a fate was equivalent to death. You could see the concept as a memorial to another death: of a fantasy. Namely, that women could ever afford *not* to undertake paid employment. But the sole breadwinner household has been unsustainable for most people, for most of history, aside from a creepy phase in the twentieth century. More often women either worked or starved (think of governess Jane Eyre or the hard-scrabble fortune hunters in Jane Austen novels).

Whatever its authors' intentions, the expression landed on US lips in 1986 and steadily spread, democratically making everyone – from retirees to students, workers to stay-at-home parents, grannies to

122

gymnasts and quite possibly monks – fear they might be failing to get this mysterious balance right.

The difficulty with this prescription for a happy life is what does a work-life balance look like? Picture this precarious balancing act and you might see yourself on life's tightrope, like a milkmaid: yoke across your neck, slop bucket either end, one marked 'life', the other 'work'. But does this mean that work is somehow equivalent to death?

Behind this idea squats the assumption that life consists of two opposed activities, work and leisure – another belief that feels like a timeless truth but is in reality a fairly recent cultural development.

Perhaps you congratulate yourself that your working lot beats that of a medieval peasant. But compare holiday entitlement and he probably had more. In fifteenth-century France one in four days was an official holiday – a medley of religious ceremony and public merriment – excluding the days of feasting and foolery set aside for marriages, funerals, saints' days. (Check out *The Peasant Wedding* by Pieter Brueghel the Elder for an idea.) One sixteenth-century parish spent a week and a half celebrating its new church.

Such jolly scenes began to fade when John Calvin (1509–64), a glum French Protestant, began banging the drum for the Christian doctrine of work. His horribly successful thesis was that we could slough off the shame of Adam and Eve's original sin by working our way to paradise. Just one catch – no amount of graft could be enough to earn God's grace.

The Protestant work ethic had lift-off. Not coincidentally, as Barbara Ehrenreich points out in *Dancing in the Streets*, the nature of free time in Europe changed. As puritanism blossomed, suicide went up, theatres closed, maypoles were burnt to ashes, dance and song were banned. Leisure became less communal and unruly, pleasure increasingly suspect.

Before the puritans, time had a seasonal swing, pivoting around festivals – cyclical high points that exerted a strong emotional pull and set off weeks of excited preparation. This capacious, merry-go-round type of time was replaced by seven-day-week time – six days on, one day off; a flat tempo that summoned 'the modern notion of time as even in quality as opposed to the primitive sense of time's unevenness and irregularity', wrote historian Keith Thomas. Time was manageable; indeed it was something to micromanage.

The division between work and pleasurable life was consolidated by industrialization in the mid-1800s, as Europe's weekend streets reeled with factory labourers, carousing in pubs during their scant time off. Meanwhile the gentleman class cultivated elegant, white-gloved pursuits, the better to display that their hands were unsullied by earning money. Puritan working values followed the Pilgrim Fathers to the United States, infusing the DNA of the American dream. Many cultures are wedded to the binary assumption that work and productivity are the opposite of relaxation and pleasure. Life is segregated between joyous, naughty hours and grinding work. What an effective way to drain enthusiasm for one of the most important activities in life.

Many, not only working parents, tussle with the tension between how we actually spend time and how we feel we should. Some hold a candle for a fantasy – of a decorative domestic angel, like her Victorian counterpart, tending home and brood with a permasmile, all the while breathing gently in her corset, Spanx or toned torso. Working parents who repudiate guilt may yet feel, if not torn in two, then pummelled by logistics and demands. Ideally life is not about dividing yourself in two. But if work and home clash – or there is no boundary between them – serving two masters becomes a tug of war.

Thinking about work-life balance is useful not because it offers an answer but because it prods us into doubts, reminding us that daily time choices deserve attention.

Is a 50–50 split between work and leisure achievable – or desirable? Only you can say. Seek a one-size-fits-all recipe for living and you will sooner find a crock of gold in Poundland.

Four-hour work week or fourteen-hour labour day? Arguably the former indicates greater productivity, although government policy quants and line managers may demur.

Those seeking inspiration might look to Australian singer-songwriter Sia, who has confected chart-busters in as little as fourteen minutes, scarcely longer than some of her tracks. (If such a ratio between input and output seems preposterous, add a few months per hit, since she spent years investigating heartbreak and addiction as she honed her lyrical craft.) Or to novelist Joyce Carol Oates, well into a century of published books. She once denied being 'fanatic or obsessive' (although her editor said: 'Wherever she is, she's writing. In cars, in airports, on planes, if she's at a party and no one's talking to her she's writing').

If you enjoy desk-epics, carry on. But try not to be a schedule flunky, locked in a doomed race with runaway to-do lists. How much better work could be if it felt like play.

5

The Good, the Bad and the Ugly of Procrastination

And how to stop

Compulsive procrastinator Leonardo da Vinci called impatience 'the mother of stupidity':

> Men are in error when they lament the flight of time,
> accusing it of being too swift, and not perceiving that
> it is sufficient as it passes.

He would say that, wouldn't he? An artist whose legacy numbers but fifteen paintings, not to mention notebooks littered with discoveries that sowed no seed in the development of science because he never got around to publishing them, can hardly be deemed an authority on time management. Or can he?

Leonardo's dallying incensed his patrons, denied us masterpieces and dismayed the man himself, yet it was not unjustified. He lived in an age of feuding princes, plague and war. Strife and interruptions were inevitable. But the root of his problem was the walkabout nature of his genius.

Way beyond art, his interests roamed from maps to music, dams to philosophy, anatomy to aeronautics, architecture to war. Outstandingly innovative, surviving on four hours' sleep a night, he designed everything from churches to flying machines to the largest equestrian statue ever – but sadly none were made (the bronze his then employer, Ludovico il Moro, set aside for the horse ended up as cannonballs). Despite this litany of stillborn potential, he produced many marvels, including an ambulant mechanical lion with a bouquet of lilies that burst from its chest, and the *Mona Lisa*, between four and thirteen years in the creation and an enduring object of fascination five centuries on. More work might have survived had he experimented less with new-fangled paint. But what remains is breathtaking.

Would he have done better to focus, the acme of twenty-first-century praise? People of 'genius', his first biographer Giorgio Vasari remarked, 'sometimes accomplish most when they work the least, for they are thinking out inventions and forming in their minds the perfect idea'. Waywardness laid his path to perfection.

Leonardo personifies procrastination's two faces: it can be a creative force but it inhibits productivity. If you share his habits of delay but not his gifts, you may strain to sort the good from the bad and the downright ugly. I certainly have. And the situation has changed. In Leonardo's day, it was a relatively high-class problem – in his case, a symptom of rare talents and the resources they brought. Our rushogenic era is ripe for an epidemic of procrastination. Who needs a wayward imagination? Just buy a TV. Make it a smartphone, and a godlike ability to surf the world's wonders is yours.

The rise and rise of procrastination is traced in a study by Professor Piers Steel. In 1978, 5 per cent of the population were chronic procrastinators. By 2007, the figure had risen to 26 per cent. With the subsequent escalation in distractions, the proportion of inveterate timewasters today must be, if still a minority, a significant one. Steel estimated that, even back in 2007 – a dark age before the credit crunch or Instagram, as smartphones began to take off – social media taxed businesses $70 billion a year in lost productivity. Today, one dreads to think.

Let us concentrate on what procrastination costs you. Can you count the daily minutes that vaporize in tangents? If they are too many to number, this chapter is dedicated to you.

1. Tortoise or hare? How to tell if you are a procrastinator

Procrastinators are skilled at self-deception. So do not dismiss the possibility that you share my vice.

Do you ever delay things that you ought – you know – to crack on with?

The best way to beat this impulse is to intercept it. So ask yourself: 'If I do not do X now, then when?'

Can you spin a ready yarn of answers?

Congratulations. You have a fine working knowledge of procrastination and its defensive technique, spurious rationalization. Here are further clues: do you find time booby-trapped? Do you fail to meet goals that looked viable a month ago? Do you dart from idea to idea? Do you never get around to making plans for your most heartfelt desires? If so, the odds are that you are one of us.

Procrastinators tell themselves they are creative, original, intellectual adventurers, yet their patterns are predictable. A six-year study by Robert Boice tracked 104 new professors and diagnosed the telltale signs. Efficient professors worked regular, steady hours, skilfully predicting and planning projects. But chronic procrastinators binged, showed consistently poor judgement in allocating time, claiming 'I work better under pressure'. Many started at the last moment, undertook too little research and found it difficult to structure effort, so feeble was their grasp on how long work would take, devoting less effort to what they could do well at than work likely to fail. Like the hare in Aesop's fable, they soon lagged behind their steadier colleagues, producing less, to less acclaim.

Boice broke down chronic procrastination into six traits:

1. Hectic busyness, rash rushing.
2. Putting product orientation (dwelling on the quantity of work produced) before process orientation (how it is produced).
3. Anxiety (being easily distracted, tense, fidgety).
4. Unrealistic expectations about how work will get done.
5. Hostility to methods for imposing order or punctuality.
6. Disappointing results.

These depressing tendencies are also what happens when we rush and fall hostage to a time-poor state of mind.

If this seems horribly familiar, read on. And take your time. *Festina lente* – hurry slowly – won Aesop's tortoise his race.

2. What procrastination is, how it self-perpetuates – and what it is not

Let us start with the word. It sounds like an embarrassing medical condition, its overload of consonants forcing you to snarl when you say it aloud. Technically, 'procrastinator' means 'tomorrow pusher' (from Latin *pro* or 'forward' and *crastinus*, 'of tomorrow'). Often confused with 'prevaricate' (to speak or act evasively), this does nothing to improve its reputation. Still, it could be worse. The Latin for habitual delayer is *cunctator*. Try saying that in a hurry. Can you see why it did not catch on?

In the real world, procrastination is generally recognized as the practice of piffling about instead of doing what you should – all the shilly-shallying indulged under pretexts of preparation (such as that favourite displacement activity of the line manager, catching up with your team). In my case, nobody need ask how work is going. A glance at the kitchen tells all. A sparkling counter bodes ill.

Procrastination is an ancient insult, especially among men of action. Understandably: in war, havering can be deadly. In the fifth century BC, Archidamus II, a diplomatic Spartan king, did his best to stave off conflict with Athens: 'We can afford to wait, when others cannot, because we are strong.' Oh dear.

According to the historian Thucydides, the Corinthians chided hesitant Sparta: 'There is promptitude on their side against procrastination on yours ... They are swift to follow up a success, and slow to recoil from a reverse ... you still delay, and fail to see that peace stays longest with those who are not more careful to use their power ... let your procrastination end.' Roman statesman Cicero summarized the prevailing view: 'Slowness and procrastination are hateful' ('*Tarditas et procrastinatio odiosa est*'). Proving himself more hare than tortoise.

The classical chorus of disdain for procrastination also hailed from a place of private pain. In youth, Cicero, like all seeking advance in the Roman Empire, would have done so by preferment. That meant dreary days loitering in vestibules, hoping to worm his way into a powerful man's circle, years of errands until a serious commission came his way. Horace, famously associated with the motto *carpe diem*, described the anguished first encounter with his patron:

> I said a few faltering words, for speechless shame
> stopped me from saying more. My tale was not that I
> was a famous father's son, nor that I rode about my
> estate on a Saturian steed; I told you what I was. As is
> your way, you answered little and I withdrew; then,
> nine months later, you sent for me again and bade me
> join your friends.

Nine months of blushing recollection, one imagines.

Over the centuries, as time management became a concern for a broader constituency than kings, philosophers and warmongers, the insult of procrastination was hurled more widely, its intention invariably to encourage people to conform with current orthodoxies – often with the whiff of a parent bullying a truculent teenager. It is this whiff that lends procrastination its appeal: it becomes a way to rebel. The term sidled into the English language via Middle French in the 1540s, when angry clerics used it to castigate congregants late to church. The word went mainstream in the eighteenth century with the industrial revolution, as life sped up and the necessity arose to boss workers en masse. Workaholic Charles Dickens brought it to its widest audience in *David Copperfield*: 'Procrastination is the thief of time,' he wrote, filching an unbeatable definition coined by poet Edward Young in 1745. 'Collar him!' But Dickens' early death from exhaustion was not a convincing argument in support of the notion.

Procrastination is invincible unless you understand what it is, since it is easily muddled with other behaviours. Here are some things it is not:

- delay
- impulsiveness
- unreliability
- idleness
- caution
- patience
- slowness
- working well under pressure

The chief difficulty of defining procrastination correctly is that it entails something we do constantly: delay. And delay is a paramount human virtue, unique among creatures, allowing us to plan, up to years ahead, and prioritize.

The distinction between prudent delay and foolish procrastination is clarified by two ancient Egyptian verbs, both of which tend to be translated as 'procrastinate'. One was positive – it meant avoiding 'unnecessary or impulsive efforts'. The other was negative – it referred to the 'harmful shirking of tasks' (such as ploughing fields in time for the Nile's yearly flood). So procrastination is about putting off unpleasantness – it is the mirror image of lusty impulsiveness, which is all about grabbing what you can.

What could be more natural? Humanity's survival once depended on avoiding pain while seeking payoffs like sex, food and happiness. But over time civilization evolved a conflicting framework of temporal virtues, rewarding prudent souls able to prioritize long-term gains: those who remained monogamous, paid their mortgages, studied, or could butter up rich patrons. Procrastination embodies the basic tension between the rewards our nature craves and those imposed by our culture. Satisfy both – find a happy balance – and we thrive. (Although less so if society defers rewards too long: the deplorable prospect of having to work two lifetimes to save up for a home, for instance, makes prudence seem less sensible.)

Delay becomes procrastination if you fail to act in what you see as your best interests at the time you intend. The best word in any language to capture this is the Arabic *taswif*: 'to say, "I will, I will"'. This sham optimism is what is so disturbing about procrastination, and what corrodes self-respect.

'Life is languished away in the gloom of anxiety, and consumed in collecting resolutions which the next morning dissipates,' wrote Samuel Johnson with feeling. According to his friend Mrs Thrale, this masterly essay on the subject was 'hastily composed, as I have heard, in Sir Joshua Reynolds's parlour, while the boy waited to carry it to the press'.

I first heard this story from my tutor, who felt I too would benefit from the imposition of deadlines and should consider journalism. Procrastination cratered my final year at university, as, desperate to do well, I felt paralysed to try. Somehow I passed the exams, but after relief, guilt took up residence. What was wrong with me? What could I have achieved with the application of a little common sense? Soul-nibbling self-doubt lived on, although deadlines helped me to break the pattern.

Today, watching hurry abbreviate people's pleasure in life, I find it hard to distinguish this response to time-pressured living from procrastination. It also makes me wonder why we distract ourselves willy-nilly, whether by rushing or procrastinating. The trouble with either approach is that no time in life feels free if a guilty conscience is breathing down your neck.

Start looking for procrastination and you find it in all sorts of places. One is failure to form an intention. For example, my husband favours 'keeping our options open'. This passes the buck of decision-making onto time – an effective way to ensure choices pass you by. But fatalism (a negative perspective on time, discussed in Chapter 2) can become entrenched.

Then again, what looks like culpable delay may turn out to be canny. Take Charles Darwin, the ultimate intellectual tortoise. He waited twenty years, until 1859, to publish his epoch-defining work, *On the Origin of Species*. It has been alleged that he wavered – for fear of upsetting his religious wife as much as of scientific ridicule. But during the intervening decades he did not idle. Unlike a chaotic procrastinator, he was not pulling all-nighters in crises of last-minutitis; steadily he adduced hillocks of data to back his ideas, profiting from delay. Had he not taken such pains he risked being dismissed as a crackpot atheist. That he was pricked into print after Alfred Russell Wallace independently proposed the same theory just made it more convincing.

Darwin's triumph recalls an epigram by the French revolutionary Hérault de Séchelles: 'Genius is only a greater aptitude for patience.' In a similar way, notoriously patient fund manager Warren Buffett bet against stock markets' irrational surges of exuberance, giving his investments scope to grow, and bringing himself billions (much of it ploughed back into charitable causes to serve the long-term good of all).

Hesitation is often condemned as procrastination. The most ridiculed manoeuvre in politics is 'kicking something into the long grass' (a stratagem for deferring a problem to your successor, or until events reach a pass where tackling the delayed problem becomes an opportunity to demonstrate strong leadership). Frequently politicians are goaded into announcements to service the mill of the twenty-four-hour news cycle – or to defuse other awkward headlines. But caution is a political imperative. Waiting clarifies the judicious path in any situation – whether you are a tennis player returning a volley or a prime minister plotting your country's exit from an international federation.

Many matters, left alone, take care of themselves. The crowning policy of Elizabeth I's reign was to resist decisions. The queen flirted with suitors but would die without husband or child, flouting the advice of those who wanted her to beget an heir or marry to form a useful alliance that would stabilize the kingdom. But surely this was prudence not procrastination. Forty-four years of unbroken virginity seems preferable to the Scylla and Charybdis of marriage and Tudor obstetrics, especially to the daughter of Anne Boleyn, beheaded at her father's order after failing to bear a son.

Procrastination can sometimes be identified only with hindsight. Outcomes are unpredictable. Some say it is best to delay a decision until the last possible moment, and that identifying that moment is the art of timing (see Chapter 9). But even microscopic delays may vastly enhance performance.

A study of schoolteachers invited them to wait a little longer after asking children a question before moving on to another child or answering the question themselves. Just three seconds instead of the usual one. This tiny tweak – the gentlest touch of time pressure – elicited noteworthy improvements. Children previously considered slow or unwilling to participate now answered, and every child's response – even of those children who had not been backwards in coming forwards previously – was richer in detail and length.

Good things come to those who wait. If only for two patient seconds.

Serial offender: why we don't get on with it

'I'll only watch five minutes of car racing, to relax before that difficult call to my girlfriend,' he tells himself. Then, five minutes later: 'Or maybe it would be kinder to ring tomorrow. She loves Formula 1 too. Why spoil her fun?'

Everybody knows that tomorrow never comes. What is worse, the conversation will only be more painful (for both) if he waits. In this way, a choice between a smaller, present pain and a larger, future one can mean that deferring short-term pain always appeals more – even though, overall, vast pain inflation results. This is the guilt-magnifying mechanism that allows people to convince themselves that breaking up by text message is fine (or to do a Daniel Day-Lewis, who back in the day dumped Isabelle Adjani by fax).

Behavioural psychologists attribute such lunacy to a mental kink called hyperbolic discounting. What this means is that we place a different value on a preference according to when we will benefit from it. For instance, if offered £100 today or £110 tomorrow, most people will pick the first (this is present bias: we prefer happiness today over the possibility of it tomorrow). Switch the choice to waiting twenty days for £100 and twenty-one for £110, and most will pick the latter. Ostensibly it is the same choice, yet it is also not. After all, both twenty days and twenty-one lie in the uncertain future, whereas the gulf between right now and tomorrow is infinite. For this reason, when people are offered the choice between a small, short-term gain and a larger, long-term one, the nearer in time the smaller gain is, the harder it becomes to resist. This is preference reversal.

Worse, we repeat a seemingly small concession to present happiness – like watching Formula 1 – again and again, because our brain uses past actions to decide future ones. Having done something a certain way once becomes a licence for repetition; thereafter we adopt self-justification motives, telling ourselves it is okay (she likes Formula 1 too). A habit then calcifies.

Resist difficult decisions too long and life bends out of shape. You see this among those seeking love without compromise. As the years pass and the quest for a partner grows more urgent, their list of demands lengthens, even as the pool of available suitors shrinks. But the longer they have invested (as they see it) in finding the One, the less willing they are to compromise. This is temporal false accounting (economists term it 'the sunk costs fallacy'). On the other hand, if they were less choosy, they might be lumbered with a costlier divorce.

....

3. How to delay better

Like love, it begins in understanding.

To ask why you procrastinate is to ask, 'Why do I not act in my own self-interest?' To which there are seldom clear-cut answers. The roots of self-sabotage are internal, sometimes painful, and resolving them may demand prolonged reflection, even therapy, but they are eminently worth exploring. Your procrastination conceals your self-portrait and you might discover things you like (see page 144).

Beware the label, however. By calling yourself a procrastinator you give an inconvenient habit the distinguished status of a pathology, and this can prove contagious since labels are often self-fulfilling. Identify with a label and it becomes part of your self-image. Unconsciously, you conform to it, due to what psychologists characterize as consistency bias – a weakness that marketers love to exploit. Negative labels are particularly unhelpful because they highlight what we should *not* do – neatly reinforcing the behaviour that they seek to discourage. According to Professor Robert Cialdini, multi-million selling author of *Influence* (he is very persuasive), this is the single biggest mistake many policy experts make. For instance, if you want a public health campaign to fail, a great tactic is to behave as follows: inform teenagers that one in five will try drugs by the age of fourteen. 'Shit!' they think, 'I'd better hurry.' For this reason, you might want to avoid calling your partner a lazy git who never tidies up.

Call yourself a procrastinator and effectively you have said yes to procrastination. It is a bit like inviting Count Dracula over for drinks then expecting him to forego the jugular for a nice cup of tea. The moment you pin this label to your chest, you are bleeding. Instead, stop believing in procrastination. It is not who you are, and it is not a monster; it is merely a disorderly pattern of delay. The easiest way to break from it is to establish positive habits. These can also become contagious, countering a negative self-image with actions that present compelling evidence that yes, you can take charge of time and fulfil your commitments. No more 'I will, I will'; instead, 'I did'.

Identifying your trigger or type of procrastination reveals where to seek change. There are five such triggers:

1. **Incapacity** This is the greatest cause. Lack the means and completion is impossible. To resolve it, work on your skills and realism – about how long things are likely to take, the processes involved – and on reducing your anxiety.

2. **Situational** The second greatest cause. Is your environment disorderly? Are your days littered with interruptions and mess?

3. **Arousal** If crisis hits like a drug, your problem is hedonism – afraid of boredom, under-invested in the future. Procrastination offers dollops of drama. So change the supply: make more exciting plans, and seek your kicks elsewhere.

4. **Avoidance** Wrestling with low self-worth, procrastinators classified as avoiders fear missing goals, and so create alternative excuses for failure. People of this type, according to a Spanish study, are often fatalists who feel unable to control the present. If this is you, focus on plans and shoring up the belief that you can reach your goals. Your starting point should not be what you think is possible, or what you imagine others want. See yourself as the active party: what do *you* wish to achieve?

5. **Indecision** Lack of resolve lets us dodge responsibility if things go awry, but also denies us the joy of autonomy and accomplishment, depleting motivation. Like avoiders, indecisive procrastinators need an infusion of courage. If this is you, remind yourself what happens if you never try. Practise making decisions. Even trivial ones, like trying new foods, help to establish the habit of choice.

The lasting answer to procrastination is to put your desires at the centre of your life, to live by priority, not urgency. Reducing the pressure to stop makes this easier. So lower the stakes. You are not slaying a procrastination monster. You simply want to get better at delay.

Ten ways to delay better

1. **Plan** Spare your willpower. Put your sensible, long-term planner self in charge, using advance commitments. For instance, a shopaholic after a deposit for a flat should set up a direct debit to leave their current account on payday – ideally to a savings account requiring thirty days' notice.
2. **Intercept** Make a habit of carrying out a cost-benefit analysis when temptation arises. Ask what happens if you do not act now. Is delay necessary or useful?
3. **Get wise to your self-deceiving lies** Keep a list of these and learn to laugh at it.

4. **If deferral really makes sense** Make a specific commitment when you will do the task. Write this down.

5. **Track patterns** Does procrastination set in when you commence a task, or en route? Strengthen your resolve at these weak points, e.g. by planning, or excluding distractions.

6. **Tackle time thieves** Weed them out, or turn them into rewards. See Chapter 9.

7. **Make not procrastinating easier** Erect barriers to digression; remove barriers to optimal behaviour.

8. **Replace procrastination with a new habit** See Chapter 11.

9. **Believe in goals** Are they real, achievable, necessary or desirable?

10. **Start sooner!**

....

Occasionally procrastination throws open the door to fresh ideas or serendipity, happy accidents that stitch wings on life. Acclaimed novelist Hilary Mantel described how it served her:

> I used to think when I set out that doing the research was enough, but then the gaps would emerge that could only be filled with imagination. And imagination only comes when you privilege the unconscious, when you make delay and procrastination work for you. For me – I'm a now, now kind of person – that was hard.

There are two methods of tactical procrastination.

Method one: noodle on something else if you hit a creative wall

Original ideas seldom wait where they are sought, because pressure to perform is inimical to creativity as the mind's horizon becomes narrowed inside its cognitve tunnel. Procrastination can evoke a relaxed mood, setting playful thoughts free.

Neurologist and author Oliver Sacks tickled his mind into creativity with a daily routine that involved circling the actual act of writing for as long as possible. Pre-writing rituals included taking a walk, playing the piano, then 'lying on my couch … [to] put my brain in an "idling" or "default" mode. I let it play with images and thoughts on its own; I come to from these altered states, if I am lucky, with energy renewed and confused thoughts clarified.'

This ploy exploits what psychologists term our 'default system'. By that they mean that our brain unconsciously ruminates on unresolved problems if we break from a task and direct our attention elsewhere. As a means of encouraging lateral thoughts, Sacks's couch tactic is equivalent to a dog playing dead and hoping a rabbit will come closer for a sniff. But it works. Deaf mathematician Dame Kathleen Ollerenshaw also claimed overnight success at solving intractable problems by writing them on a piece of paper, then popping it under her pillow before bed. By morning a solution invariably came.

Method two: use procrastination as a lever to action

I do this all the time. It is an entirely conscious act of manipulation, but no less successful for that. The idea is simple: since procrastination aims to defer unappealing costs, recruit this bias to help you. Think of a less appealing alternative to whatever it is you need to do. Then offer yourself a choice between the two. Suddenly the unappealing thing becomes more appealing. Shed need a lick of creosote? Set yourself the task of tackling your tax return and you will be outside in a jiffy.

Definitive proof that procrastination may be a fount of invention is *Hamlet*. Aptly for a play about indecision, Shakespeare becomes carried away by his hero's psychic pyrotechnics. As the Danish prince deliberates on revenge, the plot congeals and poetic tangents take over. But what finer justification for creative dither than the question, 'to be or not to be?'

What are you waiting for?

Peer behind the arras of your procrastination habit and much can be learnt from your tendency to inconvenient delay. You will meet a veritable circus of acrobats of false logic, high-wire artistes of self-deception and contortionists of common sense. Prepare to be amazed.

Understand these biases or flawed intentions and you have a direction for change. Better yet, occasionally the intention can be positive, just waiting to be coaxed out of its stubborn shell. Then you can harness it to a more productive pattern of behaviour.

Our foremost reason for procrastination is **ingrained habit**. It simply feels like who you are. (According to the law of arbitrary coherence, having once done something a certain way, we do so again – the tendency known as familiarity bias. To avert it ask 'Why?')

The other reasons fall into three categories:

- (dis)organization
- game-playing
- aversion

(Dis)organization

- **The planning fallacy** Miscalculating the work/time/skill required. This is easily done. An oddity of time perception is that the more complicated a task, the longer you imagine you have to complete it.
- **Being railroaded by a time thief** But who forced you to leave the Wi-Fi on/the door open/the phone on the hook?
- **Poor priorities** e.g. tackling easy items first, endlessly deferring the hard ones.
- **Options paralysis** Being blinded by the blizzard of choice.
- **Ineffective routine** Otherwise known as pottering …
- **Mañana-itis** Does tomorrow ever come?
- **The composting approach to work** Surely it will ripen to fruition all by itself if left in a cringeing heap in your filing cabinet.

Game-playing (conscious or not)

- **You like saying yes** It's considered polite to do so in many countries.
- **Saying no without having to say it aloud** Passive assertion, you might say.
- **To finagle someone else into doing it for you**
- **To create urgency/drama/suspense** Mark Twain wrote in *Tom Sawyer*: 'To make a man or boy covet a thing, it is only necessary to make the thing difficult to attain.'
- **To have something to reproach yourself for** The peculiar companionship in being haunted by undone tasks is that you feel in demand.
- **To appear more cautious, painstaking or creative** This is phoney perfectionism.
- **Because you believe that later is better** Punctuality is overrated, right?

Aversion

- **Fear** If action = consequence, it is surprisingly easy to kid yourself that inaction = no consequence. True perfectionism means that if nothing is ever good enough, the pain of failing due to not trying may seem preferable to the agony of a genuine failure. Then your ego can hibernate in the illusion of your untapped potential.
- **Because you do not want to do it – or not enough, or not as much as something else, or just not yet** A risky gamble. Wait too long and motivation stales, to be replaced by the scourge of panic.

146

- **To resist making a decision** This is the fallacy of keeping your options open.
- **Because you do not have to do it** Will the world end if you wait another day, two, three, four ...?

CLOCKWATCHING

Living by the clock can be exhausting. Ever tried making love by it?

Amid the ruins of wartime Naples in 1944, intelligence officer Norman Lewis had an unusual assignment: to act as romantic interpreter for an English captain and his lover, a vigorous Neapolitan widow. The source of the couple's confusion was less the language barrier, than the exacting erotic timetable in a city where sex was the one thing still expected to run like clockwork.

In as tactful a way as possible, Lewis told Captain Frazer that his inamorata's neighbours were whispering: 'Conjugal visits at midday are *de rigueur* in Naples. This I explained, and Frazer promised to do better.'

Alas, the captain struggled to discharge his duty. His lady had a habit 'which terrified Frazer, of keeping an eye on the bedside clock while he performed'. Speed was of the essence. Apparently her late husband had 'never failed to have intercourse with her less than six times a night'.

Stopwatch sex might turn you on if you were being paid for it (cockwork?), but time pressure is seldom relaxing. When we stare at clocks, usually it is because time pressure is lacking – we have a deranged hope that by sheer force of desire, we can speed up time.

Clockwatching became widespread enough to enter the dictionary in the 1880s, the epoch of factories with clocking-in machines. A clockwatcher was a pejorative nickname for someone unwilling to exceed their paid hours by a single minute (a concept dating at least as far back as 1600, when an idler was known as a 'tell-clock'). In succeeding generations the clockwatcher acquired a new title and social respectability: trade union shop steward. But clockwatching itself is an existential futility – as pointless as staring at saucepans in the hope of making water boil. Actually, it is worse.

Thinking about time makes it seem slower – either because it is depressing (causing your dopamine levels to sink) or because wishing and wishing for speed activates your brain, so that time appears contrastingly slow. Ogling your watch in hope that a windbag will wrap up his presentation only prolongs the pain (unless the windbag notices and cuts it short). The psychological error is that by diverting your attention to time, it is harder to return your mind to the task in hand. Whereas the only effective way to speed time up is instead to focus on whatever you are engaged with and try to find it more engaging.

There should be a tidy German compound noun for clock-longing – something like *Uhrbeschleunigensehnsucht* – to capture the yearning to hurry a clock's arms off. My husband was briefly enslaved by this masochism. In his first job, for a woman rumoured to show her appreciation of her employees by boxing their ears, he ran up enormous bills calling the speaking clock. It had the desired outcome when she received the bill and fired him. But as if in punishment, now he has all the time pressure anyone could want: a daily newspaper deadline.

'Clocks slay time,' claimed William Faulkner. 'Time is dead as long as it is being clicked off by little wheels; only when the clock stops does time come to life.' I learnt this bitter truth during the longest ninety minutes I have experienced, watching a dance extravaganza, *Ocean*, at London's Roundhouse.

The fault lay not with the choreography but the orchestra, which trickled around the theatre's upper circle like ribbon around a cake. This arrangement meant the musicians could not follow a conductor, and so instead kept time by means of two large digital clocks, which counted down the minutes and seconds until the end of the performance, like a timer on an action-movie bomb. These glowing numerals hypnotized me. All thought transfixed on one hope: that soon they would reach 00:00:00. No matter what cavortings fretted the stage, back my eyes coasted to the magnetic clocks, each treacly second passing more slowly than the last. Only one thing went fast in the theatre that night: the pattering of feet, as spectator after tormented spectator broke for the exit.

In my experience, thinking about time speeds it up only when you are late. That said, I met a Romanian woman, Floriana, who claimed that clocks in London ran faster than those in her home town; there was no liberty to see friends or lounge around, even though the duration of her working hours and her commute was exactly the same – because, she said, the pace of London life was so fast. But she had a solution.

'You will think I am completely mad,' she warned, before revealing what she did when racing to catch her train. 'I say "Time, go slower." And it does, I swear it.'

I am still waiting for her trick to work for me.

Part Three

How to Get it Back

Includes: the mysteries of sleep, light vampires and daily jet lag; why teenage girls do better in exams; the myth of convenience and other lies of fast; why we prefer TV to vacuum cleaners; when to play soccer in Paris; what Japanese swordsmen, weaving and Anna Wintour tell us about good timing; how Madonna's motivation is self-renewing; why 'if' and 'then' make resolutions sticky; why we are habit zombies; and how to declutter the time in your life.

6

Body Clocks

Living by your biological timetable

My mother nods off each evening, and awakens each morning, hours before my father. Often she stirs and they chat before sloping off to bed, but for at least three hours a day (aided by his naps) one is conscious without the other. After forty-six years together, this amounts to almost six of mutual solitude. They remind me of those mechanical clocks where the man disappears as the woman emerges.

'It's a miracle the marriage has lasted,' he joked one night. 'Or perhaps this is why.'

In fact they are a notably doting pair. But maybe my father is also right; their incompatible body clocks help to keep them compatible.

Few of us dwell on the peculiarities of our day's rhythms: we are too busy living. An exception was Argentine storyteller Jorge Luis Borges, who completed his tasks at a library in an hour, freeing him to spend the rest of his working day reading and writing in its basement like some literary Minotaur, wandering the wondrous labyrinth of his mind. He noticed each hour has its hue. 'Time can't be measured in days the way money is measured in pesos and centavos, because all pesos are equal, while every day, perhaps every hour is different.' Borges was correct. Each moment is unique, filtered by our ever-changing, kaleidoscopic circumstances. Yet there is a pattern, shaped by our biological timetable, which decides when energy rises and falls, and which hour suits what activity best. It can prove a stubborn form of destiny unless you understand it.

This hurried, 24/7 world often asks us to strain against our physical limits. And we are flexible; we can adjust, thrive. What could be more romantic than cocooning ourselves in a private time zone? Like singer-poet Patti Smith and her beloved husband, in a giddy 1979:

> We would stay up until dawn talking then sleep until nightfall. When we awoke we'd search for 24-hour diners or stop and mill around Art Van's furniture outlet that opened at midnight and served free coffee and powdered donuts. Sometimes we'd just drive aimlessly and stop before the sun rose at some motel …
>
> Fred finally achieved his pilot's license but couldn't afford to fly a plane. I wrote incessantly but published nothing. Through it all we held fast to the concept of the clock with no hands. Tasks were completed, sump pumps manned, sandbags piled, trees planted, shirts ironed, hems stitched, and yet we reserved the right to ignore the hands that kept on turning. Looking back, long after his death, our way of living seems a miracle, one that could only be achieved by the silent synchronization of the jewels and gears of a common mind.

Every love affair is a dance. The enchanting thing about Fred and Patti Smith is that they found their tempo even as they stepped outside the rhythm of the world around them. But how many of us can afford to be a rock star with time? A 2016 study concluded that sleep deprivation wipes out over half a trillion dollars per year in the United States, the United Kingdom, Canada, Germany and Japan – a loss to GDP of 2.92 per cent in Japan, 2.28 per cent in the US and 1.86 per cent in the UK. Britain is the least rested nation in the world, a fact blamed on overwork, technology and a lack of leisurely luncheons. But as this chapter will show, there is more to it than that. Living in sympathy with your biological timetable, understanding the jewels and gears of your body clock, is the fast track to quality time, for life.

1. How your body find its twenty-four-hour beat and why it matters

We speak of the biological clock as if there were only one – the pesky one that ticks louder and louder as women inch towards menopause. But a multitude of physiological time-keepers pattern our days. You could set your watch by some of them: the times when you wake or feel peckish, or the mid-afternoon sag as your eyelids droop. Equally significant are less obtrusive cycles: your temperature and heart rate, or for the cooking up of enzymes. The majority run for a period of twenty-four hours.

These circadian rhythms (from Latin *circa*, 'about' and *diem*, 'a day') are fundamental to all living organisms.

Mammals have around a hundred. We also have longer, infradian rhythms (such as the moon-led menstrual cycle) and briefer ultradian rhythms (the 90- to 120-minute sleep phases that patch together a night's rest).

Circadian rhythms can be seen in action. Extract a cell from your heart, liver, kidney or adrenal gland and place it under a microscope; keep it alive and its twenty-four-hour cycle will still operate, due to its 'clock' or 'period' gene (we know this is what is responsible because if you edit one from a fruit fly's DNA its circadian rhythms vanish). Or – easier – plant a flower clock, as Swedish naturalist Carl Linnaeus suggested. His day started with spotted cat's ear (open at 6 a.m.), and ended at 6 p.m. with evening primrose.

Even oysters have a private tempo, opening at high tide to feed, closing when the waters recede. Entirely logical, yet also wildly mysterious, as was discovered in 1954 after a choice selection were sent from a Long Island oyster bed to Frank Brown at Evanston University, Illinois, a thousand miles inland, for study. For two weeks they opened and closed on schedule; then, to Brown's amazement, as if by collective agreement, their clock slipped back an hour – their mouths agape at exactly the time high tide would reach Evanston, if the sea had swept that far west. How did they know? The moon controls tides by changing earth's gravitational field, so it is possible that the oysters detected some shift, but nobody can be sure how they got the message, let alone in perfect harmony.

The forces that drive your body's tempo are no less awesome than those governing the moonstruck choir of oysters. What is clear is that biological cycles constitute the working schedules of our organs: their hours of service, rest and repair. We disrupt their co-ordination at our peril. To understand why, imagine your body is an old-fashioned clock. Inside lie multiple cogs, one for each of your bodily cycles. Some are large, some smaller, taking different amounts of time to turn, but all interlock. So unless they turn steadily, the system falls out of true.

When these cycles are harmonized, so are we: we are active, digest and rest at complementary times. But if our cycles fall out of synch, we can come unstuck. For instance, when men with prostate cancer are chemically castrated to arrest the disease, very often they also 'feel they are going insane', according to neuropsychologist Ashok Jansari. (We hear little of this because old men do not whinge, or perhaps because we do not listen when they do.) Likewise, as meno-pause's guillotine severs women from their sex drive, this introduces the joy of a new sort of night sweat. Just lose sleep and circadian dips that would normally, when we are rested, gently rise and fall suddenly become extreme. Once I endured five sleepless days in a row, and it was like peeling skin off my senses: everything seemed vivid, the ground soft beneath my feet, as my emotions, temperature and appetite surged and dipped. Never again, I hope.

You become who you are in duet with your environment, so there are many ways to tweak your body clock's dials: what you eat, where you go, who you meet. Women working with men ovulate more often. Women living with women menstruate at the same time. They need not even be in the same place to synchronize: if you dab a strange female's sweat onto another's upper lip, her period co-ordinates with the stranger's, thanks to pheromones, our chemical signals. For primates living in troupes, these synergies bring mating seasons; babies are born at the same time so childcare can be pooled. Sadly, our social ties being less tight-knit than those of baboons, few of us enjoy such temporal economies.

The master clock that keeps your twenty-four-hour cycle in harmony lies just over ninety million miles away. That 1990s dance music anthem was right: the rhythm of the night is the rhythm of your life, because your body, like mine, like the flowers that open and close as the day unfolds, is entrained to the sun. Fittingly enough, just as the earliest evidence of humanity tracking time is the moon calendar in Lascaux cave, so another man would have to enter the bowels of the earth to learn that daylight controls our tempo.

In 1961 a huge underground glacier was discovered in the Alps, and intrepid twenty-three-year-old geologist Michel Siffre decided to spend a couple of weeks exploring it. 'And then this idea came to me – this idea that became the idea of my life. I decided to live like an animal, without a watch, in the dark, without knowing the time.'

The following summer, with rudimentary equipment and a primitive telephone to connect him to a support team camped at the cave's mouth, Siffre entered the dark to spend two months with perpetually wet feet, and a body temperature as low as 34 degrees Celsius (around three degrees below normal), investigating the glacier and the secrets of time in our bodies. On each occasion that he awoke after what he imagined to be a night's sleep he rang his team, told them his pulse rate and counted to 120 at a speed of one digit a second. His team were permitted to call him only once: on

14 September, when it was time to get out. He was livid when they called on 20 August – or so he thought. He emerged into the light – 'half-crazed, a disjointed marionette' – to discover that each of those two minutes counting to 120 had taken five, and that his sleep–wake cycle was between 24.5 and 25 hours. Time, in his body and mind, had slowed down.

Siffre had invented a new science, chronobiology. Afterwards he persuaded other curious spelunkers – cave explorers – to repeat his experiments for up to six months. Some fell into a forty-eight-hour sleep–wake cycle, one man dozing for over thirty-four hours without pause (they feared he was dead until they heard him snore). Somewhat jealous that he had not experienced such a temporal time lapse, a decade later Siffre descended into Midnight Cave near Del Rio, Texas, for his most ambitious test: 205 days in a dimly lit tent-laboratory, running up a $100,000 debt in the process.

Underground, some days lasted twenty-six hours, on others he stayed awake for thirty-six, yet these seemed no longer to him than a normal day. But one thing remained constant: he only felt tired enough to sleep on his mouldering mattress when his body temperature dropped. What this revealed is that a cooling body is an essential sleep trigger; however exhausted you are, tests find that you will not nod off if your body temperature does not fall on the right curve of the temperature cycle. This is why hypothermia – reputedly the kindest way to die – puts us to sleep. Fascinatingly, for every ten minutes of waking activity, Siffre enjoyed an extra minute of rapid eye movement (REM) sleep, our vivid dreamtime. This discovery prompted the French navy to investigate drugs to prolong dreams, in the hope that sun-deprived submariners could thereby be kept awake longer to work a thirty-hour day.

Siffre's other circadian rhythms went haywire: some lengthened to thirty hours, others shrank below twenty-four. His body clocks fell out of synch, like an orchestra playing to a confusion of beats, because light is the conductor that keeps us in tune. If the sun is our primary source we co-ordinate our rhythms to its twenty-four-hour cycle, but subsequent studies, including of sleep in the blind, discovered that without it some individuals naturally incline to a twenty-three-hour day, others to twenty-five. Few of us are pure circadians. Consider the implications. No matter whether your native cycle is twenty-three or twenty-five hours, you must conform to a twenty-four-hour clock. As a result, many of us are battling subtle social jet lag every day.

2. Why you sleep when you do, and what happens when body clocks and social clocks clash

On day one of Rio's 2016 Olympics, Adam Peaty won his first heat in the 100m men's breaststroke in 57.55 seconds, a new world record. Some feared the twenty-one-year old had peaked too early, but the BBC commentator assured doubters that the timing of that night's semi-final would suit Peaty better. Sure enough, he triumphed again (0.07 seconds slower, merely the second fastest performance in history). The next day, shortly before 11 p.m. Brazil time, Peaty dived into the pool once more; 57.13 seconds later he emerged with a new record and Britain's first men's Olympic swimming gold in twenty-eight years.

Did you feel weary reading that? How could swimming in the middle of the night ever be a good idea?

Because for young men – though not for the old or very young – late hours are hospitable.

Sleep is widely misunderstood. Intuitively we recognize that our patterns shift throughout life: babies obey no clock, children rise early, and so on. Yet we have been slow to draw wisdom from this insight; instead, we barricade ourselves from feeling any duty of understanding with moral judgements. We call late sleepers, or those who sleep for long hours, idle (even though you can manage on five hours a night and still be a lazy arse). Only recently has it been understood that our genes determine how much sleep we need – eight hours for most adults, although serious huggers of Morpheus prefer more (model and wit Jerry Hall averaged nine and a half most nights, twelve-plus on holidays). One to three per cent of us can be fresh on four hours' sleep, like Leonardo da Vinci (who decried slumber as 'death') or Margaret Thatcher (although the wisdom of that depends on your view of her policies). Any less and our body suffers. The late pop star Prince claimed, 'There's not a person around who can stay awake as long as I can.' He also believed that time was a 'mind construct', and stopped counting birthdays ('which stops me from counting time, which allows me to still look the same as I did ten years ago'). Sadly he only enjoyed fifty-six of them.

The hour when we need to go to sleep pendulums back and forth with age. Adolescent boys and girls rise later, and parents must yell teenage carcasses out of bed. Then our sleep's midpoint swings back; girls revert to an early waking cycle from nineteen and a half, boys from twenty-one, and many men wake later than women throughout adulthood. Hence twenty-one-year-old Adam Peaty could swim heroically at 11 p.m. But the pendulum keeps on moving, until by old age we favour crepuscular hours, rising at dawn – or, worse, we lose our circadian rhythms altogether. When the NASA Ames Research Center investigated jet lag, it found that fifty- to sixty-year-olds lost more than three times as much sleep as those in their twenties. Their temperature cycle was also weaker, explaining why they were less adaptable.

'The mind may be extremely subtle. It may work faster than the speed of light, yet often it takes longer than your body to make a journey, so that you arrive, as it were, in two instalments.' This out-of-step sensation, described by Indian freedom fighter and prince Apa Pant in *A Moment in Time*, is familiar to any long-haul traveller. But many of us experience similar disembodiment, in miniature, at our day's frayed margins. Social jet lag explains why you might crawl out of bed at 8 a.m. (making you a late chronotype) or spring up at 5 a.m. (an early chronotype). Interestingly, how long you need to sleep is unrelated to chronotype. To establish your type, note when you drop off and wake up. If the midpoint falls before 3 a.m. you are an early bird, like my mother; any later and you are an owl, like my father. But this need not be your destiny. You can reset your clock, and it can be eminently worth trying (see page 174).

Not until American sleep researcher Professor Mary Carskadon's pioneering 1990s research was it appreciated that biology, not laziness, causes groggy teenagers to surface demanding breakfast at lunchtime. Studying those woken up at school time, Carskadon found that many exhibited mild narcolepsy, experiencing bouts of micro-sleep (mini-black-outs) *without realizing it*. Surely this contributes to teenage girls' superior school exam performance: on average, their sleep–wake cycle begins to revert to an earlier hour, eighteen months before male classmates, which would let them absorb extra knowledge while the boys are micro-napping.

Do not expect different school timetables for boys and girls to be introduced any time soon. Chronobiologist Till Roenneberg campaigned for a change in this area in Germany, gathering compelling data to claim that the standard second-ary school day, from 8 a.m. to 1 p.m., was harmful. Evidence included a study of German university students, which found that late risers had performed more poorly in end-of-school exams (and this only sampled those who scraped into univer-sity; nobody knows about late risers who did not make the grade). Whereas experiments in which school start times were delayed by as little as an hour found that half of teen-agers (up from one-third) now slept for the recommended minimum of eight hours. Attendance, motivation and dietary habits improved too, breakfast being a peerless aid to concentration.

Politicians and teachers' unions united to dismiss the evidence. Change, they argued, would be too awkward: for working parents, for bus companies (who first ferried kids to school, then transported workers) and teachers (who used the afternoon to prepare lessons). The interests of adults, who vote for politicians and unions, prevailed over the teens', who were too young, or perhaps too tired, to vote for anyone. Clearly *ad hominem* judgements – such as calling boys lazier than girls – offer self-serving mental armour: they relieve us from responsibility either for wondering why exam outcomes are different, or for doing anything about it.

It seems a consolation that sleep is adaptable. For millennia, man has inhabited earth's north and south, working through dark winters rather than hibernate like other mammals. For decades, millions have flown across time zones. And goodness knows how long shift workers have toiled by night, or enjoyed siestas timed to coincide with the early afternoon drop in body temperature. (Although Spain was poised to abolish this tradition, to conform with European Union hours – a move welcomed by working parents who lived too far from their workplace to get home for a nap during their two-hour lunch break, or to kiss children at bedtime.) We can also sleep tactically. Like high-octane twentieth-century architect Buckminster Fuller, who coined the term 'ephemeralization' to describe how technology lets us do 'more and more with less and less until eventually you can do everything with nothing' (smartphones would not have surprised him). Deciding sleep was theft, he adopted a novel tactic: high-frequency sleep, snoozing for thirty minutes every six hours. This enhanced his productivity, but not his marriage, so he quit.

When London's underground rail network proclaimed its new twenty-four-hour weekend service with 'Free the Night' posters featuring a figure leaping in delight, I could not share the joy. Culture and convenience dictate our social clocks, and unending days enrich economies, but the cost imposed by inflexible sleep can be extortionate. A French investigation of three thousand workers found that those short on it had slower thought processes and remembered less.

Questioning the judgement of the sleep-deprived is tricky. Parents of young children, for instance, have it hard enough without accusations of brain damage. But one wonders whether political gambles, such as Britain's commitment to 2003's Iraq invasion or the EU in-out referendum, would have been taken had the prime ministers responsible for these decisions, Tony Blair and David Cameron, not shared their quarters at 10 Downing Street with sleep-nuking two-year-olds.

Nightworkers have it worse. Many perpetually experience the symptoms of jet lag – fatigue, headaches, ill temper, poor sleep, an irritable gut – and run a higher risk of diabetes, obesity and depression. Few ever claw back the sleep they need. Horrifying recent research has found that workers who have pulled nights for ten years or more display impairments normally seen in brains six and a half years older. If they quit, it takes five years for them to revert to the condition expected for their age. Most vulnerable are aircrew. In one study, frequent flyers working over seven time zones were found to have shrunken temporal lobes and impaired memories.

Night shifts are dangerous places, however fresh your brain may be. Alertness troughs with body temperature, plummeting to a nadir of befuddlement between 4 and 6 a.m., as a result of which people are slower: to answer telephones, react to alarms, or grasp information.

Muzziness can be countered, as brain surgeon Henry Marsh revealed:

I learned a long time ago that I can operate perfectly
well despite being tired, as when I am operating I am
in an intense state of arousal. Sleep deprivation
research has shown that people make mistakes if
moderately deprived of sleep when they are carrying
out boring, monotonous tasks. Surgery – however
trivial the operation – is never boring or monotonous.

Sadly, though, life also depends on the accurate conduct of
dull, detailed tasks, night after night. Witness the early morning disasters of Three Mile Island, Chernobyl's nuclear reac-
tor, the *Exxon Valdez* oil spill and the Bhopal gas plant,
when 500,000 innocents were poisoned in their sleep.

Can you recall when last you watched gold scarf the sky
at sunset? How often do you stay up late, then rise before
you feel ready? The healthiest timetable follows the sun. As
the Salk Institute's Satchidananda Panda explained, using the
example of the liver's metabolic clock:

When we eat determines when a particular gene turns
on or off; for example, if we eat only at nighttime, a
gene that should be turned on during the day will turn
on at night. In response to natural cycles, our body
has evolved to make glucose at nighttime. But if on
top of what you eat, you're creating excess glucose,
that damages organs, which leads to diabetes. It's like
over-charging a car battery. Bad things will happen.

Disrupt your circadian rhythms and you enter a vicious
cycle: it grows harder to stay awake when you need, and

harder to sleep when you need. Make it a habit and you can break your internal clock before old age does it for you. You could precipitate diabetes, memory loss, indigestion, altered brain hormones; heighten your risk of cancer, not to mention exacerbate effects of Parkinson's disease, multiple sclerosis, kidney disease or gastro-intestinal disorders.

Rise at dawn like a peasant, dining after the cows come home, and you are likelier to live in clover. But if that is not possible, try to protect and prioritize sleep, whenever you can get it.

Your on-off switch: how light controls sleep and gadgets pilfer it

Thomas Edison – who despised peasants almost as much as he hated sleep – credited his invention, the light bulb, with elevating human intelligence. In return all illuminated gadgets rob us of sleep. When television crept into our living rooms, we lost a lot. Now the seclusion of bed is debatable (are you ever alone with a smartphone?), the early twentieth-century paranoia about being spied on via TV screens is a real and welcome feature of our portable wonderlands. But beware these sleep vampires. Not only do they redefine the nature of privacy and keep you up late; they also bugger up your off switch.

Like a light bulb, you are powered by electricity. As darkness falls, your suprachiasmatic nucleus (SCN), a 3,000-neuron nub of tissue in the hypothalamus, located just above the optic nerve, fires a charge to various areas of the brain, such as the pineal gland. This alters how your brain synthesizes period proteins, chemicals that regulate bodily processes before sleep.

The SCN is your body's messenger from the outside world, so vital that if you cut out a rat's SCN, all its circadian cycles cease. But conflicting light messages confuse it. Neuropsychologist Randy Nelson subjected some woebegone mice to twenty-four-hour light and concluded: 'The increasing rate of depressive disorders in humans corresponds with the increasing use of light at night in modern society.'

Light, like noise, can be torture. The issue is not that light is bad: what matters is when you encounter it. A few hours' intense radiance on a winter morning helps banish depression in sufferers from seasonal affective disorder (SAD). Exposing night workers to four hours' bright light boosts their alertness, attention and accuracy at work. But if you must rise early, avoid bright light, computers and smartphones of an evening – especially the last two, which emit intense, short-wavelength blue light, damaging your eyesight and dampening your serotonin.

Serotonin is not to be squandered. It allows your brain to manufacture melatonin, a neurochemical that triggers us to wind down, slows ageing, reduces cholesterol, melancholy and stress, and suppresses tumours. Tellingly, our SCN is less effective at responding to light if we are upset, making it harder to sleep, upsetting us, making it harder to sleep … a pattern familiar to all who know the stubborn melancholy of depression.

Let us give computer and smartphone producers the benefit of the doubt. Let us assume they do not deliberately fabricate sleep-stealing, addictive devices perfectly contrived to turn us into fatigued, myopic, anxious people, primed to become addicted to apps, to panic buying unnecessary products, or to believe in adverts – ideal consumers, in fact. No, let us call it a coincidence. But it would be nice if they used non-blue light, or supplied sunglasses to filter it. Such things exist. Some kindly employers give them to nightworkers to cue drowsiness as they travel home in daylight.

If your body is out of step with your timetable, then, in the words attributed to God, 'Let there be light.' But pray there is not too much, or too little, or at the wrong hour of the day.

3. Your right times: how to chime with your biological rhythm

Our biological ebb and flow means that certain hours suit certain activities best, as I learnt by experimenting with routines when I went freelance. Patterns emerged. Mornings were slow, confident, low-pressure hours; great for demanding or creative work. Rush hour – from noon on – was highly productive, provided that I was not starving, until a slump hit at three – but not if I quaffed caffeine, avoided starchy food, or strolled and soaked up sun. Late afternoon or early evening were pacy, so long as I worked in bursts – handy for soaking up information, or mechanical tasks like admin or proofreading.

These smooth-flowing days were the easiest of my working life. Which may irritate you if you cannot set your own timetable. Then again, if you have any discretion in how you manage your workload, you can pay heed to your cycles of attention and energy, tailoring your tasks to enhance productivity. Here follows a basic biological timetable. To reflect your sleep–wake cycle accurately, shift the hours so they are in line with the time you normally wake up.

5.30 a.m.	Dreams are liveliest, cortisol (the stress hormone) and insulin rise, as blood sugar falls.	Prepare to wake.
6 a.m.	The heart beats faster; body temperature and blood pressure rise.	
7 a.m.	Open your eyes and, if you are male, say hi to evidence of a testosterone surge. If you feel low, serotonin and beta-endorphin hormones need to pick up. Men feel desire, women less so. Blood pressure rises higher and cortisol peaks.	Perform ablutions, then eat (ideally including protein, to stave off hunger). Turn up the lights. Mechanical tasks will tee you up for the day.
8 a.m.	Your brain stops producing melatonin and starts firing. Bowels prepare to void.	Time for news, radio, sudoku or to plug in. Coffee lifts the mood, water is better for hydration.

8.30 a.m.	Frequent intestinal peristalsis	Find the little room. Then seek out the sun.
10.30 a.m.	You are at your most alert, focused, logical and efficient. Willpower, balance and muscle control are at their height.	The best time for creative or intellectual challenges, or to do something scary. Exercise now – or before eating – is good for the metabolism. However, blood is thickest and heart attacks are three times as likely in the morning, so arguably afternoons are safer for workouts.
12 p.m.	Rush hour: a happy, confident time, as serotonin and beta-endorphins flood the brain. Your handshake is firmest at noon, and your physical pace picks up – making time appear swifter. You feel hungry.	A mental highpoint: focus now in order to be most productive. Snack to prolong the mood, but skip sugar and refined starch. Whole grains and complex carbohydrates keep you alert. Exercise lowers blood pressure from noon.
2 p.m.	Slow hour: energy and concentration droop as the mind wanders. Body temperature rises, physical co-ordination peaks.	A twenty-minute nap could pep you up, renewing willpower and concentration; any longer impairs night sleep. To sharpen up, act like a moth and find a bright light, or get moving.

3.30 p.m.	Back to a fast pace and swift reaction times.	Tackle routine tasks, taking regular breaks as attention shortens. Good for taking in new information.
4 p.m.	Body temperature is high, you feel strong. Heart and lungs are at their most efficient by 5 p.m., while blood pressure is low. Women feel sexiest from now onwards.	A good time to exercise and fix disrupted circadian rhythms (but don't begin too late: it takes six hours for body temperature to drop to normal, a vital sleep cue).
6 p.m.	Your sense of taste is sharp but insulin is less effective at breaking down carbohydrate and your digestion less able to process protein. Blood pressure rises.	Time for dinner nears, but go easy on carbohydrates, sugar and meat.
7 p.m.	Wine o'clock. Our liver works best around 8 p.m., so early birds can tipple without a hangover. But insulin inefficiency makes us sleepy, so overdoing it risks diabetes.	Drink – moderately – to be merry.
8 p.m.	The brain is competent for simple tasks.	Iron, sort out the neglected photo album, organize a sock drawer.

9 p.m.	Melatonin production begins, body temperature subsides.	Dim the lights, retiring all computers, large or small, *at least an hour before bed*. Read, chat, watch TV, but if you aim to sleep soon, dodge anything too exciting.
10 p.m.	The witching hour. Mood and mind lose their bounce. Peristalsis ceases.	Avoid trying conversation, checking your bank statement or dealing with anything upsetting.
11 p.m.	Prepare to sleep.	If you still have not made love, note that women are likelier to climax towards the end of the day.
Midnight	Cortisol at its lowest level.	Why aren't you asleep?
1 a.m.	Melatonin is at its zenith, blood pressure at its nadir.	Stay asleep.

HOW TO BECOME A LARK (OR AN OWL) AND BEAT JET LAG

The anti-slavery preacher Henry Ward Beecher once wrote: 'The first hour of the morning is the rudder of the day.' He did not suggest when that first hour should be.

If you know somebody is an early riser, no doubt they are also rich and famous. Why else do you remember that fact? Like Lululemon entrepreneur Shannon Wilson, who rises early to exercise, swimming competitively when not starting up business after business. Of course some conspicuous early birds, the ones who reveal their routines in magazines, may be fibbing. Maybe their staff rise at 4 a.m. to spit wit on Twitter. But if they are lying, they do so because our culture hero-worships early, regarding it as an elixir of accomplishment rather than, as in the past, the curse of peasants tethered to the bodily functions of their cattle; then, to play by night and sleep by day was distinctly aristocratic.

Those who are not natural larks may be disheartened by this reverence. My day's start, for instance, currently superintended by small imperious beings demanding milk and hugs, is seldom productive. Am I therefore doomed to be a loser?

Although early rising correlates with success, this does not prove it is the cause of it. What if today's wealthy early birds started out as pauper owls, then prospered toiling from noon to midnight, only to be forced by escalating demands to begin work nearer dawn? Could early be a price of success? Or alternatively, do naturally early chronotypes gain a competitive edge at school that helps them to leave behind socially disadvantaged late risers?

Early's chief benefits are momentum and lack of interruption: start the day confidently, accomplish your goals, and your morale will lift. Yes, our brains work well in the morning, but they also do so in the afternoon. The key lesson is that a lot can be achieved in a quiet hour, but late affords similar freedoms if you carve space to limit distractions. Gothic novelist Anne Rice completed *Interview with the Vampire* sleeping, like her hero, by day, and working after dark: 'I could concentrate the best. I needed to be alone in the still of the night, without the phone, without friends calling, with my husband sound asleep.' What matters is not when but how time is released. Late and stressed, or early and knackered, serves no one.

To change your sleep cycle, do not proceed gently: decide when you want your day to start and set an alarm. If a somnolent hand turns it off and you slither back to sleep, the following night put the alarm on the other side of the room. Persist. You will readjust. This is the basic programme, although there are further nuances. In whichever direction you want to change, your objective is to shift the midpoint of your sleep cycle: it needs to be later if you wish to rise later, or earlier in order to rise earlier.

To convert from an early to a late riser (or to recover from westbound jet lag)

This is the easiest transition. Changing your time cycle by delay pushes you in the direction of nature's clock, the sun, and it is healthier too. A study found that workers adjusting from early to late shifts felt better, were more productive and less error-prone than those switching from late to early. The same applies to jet lag: westbound passengers take one day per time zone to readjust; eastbound passengers take up to six.

To be more of an owl, extend your day: go to bed later, avoid morning sun and seek it later in the afternoon.

To convert from an owl to a lark (or to recover from eastbound jet lag)

Use the reverse strategy: get up earlier, retire earlier. Food, mood, exercise, light and rituals will cue your body to wind down. Here follows a schedule. Some of the tips may seem reminiscent of romantic manoeuvres, but your task is to woo yourself to sleep.

In the morning:

- Get up earlier (borrow an alarm clock, small child or puppy)
- Seek the sun, as early as you can, without sunglasses.
- Avoid caffeine.

In the afternoon:

- No naps or siestas, not even forty winks.
- Exercise (your body temperature remains high for six hours afterwards, so no later or you will be too hot to sleep).
- Be calm – try yoga or meditation.

In the evening:

- Avoid heavy, late meals.
- Embrace foods that make you dozy – ones rich in carbohydrates, starch and sugar, or tryptophan (found in turkey meat), an amino acid that metabolizes into serotonin, vital for the production of melatonin (another reason why you nod off after Christmas dinner).
- Skip alcohol (it dehydrates you, and as a depressant it interferes with your SCN – your on/off switch).
- Dim the lights to trick your SCN into thinking it is dusk.

At night:

- Avoid stress, anxiety, arguments and stimulants.
- Pull down blackout blinds.
- Enforce a screens curfew *at least an hour before sleep*.
- Ban illuminated clocks or chargers from the bedroom.
- Take a warm bath. As your body cools afterwards you may find it easier to drop off.
- Make love.
- Cultivate bedtime rituals, triggering you to prepare for sleep.
- Stay cool.
- Open the window (oxygen improves sleep).
- Do not go to bed before you feel ready.

7

Time Rich

How to hurry slowly, spend time better
and lose it well

Time is money. We spend it, save it, waste, lose or kill it. The virtue of this thinking is that it dissuades us from wasting time. The danger is that it turns time into a commodity, commodifying life and objectifying experience – a strategic error.

Fixate on saving time and we can misspend ourselves. Trick somebody into feeling wealthier, for example, and instantly their time feels more pressed. Placing a higher value on each hour also makes unpaid leisure harder to justify. Thus a money mentality leaches time's pleasure. At an extreme, it renders us schedule flunkies, inhaling productivity manuals as others do Mills & Boon. We may become so estranged from experience that we value it only by what it costs, like King Midas, the dimwit with ass's ears who wished that everything he touched would turn to gold.

The time–money equation is not only impoverishing but also illogical. Like money, time is disposable, yet unlike money, we cannot bank our hoarded hours. The present is a gift that exists only now, as time, alas, is non-transferable.

How ironic that the definition of luxury is to waste time conspicuously – preferably other people's. Just as soft pale hands were once coveted proof that you were a non-labouring gentleman or lady, so the albino interiors that strut inside glossy design magazines – displaying acres of cream carpet and marble – semaphore in the international language of spotless Calacatta that their owners can afford a flotilla of maids. No matter that the maids spend longer tending these temples of purity than their workaholic masters get to enjoy them.

However you spend your time, it will be richer if it feels like your choice. As Robert Levine, an expert in the pace of life, discovered amid reverse culture shock on returning to his university post after a sabbatical: 'With frightening immediacy, my future was once again filled with an abundant helping of "shoulds" and "musts." My schedule was packed.' He decided from then on, when poised to do anything – from social interaction to professional task – that he would pause to ask two questions: 'First, is this something that I absolutely must do? And, second, is it something that I choose to do? Unless there was a "yes" to one of these questions I would not invest my time in the endeavour.'

To his surprise, and pleasure, often he answered yes. But the subjection of 'should' and 'must' had transmuted into something empowering: 'I want'. He was living by his priorities. This chapter explores how you can achieve similar alchemy by making choices in time that help it to feel more like your own.

1. The case for hurrying slowly

'He who lives out his days has had a long life,' according to the *Tao Te Ching*. Today's science supports this ancient insight: sinking our senses into the moment slows and enriches time as nothing else can. But how to achieve this depth?

Perhaps surprisingly, there is no such thing as the right pace to live. Fast destabilizes us only if we react in one or more of the following ways:

- disengagement
- loss of focus
- getting stressed
- becoming disorganized

Fast is not the concern, but our response to time pressure. To be in a position of psychological strength we need a sense of control over the pace – even if this is an illusion. As was shown in studies of restaurants where, to maximize profits during busy periods, waiters needed to hasten service; however, if customers felt rushed they were less likely to return. Balancing these conflicting priorities was the profit-making sweet spot. It turned out that diners were fine with a fast pace *provided* they imagined that they were setting it themselves. For example, if waiters asked, 'Shall I bring the dishes as soon as they are ready?' the decision became the diner's.

To avoid being derailed by a fast pace does not necessarily mean slowing down; rather it means being able to make meaningful progress. But which speed to pick? Slow can be relaxing, but not if you ache for fast. In 1879 Robert Louis Stevenson toured rural France with a crafty donkey, Modestine, as bag carrier. She took full advantage of her learner driver:

> What that pace was, there is no word mean enough to
> describe; it was something much slower than a walk
> as a walk is slower than a run … in five minutes it
> exhausted the spirit and set up a fever in all the
> muscles of the leg … I tried to tell myself it was a
> lovely day; I tried to charm my foreboding spirit with
> tobacco; but I had a vision ever present to me of the
> long, long roads, up hill and down dale …
> approaching no nearer to the goal.

Fast thrills us when we can keep up. Accomplishing anything at speed, be it careering down a snow-clad hill or completing a dull report, feels like a triumph. I discovered the zest that fast lends to a task when cooking dim sum to fly into lunch-hour mouths at a city restaurant. As soon as the crowds ebbed, the pace flagged and our fun congealed. No doubt excitement also helps to explain the higher levels of subjective happiness evident in fast-paced cities, despite the pollution, stress and heart attacks.

Unfortunately our appetite for fast makes us impatient. (Fast food has this effect, even when we are not eating it.) Then we are vulnerable to manipulation by fast as a marketing tool. Think how many products are sold on debatable claims that they are quicker, better – but buy now, while stocks last …

So sensitive is our pace barometer that simply encountering an image that we associate with fast will speed us up. Sanford DeVoe, an academic specializing in organizational behaviour, exposed students to flashing subliminal images of fast-food restaurant logos for twelve milliseconds, too swift for the conscious mind to register. Afterwards they read a piece of writing 20 per cent faster than a control group. What is not clear, however, is how much information they took in. And this is the key point. The word fast has long been a euphemism for unreliable (as in the con trick, 'fast and loose', and that 1950s sexual deviant, the 'fast girl'). The trouble with a fast pace is that, because it makes us feel good, we mistake this feeling for proof that whatever we just did so speedily must therefore be right and good. Yet speed is no proof that we have a clue what we are doing.

As you move through the day you glide along using mental shortcuts – otherwise known as rules of thumb or heuristics (what Daniel Kahneman called 'fast thinking'). These off-the-peg garments of cognition are extremely helpful to our flow, reducing pauses for deliberation. And the less we stop to think, the fleeter time seems. What's not to love about that? Well, our mental autopilot can be programmed with bad habits. Then we stop noticing, thinking, when we would do better to slow down. This is why, although a bright person is 'quick' and IQ tests, considered the gold standard of mental prowess, measure rapid cognition, in reality fast can inhibit intelligence.

Time-pressured intelligence is in fact a narrow ability. IQ reveals nothing of analytical or psychological insight. (So now you know why people who broadcast their 167-point

MENSA membership seem such twits.) Robert Sternberg, a leading expert in intelligence, concluded that considered preparation and slow thinking are exceptional predictors of skill. For instance, in a test involving syllogisms, the longer individuals spent reading the first part of the task, the better they performed.

Masterly retailer Bernard Lewis demonstrates the power of slow, analytical thinking to make things happen faster. Steadily, over decades, he built a business worth billions in the flightiest trade imaginable, young women's fashion. So unafraid was he to take his time that employees were regularly kept on tenterhooks in meetings as he pondered a question in silence for ten minutes. 'Deciding is not difficult,' he told me. 'Understanding is. When you understand a problem correctly the right choice is usually obvious.'

Lewis used his prodigious focus to accelerate his decision-making. Long before computers, rather like a one-man algorithm, he devised sales, stock and on-order systems capable of capturing large quantities of information in a form that he could interpret at a glance in order to forecast trends, enabling him to tell in a trice whether a garment was taking off or nearing the end of its shelf life. This revolutionary method, entirely self-taught, allowed him to peer around the corner into the future, always staying a step ahead of the game – and thereby saving and making his business an awful lot of money. 'You have to be nimble,' he said, 'like a dancer; always on the balls of your feet.'

Lewis's thoroughgoing understanding of his trade gave him the confidence to rebrand his family's chain of stores not once but twice. In the 1960s Lewis Separates became Chelsea

Girl, Britain's wildly popular 'boutique on the high street'; then, in the 1980s, Chelsea Girl became River Island.

Understanding is the secret of any judgement, even the split-second variety. Watch a brilliant tennis player in action and their speed is deceptive, the product of years of training. This hefty time investment gives the great players lightning reactions – buying them extra time to wait fractionally longer to decide where to hit a ball. So what looks fast to us is in fact the opposite: a pause for slightly slower thought.

In the words of that well-known motto of ancient Rome, *festina lente*, 'Hurry slowly'. A considered, smooth pace produces better results than an erratic one – an ethos encapsulated in Aesop's fable of the arrogant hare, who naps and is overtaken by the stolid tortoise. Steady effort counts for more at any velocity, if the technique is right and the direction sure.

Fast can be bounteous, as novelist Georges Simenon demonstrated, locking himself away to write often excellent novels in two to three weeks, rather like a marathon *séance*. Then he spent a great deal of time recuperating in brothels, clocking up 425 books and 10,000 lovers (or a mere 1,200, if you believe his wife).

Really good work, like really good times – when we feel focused, productive, happy, relaxed – come when we know what we want to do, then concentrate. Where would music be, had Johann Sebastian Bach not been obliged as organist and cantor of St Thomas's, Leipzig to supply one cantata a week? Or literature, had Shakespeare not spouted two to three plays a year?

How to judge a good use of time

It may seem sensible to assess the benefits of a time choice using money. But money is an unsteady index of utility. The great eighteenth-century naturalist Comte de Buffon wrote, 'As soon as one passes certain limits it has almost no real value ... a man that discovered a mountain of gold would not be richer than the one that found only one cubic fathom.' But people often forget that the value they put on money is not universal. Mathematician Jordan Ellenberg identified this flawed thinking in the work of Harvard economist Greg Mankiw, who claimed that an increase in taxes under President Barack Obama in 2008 would discourage people from working, reducing tax revenues. As somebody on a sizeable income, Mankiw was right: if taxes rose, he might well decide to spend more time with his children. But if he was a bus driver, high taxes would encourage him to work harder – he would need the money.

A good use of time is also a question of point of view: of your goals and needs. When time is limited, it means more to us, but this scarcity can feed reactive, hurried thinking, making us myopic; less able to stand back, take a long view. Add anxiety to the mix and we enter the realm of uncertainty. This is unhelpful, since good decisions depend on gauging the probable: costs, benefits and risks.

To escape this mind trap, when considering a choice, assess its expected utility in terms *you* value. Ask yourself what your priorities are. Consider two things:

1. What is the hour for?
2. What are your goals, wants and needs?

Then evaluate the probable costs and benefits. Ellenberg uses the example of whether it is worth arriving late at airports:

> Showing up 15 minutes before the plane leaves is going to slam you with a very high probability of missing the plane, with all the negative utility that implies. On the other hand, arriving many hours before also costs you many utils [units of utility]. The optimal course of action falls somewhere in between. Exactly *where* it falls depends on how you personally feel about the relative merits of missing planes and wasting time.

To enhance your time choices, you could try algebra (see Ellenberg's excellent *How Not to be Wrong*). But simply making a habit of pausing to assess utility might be enough, introducing an astringent dose of calculation.

Would you gain by arriving later at airports? Or by putting more buffer time into your day, which might free you to relax if a meeting overruns and enable you to decipher the action points from your boss's monologue? If introducing extra slack means skipping lesser meetings, ask: what have you to lose? Time has no value if we throw it away.

When priorities conflict, utility is even harder to rate. Government minister Tessa Jowell faced this dilemma when an event at her daughter's school clashed with an important speech she was due to make in the House of Commons. She confided in her colleague, Alistair Darling, who offered to give the speech for her. His advice, which she would use many times, was to ask the question: 'Where am I irreplaceable?'

2. How to lose time well, find flow and make work fun

Lose your freedom and you soon savour what choices remain. In 2004 Piper Kerman was sentenced to fifteen months in prison for an almost forgotten crime, committed in her misguided youth. Full of regrets, she soon realized that time was 'a big, indolent immovable beast that wasn't interested in my efforts at hastening it'. Battling on, she learnt the truth of Parkinson's Law: any task, no matter how fatuous, expands to fit the time available. Work, friends, rituals, jogging, acts of kindness, helped her to click off the hours like prayer beads.

> In Danbury I had learned to hasten the days by
> chasing the enjoyment in them, no matter how
> elusive. Some people on the outside look for what is
> amiss ... they are always trying to hang their
> mortality on improvement. It was incredibly
> liberating to instead tackle the trick of making each
> day fly more quickly.

> 'Time, be my friend,' I repeated every day. Soon I
> would go down to the track and try to chase the day
> away running in circles.

Kerman demonstrated that time's pace, pleasure and purpose
are intertwined: the more of the latter two, the faster it spins.

Personally, I love switching off. Many nights have passed
in mute witness to the fictional misdeeds of Tony Soprano,
Betty Draper, Walter White, Stringer Bell, the Lannisters. I am
even happier tucked inside a gripping book. There, time
disappears. Film director Nora Ephron captured this joy,
describing being 'instantly lost to the world. Days pass as I
savor every word … I'm truly beside myself.' To her, such
moments were akin to 'the rapture of the deep … when a
deep-sea diver spends too much time at the bottom of the
ocean and can't tell which way is up'. If she was as ecstatic
as this when reading, one wonders how good she felt writing
her masterpieces, *Heartburn* and *When Harry Met Sally*.

Ephron was talking about transcendence – the self-escape
humans have craved since we first danced, as testified by the
prehistoric paintings of figures jiving across cave walls.
Generally we chase transcendence in sport, art, sex, drugs or
religion, but we can achieve it in a host of activities, some of
them very ordinary.

There is another word for transcendence: flow. It was
popularized by Professor Mihaly Csikszentmihalyi, the
godfather of positive psychology, who devoted decades to
investigating everyday life in order to understand what
causes happiness. His impressive body of research points to
a bald conclusion: what brings happiness is not what we

assume: 'The inertia of habit and social pressure are so strong that many people have no idea which components of their lives they actually enjoy, and which contribute to stress and depression.'

Csikszentmihalyi might give me a hard time for watching TV, less so for reading books. What he would point out is that while reading requires concentration and imaginative collaboration, both are passive pastimes: our attention is drawn along like a fish on a hook. Although at the arse-end of the day we may ache for nothing more than to sit back with a glass and tune out, or loll on a sun lounger, switching off is less wonderful for our wellbeing and brain than doing something active and tuning in. It is a view widely supported across the sciences.

In 2008, as financial cataclysm drove wellbeing up political agendas, over four hundred neuroscientists, teachers, economists, psychiatrists, psychologists, geneticists, social scientists and systems analysts from across the world contributed to the Foresight Project on Mental Capital and Wellbeing. Their mission was to supply evidence-based answers regarding how to thrive in the twenty-first century. They concluded that five actions boost health and happiness – and, by extension, productivity, since contented workers also work harder:

1. Connect.
2. Be active.
3. Take notice.
4. Keep learning.
5. Give.

If you had to sum up these five actions in a single word, it would be enthusiasm (derived from the Greek for 'possessed by god'). This energetic form of happiness lights up if we feel good about what we are doing, driving us to try harder; whenever we enter into something and feel highly motivated, whether at work, during leisure time, or – as Piper Kerman found – when helping people.

Enthusiasm is a particularly useful goal in terms of our work aspirations, and we cannot wait for divine intervention to kindle it. Sadly, employers are unlikely to wake up and start demanding less of their staff; the productivity push is set to continue. We need innovate find ways to accomplish more in less time, and the best way is to zoom in on what adds value, not burn 30 per cent of our time sifting futile email. We will also feel better if we do.

Harvard researchers demonstrated that engagement is the hallmark of happiness in an ingenious study. They gave 2,250 volunteers an app that asked questions randomly throughout the day – how they felt, and what they were doing and thinking. Surprisingly, it did not matter precisely *what* people were up to, or where – whether at work or leisure: they were happy so long as their attention was fully on what they were doing. If their mind wandered (which happened on average 46.9 per cent of the time, and no less than 30 per cent in the course of most activities, barring sex), their pleasure did too. In other words, happiness dwells in absorption in the here and now. This is why the more prone a person is to event expectancy (fixating on future occasions), the greater the odds they will suffer social anxiety. Busy minds, fretting on their tomorrows, and their to-do lists, spoil life before it has a chance to happen.

There are different ways to be absorbed. If attention is consumed by a transfixing activity – say, Candy Crush – time is apt to feel ghostly, as if we are barely there, and we are left with little to show for it. But if it is devoted to exploring, learning, we feel in charge of our life. Focus and we can even achieve the sort of rapture Nora Ephron exulted in, entering what Mihaly Csikszentmihalyi called a flow state. Like the musician Prince, who described how, late one night, alone, he played and sang for three hours straight: 'I just couldn't stop ... in the zone ... like an out-of-body experience. That's what you want. Transcendence. When that happens – Oh, boy.'

So what leads to flow?

1. Clear rules.
2. Defined goals.
3. Constant feedback.

Any game – whether mental or physical – is flow-friendly, as is cooking. But if a task is either too hard or too easy, then our attention wanders. Peak flow experiences occur when four things come together: deep engagement, efficient performance, unselfconsciousness and surpassing your limits. This can happen anywhere. For example, the engineer who glances up from her screen to notice that night has fallen, hears her stomach grumble and realizes that she last ate at breakfast, has been in flow: performing a task within her capabilities but sufficiently difficult to stretch and improve her skills. It is the ideal, relaxed mental state for creative thought, according to Daniel Kahneman.

You often see children in flow because so often they are learning. Tongue between their lips, their eyes widen, barely blinking, as the cognitive effort renders their faces still, alive only to what preoccupies them. It is a relaxed state ideal for creativity. By contrast with my little ones, I can feel my senses are cloaked, like the skin on cold custard, as thoughts of the past and future crowd out my focus on the now.

Unselfconsciousness is essential to flow. This is also why most hobbies deliver flow states. Any activity, even DIY, can qualify as a hobby; what distinguishes it from work is that it is an autotelic task – a delicious end in itself. The reward is intrinsic. But there is a quick way to ruin a hobby: add a self-conscious, extrinsic motivation. As Daniel Pink observed in *Drive*, every secondary incentive has one powerful effect: it turns play into work. Why?

Contrary to popular opinion, motivation is a delicate beast and reacts poorly to secondary incentives – whether carrots or sticks. Bribes and threats, bonuses and penalties, deplete enthusiasm by sending a subtly negative message: that this task is not itself interesting; what matters is the reward, or the avoidance of punishment. This distracting message saps focus and intrinsic motivation.

In the short term, fat bonuses or promises of lollipops do speed us up. Threats are especially effective. Marketing research finds that to persuade customers to buy, a negative – fear of loss – works better than suggested gains. Likewise, tell a child to practise the cello – because if she does so without whining, you will buy her a sticker book – and she will practise. But not with a smile, and always with an eye to the clock – at the long-term risk of neutering her delight in music. The shoots of lasting motivation only sprout if rooted within. Whereas bribes and threats make any activity less engaging, meaning that we must use up more precious will-power to stick at it – leaving us more distractible.

Rewards also inhibit risk-taking. In one study, when three-and four-year-old children at Bing nursery in Stanford were asked to draw, they proved far less enthusiastic and inventive if they knew that they would receive a smart Good Player Award card with a large gold star than if they received noth-ing at all. In another experiment, adults given a puzzle continued to fool with it in their spare moments, becoming more engrossed – but if the puzzle was presented as work (with payment attached) they spent less time on it, and also found it harder. In summary, we spend *less* time, imagination and effort on tasks if contingent rewards are attached. This is bad news, since time, creativity and effort grow skills. And being good at something makes it more enjoyable.

If you find all of this counter-intuitive, you are not alone. Corporations, colleges and schools remain wedded to the culture of prizes and bonuses. Despite consistent evidence, psychologists were slow to accept the idea until 1999, when a team analysed 128 experiments, concluding: 'Tangible rewards tend to have a substantially negative effect on intrin-sic motivation.'

Motivation comes down to freedom. Unlike work, a hobby is a chosen task, but introduce rewards or threats and this autonomy disappears: it becomes work. If you have no choice but to work for money, this context alone can make you regard paid work as a form of prison, counting the minutes until the day ends – even if the activity itself might otherwise absorb you. Hence in 2013, among the UK's least happy workers were those employed in the construction industry. Yet during the Second World War, British Prime Minister Winston Churchill found relaxation by laying bricks: a constructive contrast to the hullaballoo. Crucially, in contrast with twenty-first-century builders, bricklaying was optional for Churchill, with no time pressure, and no foreman telling him to hurry or he would dock his pay.

So let us pity the lawyers compelled to log every self-conscious minute spent on a client's account, then round it up to the nearest fifteen. Where is the fun in that?

The good news is that you can redesign any activity – even paid work – to engage you more. The most work-thrilled man Csikszentmihalyi ever met was Rico, a quality controller in a camera factory. Unlike anyone else on his assembly line, he adored his job because he saw in it endless scope to do better. Allowed forty-five seconds to check whether a camera was up to standard, he spent years improving his manoeuvres to get this down to twenty-eight seconds. The conveyor belt moved no faster, so this improvement did not boost the factory's output. But for him, it was about pride: performance, not productivity.

'The emotional rewards craftsmanship holds out for attaining skill are twofold: people are anchored in tangible reality, and they can take pride in their work,' wrote philosopher Richard Sennett. 'As skill progresses, it becomes more problem-attuned, like the lab technician worrying about procedure … At its higher reaches, technique is no longer a mechanical activity; people can feel fully and think deeply.' Sennett captured the rewards of mastery. For a violinist it begins in playing tunes, but a good player sharpens their skills, and a maestro quests for the colours in notes. Excellence is learning without end, as Rico knew.

Opportunities to enrich our wellbeing through performance exist everywhere. The Foresight Project's five recommendations provide a map for an active, learning, connected, observant and giving life. But creativity and action must be sought consciously, particularly because the ecology of leisure is changed, as creative pursuits are shoved aside by passive entertainment, made for the many, enjoyed, all too often, in solitude. For instance, my grandmother made many of her clothes, for fun and economy. She taught my mother, who offered to teach me, but I was too busy hanging out in the local shopping centre. I expect my children will buy their clothes online. Maybe an app will let them design them. Maybe they will arrive an hour later on an unmanned drone, courtesy of the local 3D printworks.

Really good times – when we feel focused, productive, happy, relaxed – come when we know what we want to do and then concentrate. You need not be a virtuoso. If doctors prescribed planting beans or knitting before anti-depressants, you have to wonder how much angst we might work out through our fingertips, producing stuff to be proud of?

How to make work feel like a hobby

Whether you are a marine tasked with building a bridge from twigs, a call-centre operator or a welder, studies find that if you are empowered by your sergeant, line manager or gaffer to design the route to reach your goals, your enthusiasm will grow. This feeling of autonomy is a prerequisite of morale and of creating a situation where 'what we feel, what we wish, and what we think are in harmony' – something vital to flow, according to Csikszentmihalyi. Design tasks to improve your skills as you work, and pace and performance will improve too.

A task that offers a learning experience could entail meeting a challenge, solving a problem or tackling something new. Approach any activity as a game and it becomes more diverting. So long as it is achievable – in balance with, while stretching, your skills. To ensure you do not head off track, it also needs:

1. Clear goals.
2. Clear rules (measures for success and failure).
3. Immediate feedback (to tell if you are working well).

Using these guidelines, review your tactics in order to bring more flow into your life. For example, if you want to get fit, attach this objective to a higher challenge (running in a 5K to raise money for charity). Then, each day of training, set yourself a new target, one that is realistic but exceeds the last. Alternatively, set challenges within your familiar routines; experiment with different approaches. If something is too easy, increase the challenge or play with sequence. If you find this too difficult, analyse the cause: are you overreaching your skills or time limits, or is your goal too hazy?

3. Stop if you want to go faster

Overwork is the enemy of flow. Stare at a computer until your eyeballs shrivel and error becomes inevitable – the greatest mistake being all that life of yours, not being lived.

The pause is the Cinderella of time management but deserves celebration. Breaks give the day rhythm – they are helpful punctuation to make you feel that life marches purposefully on. They are also pacemakers. When learning to cook game in the belly of the Ritz hotel with head chef John Williams, I recognized the value of the periodic ballet of wiping, sweeping, clearing decks. Not only did such pauses limit chaos, but like knots between beads on a necklace they kept stages of complicated recipes distinct, from plucking to chopping to boiling to caramelizing. During these breaks I refocused, kept calm and – crucially – stayed on time.

Power naps are good, but so is a stroll, or five minutes off to call a friend. Even a microbreak – standing, stretching, looking out of the window, drinking a glass of water – replenishes us, opening space for reflection to blossom. Stop when you hit a mental block and your unconscious may supply the answer, thanks to the brain's default system.

When a bright idea bubbles up in the shower – the one you needed two hours ago – it does so due to attention lag, or what psychologists call the 'hangover effect'. Put simply, the brain works overtime if left alone: break from something mid-task and it continues to brood, often unconsciously, on that incomplete thing, exerting a cognitive load that colours our thinking if we direct it elsewhere.

Hangover effects can be either positive or negative. Overwhelm your mind with incomplete tasks – take on too much, or keep switching focus – and the cognitive load drags on us, like an undertow. It is for this reason that multitaskers are slower, and less accurate. Given how bombarded many of us are by a constant influx of requests, the diabolical mental weight of incompleteness is a recipe for angst on a grand scale – something that surely explains the increase in anxiety today.

Keep a single purpose in mind, however, and the hangover effect bears fruit. Then, when you take a break, your default system can reward you for reducing the mental pressure. For instance, Russian composer Pyotr Tchaikovsky, like many artists and thinkers, went for a walk after each morning's work, always with a notebook in hand, since inspiration would inevitably hit as he ambled among the hedgerows.

The more peace a mind has, the more effective its processes. Even the intolerable becomes acceptable. Neurosurgeon Henry Marsh described his terror upon learning that an urgent operation was required to save his eyesight:

> I walked out of the building twenty minutes later in a
> state of panic. Rather than take the tube or a taxi
> home I walked the six miles back to my house
> rehearsing all the terrible things that might happen to
> me – starting with having to abandon my career …
> and going on to complete blindness … I cannot
> remember how my thoughts ran as I walked but, to
> my surprise, by the time I got home I was strangely
> reconciled to the problem.

Perhaps it helped that he forgot to switch on his phone upon leaving the clinic, and hence did not immediately talk to his panic-stricken wife and amplify the dread.

Here follow six ways to tune in:

1. **Be less available.** We all need do-nothing time: time out of time. President Barack Obama routinely scheduled slots of what he described as 'thinking time' into his day-to-day routine.

2. **Be enthusiastic.** What turns you on? Seek your divine spark.

3. **Choose absorbing activities.** How could you be more active, learn, notice, connect and give? Go dancing, ride a bicycle? Try slow activities too: fishing, painting, gardening, darning, kneading dough, peeling potatoes, making risotto from scratch. Who has the time? You may be surprised how much more time there appears to be if you lessen the pace. Better yet, launch yourself at other people, my favourite waste of time.

4. **Pay attention.** I am not about to tell you to study a raisin (although it looked hilarious on *Cold Feet*). But being mindful is always worthwhile. Anna Shepherd, author of *The Living Mountain*, observed: 'This is the innocence we have lost, living in one sense at a time to live all the way through ... The hands have an infinity of pleasure in them. The feel of things, textures, surfaces ... the scratchiness of lichen, the warmth of the sun, the sting of hail, the blunt blow of tumbling water, the flow of wind.'

Another expert attention payer was French vaudeville artist and novelist Colette, who approved of boredom as it 'helps one to make decisions' (by incentivising you to unbore yourself). Her vices – such as seducing her stepson – were many, but dullness was not among them. She once chided a friend: 'You must not pity me because my sixtieth year finds me still astonished. To be astonished is one of the surest ways of not growing old too quickly.' She cultivated this faculty, advising a writer: 'Look for a long time at what pleases you, and longer still at what pains you.'

5. **Resist the impulse to fill every second.** Take longer routes, make space for serendipitous discovery, daydream.

6. **Go outside.** According to a 2012 National Trust report, UK children have 90 per cent fewer spaces near home in which to wander unsupervised than those reared in the 1970s. Author Richard Louv, who claims we suffer 'nature deficit disorder', cites studies showing that patients in hospitals whose windows look onto natural landscapes recover faster than those who see urban vistas. Whatever your environment, it can supply a ready store of wonderment. Be inspired by sharp-eyed tenth-century lady courtier Sei Shonagan, a connoisseur of the fugitive present, such as the evening hour 'when the glittering sun sinks close to the edge of the hills and the crows fly back to their nests in threes and fours and twos'. Or Gilbert White, curate of Selborne, writing on 1 February 1785: 'On this cold day about noon a bat was flying round Gracious

street-pond, & dipping down and sipping water, like
swallows, as it flew: and all the while the wind was
very sharp & the boys were standing on the ice!'

Perhaps the miracle of existence was easier to access in the
past, with fewer distractions competing to catch the eye. But
any instant can be captivating, if you look hard enough. Like
singer-poet Patti Smith, watching heavy mist fall on
Monmouth Street: 'I caught the moment when drapes of
cloud dropped upon the ground. I had never seen such a
thing and lamented I was without film for my camera. On
the other hand I was able to experience the moment
completely unburdened.' And by reflecting on the liberty she
felt in that instant, Smith found a different way to create art
from it too.

How meditation fattens the brain

Twenty-five centuries ago a young Nepalese prince
renounced his privileges in order to seek enlightenment.
He found it sitting for seven days under a fig tree in Bodh
Gaya, India; thence he ascended to Nirvana, where time
and space melted away. Five centuries after Siddhartha
Gautama became the Buddha, another youth went on a
journey, spending forty days in the desert, re-emerging
with a hollow belly and a mouth full of parables.

Both Jesus and the Buddha withdrew from the world in
order to transform it. But their techniques for self-tran-
scendence can be used for more prosaic purposes.

Mindfulness is meditation shorn of its religious dimension. It trains you to differentiate between awareness (being conscious) and thought (your inner monologue). 'Many people find that meditation liberates them from the pressures of time, so they have more of it to spend on other things', write Professor Mark Williams and Danny Penman in their book *Mindfulness*. Further benefits include reducing depression, stress, pain and addiction, and improving health, memory, creativity and reaction times. Brain scans of regular meditators show they have a thicker cerebral cortex, greater blood flow and a larger hippocampus than non-meditators, with more electrical energy discernible in areas linked to empathy and happiness.

Rather than worry about events that have yet to occur, or the irretrievable past, you can use the tools of mindfulness to control your mental processes: to interrupt negative self-talk and insert a pause between feeling, thought and action – thus breaking reactive-panic cycles to liberate the present. Here is a simple meditation:

1. Sit on a comfortable chair and close your eyes.
2. Concentrate on breathing. Notice breath coming in and out.
3. If thoughts intrude, acknowledge them, let them go if you can, but do not fight them. Focus on breathing.
4. Your mind may feel still. Or not. Do not worry: there is no right or wrong way to do this.
5. After a minute – or will it turn out to have been five? – open your eyes.

NOW TRAPPING

I love being in the moment. Especially if I can photograph and keep it for ever.

Watching myself, or my friends, snapping and filming, I often think of butterfly catchers, romping in the meadows, getting hot and bothered and missing the view as they attempt to capture beauty and pin it to a board. Our prey is similar. We are now trappers.

Most of us paste photos online in order to keep connected with friends and family marooned in far-off places, such as half an hour up the M3. I am too lazy to post or print, and seldom inspect my bounty. But I still take pictures, in case I miss the perfect shot. I want the impossible: to take the party home, stop my parents getting any older, snare the emerald blaze of a sunlit tree, immortalize the curve of a child's cheek in something sturdier than memory's aspic; to gather up the happy times and fold them somewhere safe. I seek the irrevocable in flattering 2D.

Now trapping is seldom a private pursuit. It is hard not to judge that Instagram fanatics display their wares like so much shed skin in order to boast. To the very famous, these streams of images serve the same purpose as saints' relics did for the church: followers pay homage, drumming up business. A few – those who claim to curate their lives – might call their output art. But the underlying impulse, as old as art and religion, is identical to mine: to freeze time. Yet, as we do so, we lose time, standing at a remove from our experience in order to objectify it – like a writer with the necessary splinter of ice in the heart who panhandles every tragedy for potential raw material.

Those who once feared that the camera might steal their soul had a point. Attempt to halt time and we lose the joy of its movement, like elderly plastic surgery addicts, their taut vellum skin and faultline smiles a rictus of ersatz youth. Preoccupied by wrinkles and fat, followers and likes, we can begin to live from the outside in – making our choices to accord with external perceptions, projected standards that relate to nothing inside us. Then the quest for the image can begin to lead the life. Like those celebrity seekers whose existence seems to pass in a comic strip of carefully lit moments, the speech and thought bubbles replaced by the graffiti of others' envious or admiring comments.

The carnival of images is the great art of our age, both a product and driver of digital technology. But it is tempting to ask whether there is something especially thin in the quality of time today that is encouraging us to compile dossiers of evidence that we have lived.

Only if events stir us, if we live attentively, does the developing fluid of emotion form memories vivid enough to compete with pixels and video. Think how many of your childhood recollections are uncanny echoes of images yellowing in a family album – false memories, in a sense, planted by those pictures. Are all these gadgets we treat as our sixth sense – designed to relieve us of our terrifying solitude while extending our memories and knowledge base – perhaps also depleting our ability to live memorably?

8

Time Thieves

A handler's guide to bogus convenience,
meetings, email and other botherment

You can spot a time thief by its impact on you. Anything that
slows you down, or sends you spinning in an unhelpful direction, is a time thief.

Time thieves lurk everywhere. Like stage magicians, they
work by misdirection. Their weapons are delay, distraction
and interruption. I am talking about the booby traps that
shatter your attention, the bamboozlers that hoodwink you
into activity that seems purposeful, only to burn a hole in
your day. Like true parasites, they deplete our drive – the
force we need if we are to resist.

There are two types of time thief: latent (slowing or clut-
tering you, like mess) and active (botherers that pull you off
course). But time thieves are also situation specific. In a
library, for example, music is a time thief. Elsewhere, it
hastens dull work. 'Sorry if it sounds like a nightclub,' apol-
ogized reporter Jane Hill, broadcasting live from the EU
referendum vote count in Swindon. 'They had turned off the

music but they had to turn it back on again because people were counting much slower without it.'

The worst time thieves are other people. Like the nameless 'person from Porlock' who visited Samuel Taylor Coleridge, causing him to break at line 54 of *Kubla Khan* and forget the rest of the 'dream vision' (i.e. the opium stupor) in which the poem appeared. But sometimes people are accelerants. An intriguing study conducted in 1898 by Norman Triplett, 'The Dynamonegenic Factors in Pacemaking and Competition' (unearthed by technology expert Ben Hammersley and pretty much the foundational text of social psychology) showed that when we are watched it is easier to accomplish easy things, whereas challenges grow difficult. This seems also to apply to cockroaches. Whatever is going on with the cockroaches, in humans the phenomenon is a question of motivation: having an audience is an incentive to show off doing something dull; however, when doing something tricky, self-consciousness scuppers concentration. So if you must bash a thousand nails into a thousand planks of wood, do it with friends. But for a hard task, lock the door.

You may blame your weak will for the theft of your time. Yet many personality traits that appear robust – the psychological term for the essential fibres of our being – are in fact local, dependent on where we are. In other words, our habitat shapes many of our time habits.

Take the case of mess. Not simply the product of an untidy person, it actively hinders him from being orderly, and may muddy his scruples. A Dutch study found that if passers-by happen upon a half-sealed envelope that obviously contains money, they are less likely to seal and mail it if it lies beside a post box in a dirty, graffiti-vined street than in a clean and tidy one. If living amid mess makes us misbehave, consider its effect on self-esteem. Your chaotic workstation may draw you to live down to that standard – to be unreliable, confused or even, yes, to procrastinate.

This is the opportunity: reshaping your habitat alters habits. Declutter time thieves and much timewasting disappears. Be ruthless. The drip-drip-drip of distractions leaches not only energy but willpower, making us even less able to resist. Any lure on our attention nags, be it a heap of pending invoices or a fly headbutting a skylight. For example, illustrator N.C. Wyeth used to sequester himself to paint in a studio, then would glue card on either side of his spectacles to block the enticing view from its window. A twenty-first-century equivalent of this would be to select 'focus view' on Microsoft Word, turning your screen black but for the document you are working on. Or to don earplugs and blindfold, like Jonathan Franzen writing *The Corrections*, or retreat to a cork-lined room like Marcel Proust, whose life's work was to pickle time in his forensically attentive prose.

To wrangle time thieves, heed two rules:

1. Your habitat forges your habits, so streamline it.
2. If motivation is low and concentration inessential, let distractions enhance your performance; if the reverse, banish them.

To apply these rules, be wise to the thieves in your midst.

1. The convenience myth: how time thieves pose as friends

We can be reluctant to recognize time thieves. But to identify your worst, simply find a mirror.

We believe we want to spend time wisely, yet in practice often we squander more. Take those mod cons we would sooner eat our fingers than be without: washing machines, vacuum cleaners, hairdryers, lawnmowers to discipline grass into prayer mats of suburban rectitude. All speed up chores. Yet in so doing they elevate standards, spawning new tasks; we buy more clothes or carpets, evolve fussier hairstyles and gardens. Anthropologist Allen Johnson highlighted this pattern in 1978, comparing the lives of the Amazon's Machiguenga tribe with French workers. The Machiguenga spent four times longer producing goods (weaving cloth or baskets) than on chores. Whereas the French spent four times longer on maintenance and consumption, had longer working days, produced little and had four fewer hours of leisure. Is making cider or knitting socks less satisfying than loading and unloading crockery?

Yet convenience is a beguiling proposition and peddles countless goods. Fast food, for example, claims to save time and yes, fat- and sugar-laden breakfast bars and smoothies can be scoffed on the run, as we text. Come evening, we can dine on ready meals: nothing to cut, no bones – ideal for stabbing with a fork while flicking the TV remote. But is it actually significantly less time-consuming to queue to buy a sandwich than to make one? Or to exhume an oven-ready frozen jacket potato from its box and stick it in an oven than to bake a fresh one? And which costs more? On closer inspection, the key time saving of most convenience food is the months it can sit on a supermarket shelf, as imperishable as Snow White in her coffin. This is not time that profits us.

When we interrogate claims of convenience, the difference between a fast and a slow choice frequently turns out to be marginal in terms of time, but massive in its value to us. How much longer does it take to write a note of thanks than to text – and how much more does it mean? Purchase something by tapping a plastic card on a plastic device, and you lose that moment to wonder: is it worth it? Kitchen designer Matt Chambers called his Quooker (an instant boiling water tap) 'the best thing I've ever bought … I drink six cups of tea a day – that's twelve minutes a day saved'. Yet he also regretted it: 'We're all used to putting the kettle on, waiting two minutes, then pouring. You can miss that quiet time.' Effectively he had culled his pauses for thought – three restorative days' worth per year.

Generally, fast is best at wrapping stuff in plastic, estranging us from experiences that could be our friends. Somehow we managed before Cup-a-Soup or jars of slime-stink masquerading as chopped garlic. The real stuff takes little longer to prepare; what is required is planning. In return we gain pride and relaxation, since cooking compels us to focus, to be in the moment – a prerequisite for feeling happy.

My favourite contemporary time-sparing scam is the speedy boarding service on economy airlines. Often it enables passengers to be first in the queue – and then to shiver or roast on the tarmac waiting for non-speedy boarders to catch up. This mendacious policy is characteristic of aviation in general. Airports are digestive tracts, contrived to agitate, divert and squeeze out of us our last drop of cash. Full of delays to make us bored, then late, then panicked, they prime us to buy or eat cack to cheer ourselves up.

History reveals that despite our love of mod cons, we are far more devoted to those that fill our time than those that set it free. In the twentieth century, disposable income in the UK lagged behind the United States' by thirty years. In line with this, British households lagged behind those in the US by thirty years in adopting time-saving washing machines and vacuum cleaners. Yet when it came to time-guzzling devices – radio, television – take-up was only five years behind. Maybe in those days men, not women, controlled the purse strings, and so abbreviating chores was not considered a priority. Whatever the truth, our appetite for distraction clearly exceeds our hunger to save time. Tellingly, British take-up of the telephone was just as slow as that of vacuum cleaners – until telephones mutated into entertaining, TV-like smartphones.

Despite these facts, our conviction that we want to spend time wisely is strong. So much so that it is used against us. Marketers lure us into committing unnecessary time, and then this itself becomes a lever to persuade us to buy things. The wait for the sold-out Christmas toy, the queue at the velvet rope for the half-empty nightclub, the pavement snarl outside the restaurant that refuses to take bookings – all aim to secure time investments, which then bias us to believe that the goal merits the bother (the sunk costs fallacy again). 'X must be good,' we tell ourselves; 'look how long I've waited.'

Next time somebody offers to save you time, ask what price you will pay.

Nine ways to cuff time thieves

1. **Notice where time leaks.** Such places might include physical spaces, or twists and turns in routines. What regularly makes you late? Is it easy to find your coat or umbrella?
2. **Erect ladders to distraction.** Create boundaries – physical and metaphorical. Turn off the Wi-Fi. Put the biscuits on a high shelf.
3. **Create gateways to desirable behaviour.** Create set-ups or chutes to ease desired actions. Wise author and agony aunt Virginia Ironside never failed to reciprocate unexpected Christmas cards, by the expedient of keeping spare cards and stamps by her front door.
4. **Smooth the flow.** Could switching between tasks be easier?
5. **Go on a distractions diet.** Send each of yours to Coventry for a week. How much more did you accomplish? Can you quit any of them altogether?
6. **Make them useful.** Treat your favourite distractions as rewards for sticking at dull tasks.
7. **Bundle and quarantine interruptions.** If you cannot excommunicate a distraction, do not let it come at you in scattershot fashion and throw you. Instead, chunk it into

211

a task and domesticate it to a set timeslot – with a strict time limit.

8. **Make time thieves less attractive.** The power of a stimulus lies in how it arouses us. This is why thinking of temptations as good (as in, green is good for you) or bad (but delicious) is self-defeating, because temptation only seems more tempting. Instead, focus on a distraction's less appealing qualities. During the tests of self-control conducted by Walter Mischel, children as young as three and a half found marshmallows and similar treats easier to resist if they had been given tips to render them more remote or less real-seeming. For example, imagine a picture frame around the marshmallow, or consider its less delicious qualities (how cloud-like it is). You too can use this tactic to neuter time thieves' appeal. Before an eBay graze, ask: do you have forty-five minutes of finite life to gawk at lampshades? Before hitting the shops, ask: is your wardrobe full of costumes for a life you have no time to live?

9. **Hit refresh.** When your mind wanders towards a distraction, imagine a button inside your brain marked 'refresh'. Hit it.

....

2. Time theft in the workplace

Is it Gina's spreadsheets, or Andrew – always so generous with his thoughts – on speakerphone, or the latest instalment of Al's Incredible Life Story?

At work, time drains are as varied as life's rich tapestry. Not all are preventable, but there are common threads between them, and tactics you can use to cauterize them.

Meetings

The first problem of meetings is their volume. They take up more than a third of employees' time, studies find, and up to two-thirds of CEOs', because a meeting culture metastasizes in proportion to an organization's size and an employee's status. It is as if there is a conspiracy to ensure bosses have no leisure to reflect and wonder what all these managers are for.

The second problem is conduct. I have been to meetings convened to discuss inconclusive meetings. Woolly agendas, no structure, waffly chairmen, zero action points, no follow-up: hour upon hour of pointlessness.

The third problem is people: too many, or they ogle phones, or see meetings as podiums. I remember one monologuing colleague who would, if a brave soul ever interposed a remark, squint then say, 'I take a Brechtian stance on that.' Whatever he meant, this had the desired effect. The floor was his.

The solution to these problems is to keep meetings purposeful, and to have as few as possible.

As productivity expert Carson Tate notes, there are six types of meeting: for information sharing, instruction, team building, brainstorming, decision-making and problem solving. The first two are eminently avoidable, as information and instruction can be shared in other formats. If your department must attend, delegate juniors to take notes. Team building requires team presence, but is best if timed to a slack period. Brainstorming also needs bodies in the same room, yet is more effective if any relevant material is circulated – and read – in advance. This also applies to decision-making and problem-solving meetings. So if such material is not forthcoming, request it.

To whittle down the number of meetings, ask: Is my presence irreplaceable? Is this meeting necessary? If the answer to both is yes, go. If not, wriggle. Explain you do not want to clutter the room. If possible, question the meeting's purpose.

If a meeting must happen, be sure you actually meet. (Teleconferencing reveals far less than other people's faces do.) Be clear as to the meeting's purpose, the attendees' relevance, the expected outcomes, and who will be executing any action points or follow-up. If there is no agenda, seek one. If action points and responsibilities are unclear, ask while people are in the room.

Many meetings vaporize into chit-chat until the second half, so jump to that half. Use time pressure to focus minds by shortening the meeting time, or deploy devious accelerants. Coca-Cola conducts meetings standing up. Why not banish chairs and book a chilly room?

The paper avalanche

Drifts of paper on a desk are cold comfort. Usually they are monuments to indecision. The solution is to decide: is this paper to be actioned, filed or ditched?

Process paper in bursts. If the information it contains is available elsewhere, does not need to be retained or require action, bin it. Otherwise file it, act now if you can, or add the task to your to-do list.

People

People are quick to seek our time but never give it back. Like my friend. Let us call him Dan. Mostly he works for a sales department. The sales people love communicating with him. Once a week they ask him to compile a pack in preparation for a deal. He does. The next week the deal is off. He bins the pack. The week after the deal is on again …

Once you are wise to time-wasters, strategize for their deficiencies (Dan no longer bins work asked for by sales). And ration access. If you have no office door to close, use a sign, or schedule time when people know you can and cannot be interrupted.

If lateness is an issue in your office, find a way – covert or overt, depending on your seniority – to ensure that managers (often the worst offenders) understand the impact on morale.

Managers

So often the conveners of meetings, managers are less frequently seen actually doing. Middle management's primary function can appear to be to remind colleagues that they exist: by issuing vague briefs, or firing late-night, tinkering emails on topics they do not grasp, or trying to micromanage staff.

Managing up is a verb that has yet to find a satisfactory definition. As we await such a definition, you can help managers to help you. Ensure that your role and responsibilities are clear regarding goals, detail, expectations and deadlines; establish specific measures of success, explicit limits on autonomy, and definite timeframes. Seek regular, timely feedback – not last-minute approval.

Noise

Noise, however dulcet, drains the brain. If your workplace is loud, investing in expensive noise-cancelling headphones may prove cheaper than lost productivity. If achieving quiet is not feasible, ask to use a meeting room or to work from home (though be warned: it will be seen as skiving).

The email deluge

A recent study reckoned that managing email consumed 28 per cent of the average person's working week – and email traffic is growing all the time. This vast issue, expanding faster than the universe, needs its own space.

3. Unnecessary communication

I am drawn to a tactic proposed by the busy MD of a communications company:

> It is a simple idea but will need new technology. When people send an email they will receive a mild electric shock. Its intensity will grow according to the length

of the email and how much time it takes the person
who receives it to deal with the contents.

Does this seem extreme? Email is not a victimless crime.

Inessential communication has been with us since
Babylon's scribes started poking cuneiform sticks into clay.
But today drivel is an epidemic because masses of us can be
bothered, 24/7, at little cost to the botherer. No need to stuff
envelopes or sour our tongues licking stamps.

Sadly, the accessibility of others makes us trigger-happy.
People forget that the immediate effect of each communication, no matter how cogent, witty or pretty, is to lay a burden
on someone else. Even if that person ignores our message,
they pay a tax in mild guilt.

At work, email silt is a torment. A friend pitched into
depression because his insomniac new boss sent contradictory missives all night long, then became furious when the
results were equally contradictory (my friend should have
pointed out the problems – always easy, with a new boss …).
Another pal leapt for redundancy from a prestigious car
company after work became no more than a trudge through
meetings and email treacle requiring hours of ministration,
after dark, if she was to accomplish anything by day.

Occasionally I wonder how this deluge came to pass. I first
encountered email when I worked on a listings magazine
(remember them?). For some, it acted as a carrier pigeon for
passing work to colleagues ten metres away, but they were
thought odd and lazy. Most of us flung email about to gossip
silently or avoid people with halitosis (an advantage in 1990s
journalism). Until, that is, we learnt that email was company

property, and that vaporous messages constitute binding contracts, and their improper use could be an excuse to fire us. Clearly we had to take email seriously. Unfortunately, shortly afterwards the world decided sending email was a purposeful activity all on its own.

You can see why it took off. Colleagues agree to do things, then deny it. Whereas email promises traceable decisions.

The difficulty is that people are so careless; they fail to include relevant information or identify the issues, and thus email breeds more of itself, as simple questions that could crystallize into a decision during one face-to-face meeting instead clot into back-and-forth exchanges between multiple people. We can express this situation in the following formula:

ill-expressed message + hit send too fast = confusion = ill-expressed message + hit send too fast

Even if a message is well-expressed, without a voice or face to go by, its interpretation is coloured by the recipient's mood. So when we are grumpy, a businesslike request appears rude. Worse, since emails are quick to send, they encourage us to expect an instant response.

Despite these shortcomings, when we write an email we can kid ourselves that our time has been spent profitably: there is demonstrable proof, we did something! Those neat letters, in straight lines on virginal virtual paper, can also delude us that confusing messages are clear and orderly – as a fair face can be mistaken for an outward sign of a beautiful soul.

Email also has a handy time-code to show when you sent it. How better to display commitment, or terrify your underlings, than to press send at 3.48 a.m. and let those numbers do the talking?

Nobody makes a phone call at 3.48 a.m. But of course that is the joy of digital communications: you can respond whenever it suits you. If only people did that, instead of rushing to reply because they feel they should.

The textual deluge has myriad consequences, personal and political. Amid the blizzard of data, vital information can be missed. We can grow into casual, lazy communicators, making heedless requests or promises we cannot keep. A single mindfart on Twitter can kill a career. A solitary misfired email can endanger national security, cost an election or your job. So let us kill the blizzard and reclaim digital communication as a vehicle for meaning.

How to tame digital communication

1. **Consider the alternatives.** Is your message worthy of the recipient's time? What if you met face to face? Waited? Did nothing?
2. **Be concise in order to focus attention.** The less you say, the more the recipient will take in: have a clear subject heading, spotlight the relevant information, be specific.
3. **Never reply instantly.** Ever.
4. **Demand less.** My friend's boss would reply to arse-covering emails with two words: 'Too long.'

5. **Chunk it.** Allocate a fixed slot for dealing with digital communication. Ideally not first thing in the morning, as it will divert you, loading your mind with incomplete tasks.

6. **Scan.** Carry out an hourly box scan to catch any emergencies. (And is it an emergency, or is someone just being hysterical?)

7. **Declutter.** If you cannot delete emails, file them. If no category springs to mind, why keep it? For the archive in the future museum of you?

8. **Abolish cc and bcc.** Either somebody is the target of your message or not. Invoking others' surveillance is passive-aggressive.

9. **Go on a text fast.** The out-of-office assistant message reads: 'I am not available on email. Call if it is important.' Take a day off. And another. How long can you last?

10. **Respond at a time that suits you.**

---

4. How to unplug

Film star Eddie Redmayne once retired his smartphone, but not for long. He found it more objectionable to spend two hours a night servicing his email on a laptop. Supermodel Christy Turlington cast her BlackBerry (remember them?) in bronze because her husband grew so fed up with it – then helped to launch the Apple watch. If digital opt-outs proved unsustainable for them, they probably are for you. Instead, try becoming a part-time techno-hermit.

Find a large hill, spend a week in Herefordshire, or head to Hove, Brighton's peaceful sister town, where The Gin Tub has installed a Faraday cage (a copper screen that blocks mobile signals). 'Mobile phones have killed pubs. I hate seeing a whole group of people, sitting there on their phones,' explained its owner. 'Rather than telling people they can't use their phones we've basically disabled them.'

For a demi-detox try the Altruis jewel, a synthetic gem that hooks into your smartphone and vibrates only if messages arrive from VIPs on a pre-set list. Developer Kate Unsworth came up with the idea after waiting two hours in a restaurant for a friend who was late. 'I thought I would just catch up on work while I waited. Then my battery died and I remember feeling so angry. But I ended up having a glass of wine, relaxing, and thinking, "This is what I should have been doing in the first place."' Afterwards she quit her phone, rationed her internet use to work and began leaving the office at 5 p.m.

> It didn't affect my work. In fact it made me more focused and productive … I vividly remember sitting on a bus behind a couple in their seventies. She leant over and kissed him on the cheek, and he turned to her and smiled. I burst into tears. For the first time in ages I was present enough to witness these small things that happen around us.

Alternatively, cocoon your technology. Use the Blokket pouch, a nylon-silver smartphone slipcover or mini-Faraday cage. I would recommend the Focus clothing collection, whose metal fibres shut down phone frequencies. 'It protects us from social media that eats up the time we spend in real life,' said designer Masashi Kawamura. But unfortunately the range was not put into production. And switching off is cheaper. To make it more fun, digital consultant Martin Talks suggests a game called phone stacking. At a meeting or meal, everyone puts their device in the middle of the table. The first to reach out pays a forfeit.

CARPE DIEM

The most enduring answer to the question of how best to use time is succinct. *Carpe diem*. Seize the day.

I first heard it hollered by Robin Williams, playing a liberating schoolmaster in *Dead Poets' Society*, but this maxim has a long pedigree. For centuries, men, especially, embraced it. Such as Robert Herrick, a Tudor priest who counselled 'gather ye rosebuds while ye may' – which sounds enchanting, until you learn it is a chat-up line designed to prise petals off young blooms in his randy poem, 'To the Virgins, to Make Much of Time'. ('Old Time is still a-flying;/And this same flower that smiles today/Tomorrow will be dying.')

The expression *carpe diem* is first found in another poem. It, too, seems less celebratory if you read the words that follow: *'Quam minimum credula postero'* ('Trust as little in the next day as possible'). But this gloom is understandable, since its author, Horace, was a soldier who survived war and disease in an era before antibiotics to become spokesman for Rome's fledgling empire. In his day, with the past so fraught, the future doubtful, the present was the only sure time to rely on. Arguably this is always true for us all.

'Seize the day' recalls the command to live 'in the moment', but there is a distinction: *carpe diem* is about grabbing what you can, which seems a narrow life philosophy. Yes, existence is an irretrievable stream of minutes. Yes, abandon ourselves to experience and we are also likelier to notice the optimal moment to act – which is handy for improving our timing. But we can expect to live far longer than Horace, who died in 8 BC at the then grand age of fifty-six.

Anointed the last of Rome's so-called Five Good Emperors a century and a half later, Marcus Aurelius witnessed the first crumbling of Horace's beloved empire. During the long military campaign that ended with his death, Aurelius somehow chiselled out the leisure to write *Meditations*, a masterpiece of Stoic philosophy. One imagines that, in his uniquely isolated position, his writing was his chief companion. Sure enough, it captures the misery of an existence rated solely by the now: 'A man's life lies all within this present as 'twere but a hair's breadth of time; as for the rest, the past is gone, the future yet unseen. Short, therefore, is man's life.'

How like a prison his short life sounds. By contrast, the advice of Buddhist teacher Thich Nhat Hanh – 'the past is already gone, the future is not yet here; there is only one moment for you to live: that is the present moment' – a near identical idea, invites us to be active: to wake up and live.

To seize every day and give it your all, it is wise to keep faith with tomorrow. The span of life is a bridge through time. Our past, our expectations for the future, lift us above the waters of unknowing, opening up a further horizon.

9

Timing

Making time serve you

Some day around 1612, Francis Bacon,* the wily philoso-pher-statesman and granddaddy of empirical science, wrote: 'To choose time, is to save time ... an unseasonable motion is but beating the air.' His point was simple: pick the right moment and you control a situation.

Bacon knew whereof he wrote, having survived long years at Elizabeth I's vicious court to become Lord Chancellor to James I. But his downfall was curiosity. One winter's day he plunged a chicken into a pile of snow, to investigate how freez-ing preserved meat. His calculations overlooked the possibility that he too might catch cold, and he died of pneumonia.

Bad luck, or bad timing?

In ancient Greece there were two conceptions of time. There was *chronos* – sequential time, the one-damned-thing-

---

* Not to be confused with the twentieth-century painter, whose temporal expertise consisted of staying up very late, imbibing heroic quantities of wine and anything else to hand, then rising at dawn to squirt out another masterpiece.

after-another variety (as seen on calendars and clocks). Then there was *kairos* – the right time, otherwise known as opportunity. Both were worshipped as gods, and their image pops up all over the ancient world.

You already know what Chronos looked like; remote, beardy old Father Time. Kairos was a livelier if slippery character. Zeus's beautiful youngest son and a lover of Tyche (luck), he was usually depicted on tiptoe, his heels winged, his head bald but for one fat forelock. This ugly hairstyle expressed a moral precept: life offers golden moments, but grab them before they fly or you will be left grasping air. The point would not have been lost on the athletes who passed the altar dedicated to Kairos on their way to the stadium at Olympia. Timing is time at its most personal.

When timing works it is a delight to behold. We see it as dancers swoop in harmony and skaters arc runes across ice. Chef Anthony Bourdain found its enchantment in sweat-fugged kitchens:

> Few things are more beautiful to me than a bunch of thuggish, heavily tattooed line cooks moving around each other like ballerinas on a busy Saturday night. Seeing two guys who'd just as soon cut each other's throats in their off hours moving in unison with grace and ease can be as uplifting as any chemical stimulant or organised religion.

To a boxer, good timing is the difference between a knockout and a flailing fist. To a stand-up comic – or a horror film director – it is knowing how far to push a pause before sock-ing the killer punch at your audience. To a runner, it is recognizing when to dash and leave the pack behind. To Napoleon Bonaparte, it was a question of identifying when the 'least manoeuvre' could bring victory, just as a 'drop of water … makes a vessel run over … The fate of a battle is a question of a single moment, a single thought … the decisive moment arrives, the moral spark is kindled, and the smallest reserve force settles the argument.'

Many prefer to attribute timing to luck. Such as the day we met our beloved (never mind that the stars happened to align when we were at a point in life that we were ready to settle). It may be relaxing to believe, like photographer Ansel Adams, 'sometimes I think I do get to places just when God's ready to have someone click the shutter'. And certainly, the ripeness of good timing often owes a great deal to happenstance, since so much in life is beyond our control. But surrender to comforting abstract nouns with capital letters, blame Providence and Destiny for life's twists and turns, and this fatalism blinds us to how we might shift direction or learn from our mistakes.

I am more convinced by Henri Cartier-Bresson, who when taking pictures looked for 'the decisive moment', just as Bonaparte did in battle – in his case, the instant an image captured the significance of an event to give its 'proper expression'. Only he knew when to snap.

This is the challenge of timing: it is a function of skill. Your ability to tailor your actions to the instant is only as good as your analysis, strategy and technique – the fruits of time, training and adaptability. Humans have always been good at the latter – it is the trait that let us breed and hunt our way to the top of the food chain – but today we are slower to adapt than the tools and toys that have so accelerated our pace of life. Herein lies a problem. In 1961, despairing of nuclear weapons, Bertrand Russell wrote in *Has Man a Future?*, 'One of the troubles of our age is that habits of thought cannot change as quickly as techniques, with the result that, as skill increases, wisdom fades.'

Given that good timing is hardest to achieve in fast-moving situations, and that digital media are evolving so rapidly, you could say that the peril of our age is bad timing on a grand scale: that we expend so much time chasing fast – updating, surfing, monitoring, attending meetings, fizzing on Snapchat or wrangling work email – that we are always behind, running late, burning energy, messing up. The risk is that by prioritizing speed, stretching our capacity, we render something precious in ourselves – our originality, creativity, values, experience – obsolete. We need to think more, not less – to treasure our judgement, foster ethics, creativity and insight – to survive in a fast-forward world. Not least because fast is such a marketing scam, designed to destabilize us with anxiety – with the very successful effect of turning us into panic buyers of the nearest thing that presents itself as a convenience to make life easier. Or indeed a political slogan, masquerading as a solution to our fears or sense of inadequacy.

Good timing involves more than a talent for adapting quickly to situations and seizing our chances. Appreciate how timing shapes your life and you can compensate for the occasions when it is not in your favour. As this chapter sets out, even bad happenstance gets better if we seize on the opportunities of timing, or massage it to suit us better. Perfect timing is something that we create: whenever we decide what opportunity looks like and make time to go for it.

1. How timing's hidden hand warps lives

Is your birthday a birth defect? It is a serious question. Timing's sly hand steers us often silently, and the greatest accident of timing is birth.

When my mother delivered a large baby on 12 August, all those years ago, the general consensus was that I had arrived eight days late. But on reflection I may have been three weeks early. As a summer child, I was young for my year and proud of it; it only grated when I had to wait five years after my classmates to vote in an election. Since then I have learnt that far greater disadvantages come of being schooled among older children.

In an ideal world, no life would be influenced by when it begins. But nobody is immune to external temporal strictures. We do not walk solely along the tightrope of our own lifetime; this, our personal time zone, must also slot into social clocks, which have their own cycles. This leads to the phenomenon of relative age effects. We experience them as soon as we enter a group organized by age, because each selection period has a cut-off date: the start of the calendar year, academic year or sporting season. Consequently children born soon after the cut-off can be up to 364 days older than those born just before their selection period ends. The younger the child within an age group, the wider the gulf in relative maturity yawns. To a five-year-old, 364 days is 20 per cent of a lifetime; to a four-years-and-one-day-old it is 25 per cent. A big disadvantage, in terms of physical strength, as well as emotional and intellectual development.

You might expect an early head start would shrink to irrelevance in the long run; after all, 364 days is less than six per cent of an eighteen-year-old's life. Yet, conversely, it can grow if it leads to inequalities of opportunity. As Malcolm Gladwell points out in his book *Outliers*, when fresh sporting talent is scouted, large children with superior motor skills (i.e. older ones) appear to be the most gifted. If they land a spot on a team this confers on them further opportunities to practise and to shine. This means a better chance of hitting the magic ten thousand hours' practice that, according to aptitude research, it takes to master anything, from papyrology to baseball. The sooner that number is reached, the likelier we will excel. This is borne out in the life of Wolfgang Amadeus Mozart. Doubtless his angelic muse would have taken wing in a chicken coop, but being steeped in music from the cradle, inspired by his pushy papa, his talented sister and applause throughout Europe's ducal courts, leavened the boy's ambition with the heat of exposure, nourishing his hunger to compose.

The munificent and enduring legacy of a relatively early birth date is easiest to detect in sport. In UEFA's 2010/11 international youth football tournaments, the age group cut-off was usually 1 January, and four times as many players' birthdays fell in January as December. The same bias prevails in the upper echelons of adult Canadian ice hockey, US baseball and European football. In Italy's top-flight Serie

A in 2013, twice as many players were born in the first quarter of the year as the last. Relatively older ones were also better paid throughout their career.

The halo cast by perceived talent can cast dark shadows. The academic attainment of a summer-born child in primary school is around 25 per cent lower. Supposedly this discrepancy evens out by the end of secondary school, but if a dispiriting taint of being the class runt, a slowcoach, lingers in how we see ourselves and how others see us, the knock-on effect – although harder to calculate than footballers' salaries or to write academic papers about – may be immeasurable. What we can say, thanks to Canadian and US research, is that the younger members of a peer cohort gain lower grades, commit more youth crime, and are less inclined to head to university – but likelier to be diagnosed with a learning disability, ADHD or schizophrenia.

Our life prospects need not be dented by the immovable fact of a birth date. Invidious age discrimination is here to stay (cut-off dates are unavoidable), but be aware and you can balance the bad timing. If your December baby adores football, provide extra hours of practice – encourage her to join a weekend club. If your August boy falls behind, help him to catch up. Or buy a bonus year (deferral is increasingly possible in UK schools).

Now that I am wise to relative age effects, I see why I felt lost at kindergarten, and mourn not pausing to do a job before heading to university. Seasoned by real graft, studying alongside my younger peers, I might have knuckled down and procrastinated less. But understanding the legacy of a summer birth also lets me see that my left-behind feelings are out of date. If you have ever lost out because timing did not tip in your favour, tell yourself that you started late. Now it is time to run your own race.

2. How to improve your timing

We are all – with the exception of billionaires, rock stars and babies – governed by a multitude of social clocks: from train schedules to office hours to other people. The more social clocks that we juggle, the more varied our commitments, the greater the odds of conflict. Good timing, hour by hour, or day, month and year, depends on balancing them. And on accepting a simple premise: that time keeps moving. We must hit the refresh screen on our aspirations if we are to achieve them. Yesterday's opportunity – or that burnished dream, put on hold for decades – may not apply today.

Ageing is our greatest timing challenge, but the one that we are most reluctant to face. Medicine and technology can buffer or mask physical decline, yet this introduces other problems. Stand too long on the escalator from one life stage to the next and major life events concertina. Welcome children in your late thirties or beyond, as menopause grins at you, and expect to say hello to a mid-life crisis – ideally timed to collide with your offspring's puberty and the deliquescence of your beloved parents.

You need not be Napoleon Bonaparte or Henri Cartier-Bresson to improve your timing. Most of all, it requires you to take responsibility for your timing: to read situations, predict outcomes, understand others' behaviour and act promptly. Great timing comes when we cease to be an interested party in our life and become an entrepreneur.

In 700 BC the poet Hesiod, despairing of his feckless younger brother, wrote an almanac designed to instruct him how to run the family farm: 'Observe due measure, for right timing is in all things the most important factor.' This, the oldest surviving advice on timing, suggests that success hinges on being aware of the time-critical aspects of a situation. Sixteenth-century Japanese swordsman Miyamoto Musashi, whose mastery led him to a peaceful death at eighty-one, concurred: 'All things entail rising and falling timing. You must be able to discern this ... You win battles by knowing the enemy's timing, and using a timing which the enemy does not expect.' Such as a dawn raid when they are at rest.

I doubt that William the Conqueror consulted Hesiod's almanac before landing at Pevensey to invade England on 29 September 1066, but the agricultural calendar helped him spring his trap. The Anglo-Saxon *fyrd*, or militia, had spent four months patrolling the Sussex coast, anticipating just such an attack, but retreated home to bring in the harvest before it spoilt. Meanwhile the English army were hiking to York to beat off the sallies of Harald Hardrada, King of Norway.

Excellent timing was a full-time occupation for Ayrton Senna, the Brazilian Formula 1 maestro, whose superlative tactics regularly allowed him to triumph with tired tyres and inferior cars. Admiring fellow racing driver Davy Jones said: 'You know, when you take a corner, your mind goes to the turn-in, then to the apex, then the exit. You're always a step ahead of what you're actually doing. But maybe Senna is always three steps ahead. Maybe that was it. And maybe that's why he's such a great champion.'

Senna inverted the received wisdom. For instance, when taking corners a driver traditionally went in slow and came out fast – a safer approach. Whereas Senna accelerated to overtake at danger points, adopting a different mantra: he who brakes last, wins. Senna's dexterity awed his rivals. One described his car as dancing 'like raindrops on a pavement. The control …' His other tricks included brake testing (slowing down to stop others overtaking) or pulling off moves at the last possible moment. Above all, his timing was unpredictable.

Your daily tempo makes you predictable – and vulnerable. If not to dawn raids by Japanese swordsmen, then to telephone marketers who call you when you are eating or preparing for bed, when your defences are low – and you are more prone to agree to participate in a survey or receive a visit from a double-glazing rep.

Countless other currents inflect our timing. We surf or dart between them, especially when we travel. Each city has its pulse, as aspiring actor Michael Goldfarb learnt, driving a taxi at night in 1970s New York to pay his rent:

> The city was mine. I learnt its rhythms, knew where to
> be and at what time to get a good fare, knew when to
> avoid 8th Avenue and ride the sequenced lights up
> 10th … To get the job, I had to agree to work shifts no
> one else wanted. The slow nights, Sunday and Monday.
> Monday was especially grim. The streets emptied after

rush hour. Actually they were pretty empty affairs during rush hour. It was as if the whole of solvent Manhattan had a collective fit of guilt over how much money they had spent during the weekend and decided to save a few bucks and ride the subway home.

But patterns change, increasingly rapidly. In 2015 the *Economist* reported that rush hour on London's underground train network had tripled in girth. It now lasted from 7 a.m. until 10 a.m. and from 4 p.m. until 7 p.m. – reflecting soaring levels of self-employment and longer working days – and was 30 per cent more congested than in 2007, as workers and tourists flocked to the capital.

Being wise to temporal pressure points influences not only our timing but our health. In London in 2016, levels of nitrogen dioxide (a pollutant in car exhaust fumes) peaked at 9 a.m. and again from 6 p.m. until 8 p.m. Similar peaks fell later in the day in Paris, but were nearer 8 a.m. and 9 p.m. in New York City – reflecting the later hours kept in France, and the States' longer working day. Parisian parents are advised to book children's outdoor activities on Sunday, when pollution drops, as the rest of the city tarries in bed even later than usual.

Master timing, and we have the confidence to put ourselves in the right place, and then be spontaneous. There are three golden rules for this:

- Understand the situation
- Use the context
- Influence the pace

To apply them, here are ten tactics.

1. Make a habit of thinking about the optimal timing for actions

Planning will be more precise, putting you on the front foot (the attacking position for batsmen in cricket), increasing confidence for taking the initiative.

2. Start earlier

Time distortions lead us to imagine that we have longer to complete complicated tasks and to underestimate the complexity of faraway events.

3. Create extra space

Introduce ten-minute buffers in your schedule to ensure that overruns will not derail you, and knowing that you have this luxury also reduces time pressure, freeing your mind to concentrate. Think of it as the rubber laid at intervals between train tracks: when the summer heat rises, the iron rails expand, but the rubber contracts. The track does not buckle.

4. Analyse the implications of your timeframe and context

Holding a dinner to coincide with the FA Cup final might be lucky or disastrous, depending on your guests. To plan a party, pension or marathon successfully, time-critical factors must be clear. Study the relevant people, threats, advantages. If having broken down the picture, no window of opportunity beckons, can you see how to poke one in?

Think of Alexander the Great, who stood by the Granicus river in May 334 BC. Studying the Persian line on the far bank he spied a thin point at its centre, and sent his commander Amyntas to mount a diversionary assault on the left flank while preparing to launch his cavalry at the centre. Then came the wait. Attack too soon and the Persians would rumble him; too late and Amyntas would be crushed. But Alexander timed it perfectly. The Persian line collapsed.

5. Predict outcomes

Generate alternative outcomes to test your choices. What possibilities churn up if you follow option X, Y or Z? Set a timer to limit this stage of a decision process.

6. Pick *your* moment

Of China's 36 *Stratagems*, a military guide from the third century BC, the simplest is this: 'Wait at ease for the enemy'. As in, let them squander their energy: act when *you* are ready. Be opportunistic. Politicians bury bad news when bigger stories dominate. Similarly, telling a friend you cannot go on holiday together is easier if you have just done them a favour.

7. Use the tempo

Timing is a dance: feel the rhythm of the situation to sense what pace works. And respect your own tempo. What seems fast to you is probably too fast. Can you slow things down to suit you, like slick Ayrton Senna?

8. Manipulate the context

In Aristotle's *Rhetoric*, a study of persuasive speech, the word *kairos* denotes the apt time to deliver the message or 'proof' of an argument. This involves creating the right moment by massaging the social mood. A best man's speech, for instance, sets up jokes, building suspense before firing a zinger. In the same way a politician seduces a crowd. First he whips them, using repetition and other rhetorical tricks to fan their emotions about the issues that concern voters, and then he bowls his policy as a solution. Ta-dah! Even if the policy is preposterous – say, linking an underfunded NHS with membership of the EU – those waves of desire can make it *feel* credible. Then the politician bathes in a halo effect as the audience's emotions transfer to him, gilding him as their saviour. The more often his message is repeated, the more it convinces. Even if, as with Hitler, it is a filthy lie.

9. Use time pressure to make the time seem right

Simply create a sense of urgency. This idea or proposition or plan is a last chance – so hurry up, while stocks last …

10. Be resolute. What are you waiting for?

Ultimately, timing is an effort of will. Projecting will with conviction, emphatically, maximizes the impact. The origins of the word *kairos* convey this point well. In archery, *kairos* was an 'opportunity' – literally, a tunnel-like opening through which arrows had to pass. They would do so only if both an archer's aim *and* power were true. In weaving, *kairos* referred to the critical time when yarn needed to pass through a gap in the warp; a forceful movement ensured a strong weave. In any context, pace and force are critical to moving things along.

If time presses but you doubt which path to take, you could fake your way out. As Anna Wintour, of US *Vogue* and artistic director of Condé Naste, explained:

> I grew up watching [my father] lead a team of
> journalists, and being a very decisive and I think
> fearless editor. I think through that example I realized
> possibly that what people ... hate most is indecision.
> Even if I'm completely unsure, I will pretend ... The
> world we are in is about instinct and being fast and
> responding.

Similar resolve is expressed in her pre-office tennis match, and her loyalty to the same hairstyle and lunch (creamed potato and steak, if you must know) – rituals that limit the decisions she has to make, liberating her mind for more important questions, such as how to sell more magazines and, of course, what to wear. Food writer Nigella Lawson used to adhere to the same principle, but applied it differently. For years her wardrobe comprised a daily uniform of identical frocks in a range of colours.

This is the highest strategy of timing. Create space to concentrate on what matters to you and you can live in your own good time.

How to accelerate decision-making

It is always tempting to delay taking a position until you have built an unassailable fortress of information about its pros and cons. But how long will it take to dig your way out and convert that data into useable knowledge? In the meantime opportunity may fly.

Decisions are faster, and of higher quality, when approached systematically. Researchers at Stanford University uncovered best practice in this area in a study of strategic decision-making in high-velocity businesses (microcomputer companies, as it happens). Interestingly, the most rapid decision makers outperformed the slow. They also used *more* information than the slow, generating a broader range of propositions, then analysed tactical plans for accomplishing them, to see how well they accorded with business goals.

To reach speedy, creative and tactically astute decisions:

1. **Brainstorm** (while being disciplined about how long you do it).

2. **Rate alternatives:** do they support your broader strategy?
3. **Focus on relevant data.** Draw up a checklist.
4. **Reduce decisions.** Make the necessary ones count.

ON TIME

In 2012 Jim Dunbar arrived twenty minutes late for an appointment at Ninewells Hospital, Dundee. He left diagnosed with an hitherto unknown condition, Chronic Lateness. This may seem an overreaction by doctors, but all his life Dunbar had been late: for work, holidays, funerals, shedding friends and jobs with the mislaid hours. He once took eleven hours to get to a cinema. Heartily relieved to have a name for his problem, he went public, and so far did the news spread that Spanish travel company Atrápalo made him poster boy for national 'Llegaprontismo day' ('I arrived in time day') to encourage early holiday bookings. These duly rose by 25 per cent.

Dunbar's happy ending sets a dangerous precedent. Imagine the chaos if lateness were a recognized illness. Laggards could claim discrimination every time managers tapped a watch. Things are bad enough without this excuse. Up to 15 per cent of US workers arrive late at least once a week, costing their employers an estimated $3 billion.

There is little hard evidence to show that punctuality is actually declining, yet it feels as if it is, now that appointments can be treated as movable feasts (as in, 'I texted to say I would be late.' 'Yes, five minutes before we agreed to meet!'). If this is the case, Dunbar's diagnosis suggests a more nuanced explanation for why it might be. His problems recall sufferers from ADHD, for whom, according to psychiatrist Edward Hallowell, 'time becomes a black hole … It feels as if everything is happening all at once.' The same words apply when actions fall out of sequence because you have attempted too much or an interruption has thrown you off your stride – routine hazards of hurry and spiralling distractions today.

How much store to set by punctuality can be a divisive question. Playwright Alan Bennett called it the one threat to his otherwise happy relationship (he was all for punctuality). Some of us are always running late, some can take it at a stroll and some see the appointed hour as a point of honour. I am an uncomfortable mix of all three. If I am behind schedule I tell myself, 'Okay, so be late. So what?' Then off I run, jacket billowing behind me like a superhero cape, as if three salvaged, breathless minutes might save the day. I would love to be like my relaxed friend, who edits a news bulletin that starts on the pip. Meeting her socially, though, it is safest to tack an extra half-hour on to the agreed time. She believes it is a relic of childhood, which saw her and her sisters trailing their irredeemably tardy mother like kite tails – as if lateness were a form of loyalty, designed to guard her mother's way of being. To be fair, my friend improved on meeting her punctual partner: selective mating is a fine cure for this trait.

Turning up on time, finishing on time: these are social contracts, and to break them is risky. Yet be warned, passionate advocates of punctuality: the moral high ground is unclear. Wherever you sit on the punctuality spectrum, an argument exists to back your view. 'Punctuality is the politeness of kings,' said Louis XVIII of France. Anyone who has withstood the curdling wait for a minor member of the House of Windsor might regard this with scepticism, but regal standards are higher. As a princess touring South Africa in 1947, the future Elizabeth II famously jabbed her chatty mother with an umbrella whenever she tarried too long in greeting lines. And Louis XVIII himself had bitter experience of delay, having to sit through French revolution, the deaths of his brother and his nephew and the downfall of Napoleon before acceding to the throne. As a result he was a constitutional monarch, who unlike his brother (the Louis who lost his head) saw the wisdom in turning up when politicians asked.

Yet another Frenchman, the novelist André Maurois, trumpeted lateness as 'the politeness of artists'. And a chorus of arty types agreed. Oscar Wilde dismissed punctuality as 'the thief of time', and to novelist Evelyn Waugh it was 'the virtue of the bored'. 'Only the servile are punctual,' advised Rose Macaulay, terminally. As these snoots saw, the beauty of lateness is that you are unlikely to be kept waiting; the ugliness is that it suggests you do not mind wasting other people's time. Then again, who cares if power play is your intention?

Relationships set the terms and conditions of social contracts. Hence, grievously often, punctuality is a status game. Its rules can appear to be written in invisible ink, however, since they vary from place to place.

When you are abroad, consult a local before taking the words 'on time' at first sight. In Saudi Arabia, for instance, to be thirty minutes late is fine, yet checking your watch in a meeting is an insult. In Russia, foreigners are expected to be prompt – but do not expect this to be reciprocated. For Brazilian VIPs and international divas, turning up late is mandatory in order to flaunt your prestige, unless you agree to meet on 'English time', as in 'on time' (an ideal possibly out of step with current British timekeeping) – but woe betide any Brazilian underling or foreigner who is late. In Nigeria, visitors are advised to pitch up two hours late for an appointment, despite or possibly because of the 1980s 'war against indiscipline' led by the military government, when soldiers forced civil servants to do frog jumps before jeering mobs if they drifted in untimely to work.

If you abhor lateness head for Switzerland, the clock lover's spiritual home, or Germany; the two tie as earth's most time-reverent nations. In Germany, ten minutes early for a meeting is on time. This fits the theories of INSEAD business school Professor Erin Meyer, who placed Germanic, Anglo-Saxon and Northern European countries at the exacting end of the global punctuality spectrum (see below), reasoning that it was because these countries came early to industrialization, which demanded precise timekeeping, since one late worker could freeze a factory assembly line, at vast expense.

Source: Erin Meyer, *The Culture Map* (Public Affairs, 2014)

Proponents of punctuality consider it the most productive way to operate, yet even this is not universally true. Where time is linear and life predictable, to run like clockwork using sequential plans and processes is wise, and punctuality is a pragmatic courtesy to be flourished in public – a form of creditworthiness. But if life is changeable – whether due to hurricanes, poverty or bonkers politics – long-term horizons become unclear. Then it is the hospitable courtesy of patience that keeps business ticking over. As Meyer wrote:

> What matters is that your work structure is flexible enough to adapt with changes in the natural environment, and that you have invested in the critical relationships needed to keep your workers loyal in times of drought or flooding, erosion or insect infestation. In this environment, productivity and profit are directly linked to the flexibility and the relationships of the person in charge.

Meyer has identified the essential challenge of time in our world today: how to meld the fluidity and immediacy of our new ways of communicating and working with our strategies for getting stuff done. Without question, the habit of being on time helps: it is useful not only in business but as a social game-changer, shifting relationships onto an egalitarian footing. Few things are so demoralizing, in any country or company, as a boss who ambles in hours after everybody else while pulling rank and drawing a fatter wage. This is why achieving change in expectations about punctuality is a goal in many developing countries. So if you are a manager, think twice before emailing to say that you are working from home.

The culture of being on time – arriving on time, leaving on time – is an awful lot more productive than busy, hair-shredding no-time-for-me time. To propagate it requires leadership from the top and imagination from us all. If we are to seize our opportunities in this hyperfast world, every one of us must innovate our own ways to stay linear and make progress, while reconciling this with the freedoms of flexitime. Punctuality matters more, not less, when time is so high maintenance – if you want to custom-fit it to suit you.

10

Sticking at It

The secret life of routines, plans and deadlines

Wanting to do something is easy. Sticking at it is less so.

That is what my grandmother said. A nurse, she left Glasgow's slums in 1940 to join the army, sailing to Burma in order to chase the enemy through the jungle at night, armed with a hurricane lamp and pistol, and to heal prisoners of war who had been starved to the span of the railway tracks they were forced to lay across the land. So she appreciated virtues like gumption. My grandfather would have said that you do not know endurance until you have led your men through fifty miles of rainforest, while suffering haemorrhoids and diarrhoea and equipped with two sheets of bog roll. I cannot be sure what my other grandparents would have said – we never met – but my grandad piloted RAF planes throughout the Second World War, beating even odds of death, so doubtless they would agree.

Men and women like my grandparents secured us the freedom to spend time as we wish. If I could ask them how they managed it, I am certain they would laugh then say, 'We got on with it!'

Tenacity is a virtue we pin on that generation like a medal. Given few choices, they stuck valiantly by those they made. But it would be a mistake to consider that quality old hat. In our choice-laden world, the capacity to override distraction and pursue long-term goals could not be more relevant.

Sticking at it has three ingredients: motivation, willpower and time. Motivation gives willpower a destination, but time gets you there – day after day, year after year.

'Civilization advances by extending the number of operations we can perform without thinking about them,' remarked the mathematician and philosopher Alfred North Whitehead. This approach can civilize a stressful life by helping to simplify time. Although exercising choice is an act of freedom, the disadvantage is that for whatever you choose to do, something must be refused. Then opportunity costs stack up. This is why, when we face too many options, freedom can lead to paralysis. Equally, fixating on long-term goals can be self-limiting, leading to 'destination syndrome' ('I will only be happy when I am rich/old/thin/living in Florida').

There are several tools we can use for long-haul time travel: routines, habits, plans, deadlines, contracts. They can seem joy-thieving bastards. Author Edward Abbey told his editor: 'I hate commitments, obligations and working under pressure. But on the other hand, I like getting paid in advance and I only work under pressure.' (In other words, he was a procrastinator.)

Each tool deploys time pressure differently. Routines and habits impose structure, steering us from activity to activity, reducing the decisions we need to make and the pressure we feel; plans budget our time and attention, spacing out the pressure more evenly; with deadlines and commitments, pressure becomes a whip that drives us on. All of these tactics share one strategy: putting your prudent, long-term planner self in charge, so that impulse and distraction do not railroad you. This makes it easier to live by our priorities, instead of being buffeted about by demands, hurry and illusory urgency. Minimize choices by making them in advance and it becomes easier to balance your present needs and long-term priorities, reducing disruption. (This is why you devise the menu before placing the order, pick out the clothes you will wear the night before and list what you need for the trip two days ahead – long enough to dry-clean that suit.) These tools also counter our native ineptitude at estimating how much time we need.

Why busy people think there is enough time

The human brain routinely miscalculates time, due to idiocies like hyperbolic discounting, present bias and the sunk costs fallacy (see page 137). We also suffer two temporal distortions that I call the faraway blur and the complexity blur.

- **The faraway blur** If a deadline is far off, we underestimate the time a task will take and assume that it will entail fewer steps.

- **The complexity blur** The more complicated a task, the
  more involved, the further off a deadline seems.

This fatal combination means that if we have lots on, we
imagine that we have longer to do it *and* underestimate the
tasks' complexity. No wonder we can be incorrigible opti-
mists. 'Next month,' we tell ourselves, 'I'll save/diet/jog;
today it's okay to spend/pig out/loaf.' This is why, at the
start of the week, if you operate on multiple channels (say
you have a job, family, friends and outside interests, plus
surplus projects like redecorating or getting divorced),
Saturday seems remote, and you can delude yourself that
everything is achievable – then (unreasonably) feel a failure if it turns out not to be so.

These distortions explain the adage, 'If you want a job
done, ask a busy person.' Busy people evidently struggle to
assess their capacity, so are unlikely to say no.

....

1. How routines build motivation and willpower

Watching Madonna climb the stairs to the O2 stage at 2015's
Brit Awards, I felt trepidation. At the age of fifty-six, dressed
as a matador, could *Billboard*'s all-time top solo artist possibly still have *it*?

A dancer reached out to untie her cape. He pulled. She
tottered, then down the stairs she fell. But seconds later she
was up again, sawing away like a circus macaque whom

nobody has informed that singing while dancing with bruised ribs is supposed to look difficult.

Madonna has attributed her endurance to her body: 'Physicality, feeling strong, feeling empowered was my ticket out of middle-class Midwest culture.' I used to believe her secret was timing; her relentless ability to morph ahead of fashion, like her hero David Bowie, to ensure that she never went out of date. And there she was, still shimmying around fame's maypole after three decades in pop, the sector of show business with the shortest shelf life. But watching that night, I realized that she was wrong yet also right. The vehicle of Madonna's success was the very same thing that kept her body in such formidable shape: her adamantine routine, including varied workouts (bringing endorphin highs, exceptional brain health, time to think), stimulating travel, charitable endeavours, business meetings, and tri-hourly meals calibrated to the nanocalorie. This intensely disciplined lifestyle not only demonstrated her determination: it exercised it, renewing her motivation and stamina.

Madonna's relentlessness reflects the findings of psychologist Angela Duckworth, who has extensively researched the ingredients for enduring success. Only one factor consistently predicts long-term attainment in any field, from sport to the marines, from business to academe: grit. You can be a 100 per cent genius, but you will not last without passion and perseverance, the dirt about which success pearls.

Grit is easily confused with obstinacy, but the latter is about *not* doing. (The biblical Hebrew word usually translated as 'stubborn' means 'backsliding', a sin punishable, in the Old Testament, with death by stoning.) Whereas stubbornness resists change, grit seeks it: it has a direction in which to travel.

Duckworth offers two key suggestions for brewing tenacity. Commit to something hard for a minimum of two years (long enough to acquire the skills to make it interesting). And have a routine.

In a world of instant everything, routines are bodyguards against self-defeating impulse. Just as we behave better in tidy environments, so a well-structured day is a form of personal grooming, reinforcing our respect for our time and ourselves. Feel like a busy person who does, not a slob who skulks, and the circle of virtue is neat: the stronger your self-image as a can-doer, the greater your compulsion to live up to it.

Routines minimize the amount of self-control we need to exercise, because they are conga lines of habits, which constitute around 40 per cent of your waking day. If this proportion seems surprisingly large, it is because habits automate choices; once actions are habitual, we notice them less. Habits serve as cues, triggering effort. For instance, the gun that fires the day for choreographer Twyla Tharp is dressing in exercise clothes then hailing a cab to the gym – leaving no pause to quarrel with herself about whether to go. This is why musicians following the Suzuki method for mastering their craft prefer two short practices a day to one long one. Once this routine takes, they learn faster and require less willpower to sit down and play.

To ensure that determination lasts the distance, it is important to embed your priorities in small, daily acts. 'The strongest of all warriors are these two – Patience and Time,' wrote

Leo Tolstoy in *War and Peace*, placing these words in the mouth of General Kutuzov, a real-life hero who saved Russia from Napoleon. But Tolstoy practised this belief in a more prosaic vein. 'I must write each day without fail,' he said, 'not so much for the success of the work, as in order not to get out of my routine.' The habit drew him to his desk for six years until his masterpiece was complete.

The wonder of unthinking habit, like Tolstoy's steady routine or Madonna's energetic schedule, is to offer a sustainable path to our goals. Reducing our reliance on motivation or willpower can enhance those qualities – just as Madonna built her muscles. This is because motivation and willpower are interdependent. Think of them as opposite ends of a seesaw: the higher your motivation, the less willpower is necessary to perform a task. But if motivation is low, more willpower is required, and sadly willpower tires with overuse. In other words, the less motivation we feel, the less stamina we have. This is why enthusiasm is critical to long-lived success. So beware secondary incentives, bribes or threats, which deplete our intrinsic motivation. And use time pressure sparingly, by establishing plans or deadlines.

If you do not think that you have the capacity to stick at it, these exceptional people prove that tenacity is not an innate property of the soul. It is something that we do, and we do it best if we do it repeatedly. As prolific author John Updike, a proud 'blue-collar writer', said: 'Creativity is merely a plus name for regular activity.' Clint Eastwood epitomized this when he shucked off his film-star chrysalis to direct two acclaimed features per year in his seventies. 'It's just a bit of a work ethic. I get fairly decisive.'

> When I was growing up, Howard Hawks and Raoul
> Walsh and all those directors made several pictures in
> one year. There's no big deal … It's like being a
> musician. If you play every day, your embouchure is
> strong. If you play once every two years, you have to
> build up all over again.

Your routine controls almost half the time in your life. With
practice and the right ingredients it can get better – as I have
found with family life, that masterclass in logistics.

Two rules for establishing gritty routines

1. Keep it interesting

Man-dynamo Thomas Edison said, 'Genius is one per cent
inspiration and 99 per cent perspiration. Accordingly, a
"genius" is often merely a talented person who has done
all of his or her homework.' Yet he claimed, 'I never did a
day's work in my life, it was all fun.' Fun stemmed from
approaching everything as a learning experience.

The same was true of James Dyson, who had two fine
insights: that vacuum cleaners suck harder using cyclones,
and if they look cool men will buy expensive ones. But
fascination funded his success, as he remortgaged his home
to develop 5,127 prototypes until he was satisfied.
Absorption in this puzzle left no room in his mind to
doubt himself.

2. Keep reaching

Martin Johnson, who captained England's rugby team to
World Cup victory in 2003, credited his grit to his feisty
mother. 'She'd take me hill training or to a running track
and had absolutely no sympathy if I got tired.' Reaching
became his team's ethos:

> They weren't guys who had so much natural talent that
> they'd been earmarked to play for England when they
> were kids. The problem with being a naturally talented kid
> is that everything seems fun and easy, until you eventually
> come across players who are just as good as you. At that
> stage, a lot of them give up, because they're not used to
> finding it difficult and having to work really hard.

Johnson is describing how flimsy motivation can be if you
never have to fight for it. Setting goals that are beyond
your immediate grasp gives motivation stamina.

2. How to ensure deadlines are not deathly, and lay better plans

Remember those pitiless hands circling the exam hall clock?
Maybe you hated them, but you cannot deny their power.
The more time passed, the faster they turned, as did your
pen, dashing out your final answers. When we are reminded
that every second is irretrievable, every act seems to count.

As a result, few things are as powerful as deadlines for focusing the mind – or as stressful.

The power of deadlines is drawn from our ego. Commit to a deadline and, due to consistency bias (our drive to behave in a way that reflects the person we believe ourselves to be), our sense of self becomes bound up in fulfilling the promise. Fail to deliver, however, and this dents self-confidence. The lapse can even encourage us to break more deadlines in future (thus living down to our negative self-image). This is our passport to procrastination hell.

Under excessive pressure, performance can suffer. Like the author I met at a Christmas party, his one indulgence of the season, who confided that he had six weeks to ghostwrite a novel for a celebrity. 'The trouble is you only get time to have one idea,' he said, glass quaking in his hand. 'Then you are stuck with it for five thousand words!' On the plus side, fear can be productive. Witness time-haunted philosophers Albert Camus and Søren Kierkegaard. Both believed they would die young – and, spookily, both did (Camus in a car crash at forty-six, Kierkegaard at forty-two). But this gloomy prognosis propelled them to prolific feats, Camus becoming the second youngest recipient of the Nobel Prize for Literature at forty-four (after Rudyard Kipling at forty-two), pouring forth eight books and six plays in his lifetime and many more posthumously, while Kierkegaard became the father of existentialism. And rather depressing their work is too.

Don A. Moore and Elizabeth Tenney of the University of California surveyed existing research on time pressure and clarified how deadlines can undermine performance by clapping on mental blinkers, focusing the mind on getting the job done. Allowing more time enables greater accomplishment, yet at a steeply declining rate: in one study, people solved twice as many anagrams given four times as long to do so – meaning that, on average, they were half as productive. But although productivity rises under time pressure, creativity and originality diminish: people can stop brainstorming tailor-made ideas, falling back on off-the-peg tactics, which itself can harm morale.

Time pressure can also scupper concentration – as I found when writing this book. Every weekday I had to stop work at 11.30 a.m. to collect my son from nursery and drop him at his minder's. As a result, a distracting sense of expectation hovered in my mind from 10.30. But after I outsourced the task, mornings seemed twice as capacious, and I found my flow.

On the other hand, although deadlines may weaken performance, being on time and 10 per cent below your peak is generally preferable to being ten days late with something perfect. In business, when launching a new product, originality and being first to market are equally significant. But once a product exists, being fast, and selling the hell out of it, is the crucial thing.

So the strengths and weaknesses of time commitments are finely weighted: they can add urgency, but diminish enthusiasm; push up output, but lower quality. The question is not, do we need them, because we cannot avoid them (the world turns on contracts). It is: can we beat the toxic side effects?

The answer is yes – if you have a plan, distributing time pressure evenly, with achievable targets. Success hinges on the design of that plan. As chef and entrepreneur Tom Aikens said, 'It's all very well putting your head down, but without a game plan for where you see yourself in ten years, it's pointless.'

Plans cement our resolve by using joined-up thinking. This is why, if your aim is vaguely to get fit, there is always a chance that you might run on Sunday. But when you set a specific goal (that fund-raising 10K run), devise a training plan to reach it, and put out your kit on Saturday night, the likelihood that you will shoots up.

A well-engineered plan:

- picks the right goal: one that's clear, desirable, achievable
- focuses on timing, with step-by-step sub-goals and deadlines to set a productive pace
- is clear how much creativity is necessary, then enables it

The single greatest guarantee of a plan's success is to commit to a timetable – ahead of time. How many schemes run aground before leaving port because we say we will do it 'soon' rather than 'on 9 November'? Setting specific times to achieve each sub-goal on the way serves two purposes. First, ticking off the completed steps feeds confidence and momentum. Second, if for any reason you miss a time goal, it is easier to adapt the plan and get back on track – it keeps the plan flexible, ensuring that a small lapse does not lead to a dramatic derailment.

If you find time pressure stressful or compromising to your high standards, try to see finishing on time as a facet of quality – something to be proud of. Remember that less time often means more efficiency. As noted, a fast pace only causes problems if we disengage or lose focus, becoming stressed or disorganized as a result. But plans and deadlines can counter all four reactions, helping us to work confidently, attentively, innovatively – and, if we wish, faster. The trick is to keep those deadlines realistic, applying *just enough* pressure to allow you to work at a pace that suits you.

To strengthen your commitment, write down your plans in longhand. Then an aspiration will become a verifiable, black-and-white intention, both memorable and compelling (increasing your commitment through consistency bias). Better yet, the act of writing slows thinking and clarifies thought, resulting in improved plans.

There is persuasive research to support these ideas. Students who jot down lecture notes record less information than those typing on computers, but recall and comprehend more. And patients recuperating from hip operations heal faster if they write plans point by point, setting out specifics, such as when and where they will perform the agonizing exercises required for their recovery. 'I will get up from my chair without using a stick and then go to the bus stop at 9 a.m. with my wife' proved easier to abide by for one such man than 'Walk ten minutes'.

When devising plans, a sneaky tactic for enhancing success is to use the words 'if' and 'then'. Tell yourself 'I must finish this audit tomorrow' and, studies find, you are less likely to achieve your aim than if you express it as 'If I do X, then tomorrow I will finish this audit'. Why? The goals are identical; however, the psychology is different. Option one is a hard rule, its success pinned to your ego: fail to meet it and 'I' will have failed. Option two is a plan: miss the target and psychological pain is reduced because the rule is unbroken (all it proves is that 'If I don't do X, I will not finish this audit'). This nuance sounds minor but has great potential. Sticking to a diet or any other resolution is significantly less onerous with if–then plans, because if you lapse, your self-esteem remains intact. You can try again tomorrow, unfreighted by quite so great a sense of failure.

When stress bites, why not view it as rocket fuel? Stage fright galvanizes actors to take risks, and it can do the same for you. Mild stress, when your heart beats faster, readying your body for a challenge, brings physical benefits: it increases cell growth in the learning part of the brain, and boosts the immune system and oxytocin, which helps us bond, building team spirit.

Keep time pressure under your control and you increase your confidence to use it. Then, if your energy flags, you can crank your engine using micro-deadlines. Set an alarm to go off every twenty-five minutes, allowing yourself a short break, and a longer one after about four bursts of effort (this is Francesco Cirillo's notorious Pomodoro Technique, named after the tomato-shaped kitchen timer he had as a student). Time will seem swifter. You will be too.

How to stick at it

Writing a book is a study in long-haul endeavour. The following commitment fixes glued my bottom to the chair:

1. **Visible motivation.** Write down your headline reason for working today. Will it take you closer to a dream? Plant it within view of your workstation. (Equivalent to putting a 'fat bikini' shot on the refrigerator.)

2. **A mug of coffee (or similar).** Caffeine mimics stress in the brain, aiding focus. But what fills the mug is less relevant than the ritual making of it (a mini-mind-break) and the mug's size: the larger the mug, the longer I sip from it, and the longer I sit.

3. **Know you have to be elsewhere in an hour (or less).** You will hurry to finish what you are doing.

4. **Extend your attention span.** Note how long you have worked, then try to beat it next time. Or put a biscuit on your desk, giving yourself a set time at which to indulge.

5. **Fuel.** Do eat that biscuit: calories prolong the stamina we need for cognitively draining tasks. This is not science sponsored by Hobnobs. Resisting treats drains willpower and concentration. For instance, Professor Iain Hutchison, a pioneer in facial reconstruction, performed a twenty-three-hour operation aided by adrenaline, three half-hour breaks, peanut butter, chocolate, smoked salmon bagels and techno music, switching to soothing arias at the end when all depended on precise stitches a hair's breadth wide (which were inserted while he sucked

on a toffee to steady his breath and focus). Happily, the surgery was a success.

6. **Treat breaks as rewards.** Make sure you earn them.

7. **Limit your goals.** I bought a smaller diary. Writing clarified and reined in my objectives (unlike computerized lists, paper cannot expand).

8. **Find an audience.** According to myth, the terrifying hound Cerberus guards the gates of the Underworld. So find yourself a Cerberus, or work in a public place. It is harder there to hop up every twenty minutes to go to the loo, check your email or eat cake.

9. **Share your plans.** Telling somebody shores up your commitment. Could they also receive progress updates, enforcing a penalty if you lapse, or become a pacemaker? A friend and I sped up work on unrelated projects by emailing each other once a week, stating our goals, and reporting back seven days later. (Do not pick someone you live with as a commitment partner: self-interest may mean they are less likely to hold you to account, preferring that you resume smoking, for instance, rather than put up with grumpy you.)

MOMENTUM: FASTER,
WITH LESS EFFORT

Momentum is a gathering force that tilts the axis of lives. It has dashed armies to pieces and knocked kings off their thrones – and it can be yours to wield. To demonstrate its might, as well as how deeply and recently our relationship with time has changed, here follows a cautionary tale.

1. How VHS killed Betamax (or was it corporate suicide?)

Once upon a time in the 1980s there was a machine called the video player. People adored it as much as they had the Walkman portable stereo, because it liberated them from rigid TV schedules to do something new: time-shifting. Suddenly you could record *Rambo II*, go to the pub, then after closing time (c. 10.30 p.m.), instead of subsiding onto the sofa in an alcoholic sozzle as the national anthem serenaded transmission's end (c. 12 p.m.), you could watch Sylvester Stallone tear about the jungle like an angry swarm of walnuts, zapping fake guns at fake Russians. And if you nodded off, you could watch it again later.

When domestic video launched in the 1970s several formats competed for dominance, including 'The Great Time Machine' (so-called because its timer let users pre-set recordings). By the 1980s the video wars had become a duel between two rival formats: Sony's Betamax and VHS by JVC. Initially Betamax led, with nigh on

100 per cent of the market. It offered a sharper image than VHS. Sony even vanquished a Hollywood lawsuit, which argued that video was an infringement of copyright. The momentum was theirs. As Al Ries states in *The 22 Immutable Laws of Branding*: 'Customers don't really care about new brands, they care about new categories. By first pre-empting the category and then aggressively promoting the category, you create both a powerful brand and a rapidly escalating market.' But somehow, Sony lost.

Why? First, Betamax tapes, smaller than VHS, offered one hour of recording time, while VHS offered two – incomparably better for recording movies. But incredibly, the Sony bigwigs and engineers, infatuated by aesthetics, imagined that superior picture quality and chic little cassettes mattered more than what customers actually valued. And they made a second mistake: timing. While Sony resisted the sublicensing of Betamax technology, JVC was swift to share VHS with other manufacturers, meaning that many more, cheaper VHS players were soon on sale. VHS rapidly gobbled a 70 per cent slice of the world's top couch-potato market, the United States. No subsequent innovation in Sony labs, not even long-playing cassettes, would prove dazzling enough to blind customers walking into Blockbuster on a Saturday from seeing massed ranks of VHS and shrinking battalions of Betamax and stop them from concluding that sexy, premium Sony was the loser product.

Sony would not be the last company to fail to grasp that temporal flexibility formed the core of video's appeal. In 2000 Blockbuster refused to pay $50 million for an upstart online video provider, Netflix. Then time-shifting gave way to streaming. In 2013 Blockbuster went bust – the same year that Netflix was valued at $22,745,241,000. What a powerful reminder that the thrust behind every major leap in consumer technology in recent years – sweeping away analogue pastimes, businesses and jobs – has been the drive to redeploy time, and soak it up. Momentum is a force that you want on your side.

2. How to harness momentum

Momentum's rules are clearest in physics, which defines it as the force of an object's movement. The heavier an object, and the faster it moves, the mightier its momentum. To increase momentum, either you increase an object's mass or velocity, or reduce the obstacles and friction that drag on it. When it is on a roll, this force is hard to send in another direction.

Similar principles apply to psychological momentum. For instance, if I say that the momentum in a tennis match is heading Roger Federer's way I am describing a perception: my favourite appears to be racing to victory. This should not influence his ability to win point after point, but since tennis is a mental battle, to succeed a player must play each point in isolation, forgetting its significance to the match, and this ability depends on his morale. So if Federer's opponent loses point after point, well may his hope fade. At this moment the game is over.

Momentum turns us on because we adore a sense of moving forward. It is embedded in our language of time, of life as a journey – and is perhaps natural to a species whose ancestors spent their lives roaming from place to place. So physical is our feeling for time that a study of mind-wandering found that if people watch a screen whose images generate a sense of moving backwards, their thoughts drift to the past. But make them feel they are moving forwards and their mind shifts to the future.

Anything that conveys the sensation that we are charging towards a goal makes us feel in charge. Momentum delivers this motivating sensation on steroids. See it in others, and we like them more. Take the 1988 nomination race for the Republican presidential nomination. Vice-President George H.W. Bush began as favourite only to come third in Iowa's first primary caucus, revealing that his popularity was lower than expected. His team put all their effort into the next battle, in New Hampshire, attacking his chief rival, Bob Dole. Bush won. From then on, he attracted more campaign funds, spent more on advertising and won caucus after caucus, raising still more funds. Soon victory seemed inevitable. Yet a study found voters liked Bush no more than at the start; those who had fancied other candidates hopped onto his bandwagon, rallied by the perception that he was winning – either because they wanted to back a winner or had lost faith that anyone could beat him.

To build momentum into your daily life, smooth the path. Reducing sources of conflict, friction or distraction multiplies the output gained by effort, especially if you concentrate it at a point where it makes the greatest difference. Like Usain Bolt, the world's fastest man in 2017 and set to remain so for years. What made him unbeatable was not just the skyscraping limbs – which allowed him to take forty-one paces over 100 metres compared to his competitors' forty-four – but his economy. His legs moved no faster than those of other good sprinters as they sliced the air; however, hitting the ground they were significantly quicker, pushing him forwards with more vigour than any rival.

The psychology of momentum is overwhelmingly positive. When our mind is primed with positive expectations from positive past experience, success breeds success. So link a small, positive action today (you began work on time!) with hope of good to follow.

Here are some tips for enhancing your momentum:

- **Increase the mass of your effort** Focus on what a task requires, casting aside irrelevance.
- **Boost the pace** Use time pressure sparingly, maximizing motivation by, wherever possible, doing what you want, in the way that you prefer.
- **Reduce obstacles, distractions and drains**
- **Seek feedback to stay on course**
- **Refuel** Take breaks to maintain energy.
- **Talk yourself up** If your inner monologue harps on the negative, change its tune or silence it. Do something absorbing with someone fun. Or why not go for a run?

11

The Life Edit

Refurbishing habits, decluttering your day

Everyone knows that changing our habits is difficult. Changing our routines – whole chains of habits – seems especially daunting. For a start, we are so attached to those routines that we may not wish to try.

In an attempt to explain neighbourly hatred, Sigmund Freud wrote of the 'narcissism of minor differences', and it is true. We cling to certain rituals, however bad or petty, because we recognize ourselves through them. My friend's grandfather, Sir Narayan Pillai, the distinguished first Cabinet Secretary to India's first independent government, insisted on sitting down to an elaborate table setting, with families of knives and forks to keep his plate company, at the age of ninety-three, when he was able only to sip soup from a spoon. Suggesting that he stop would not have been merely rude; it would have been like asking him to cease being himself.

Most of us are control freaks about our habits, as if any affront – such as when our flatmate always washes up in his own special way and will never, ever try ours – represents a trespass on our territory. In reality, our routines control us, like zombie software locked on repeat. Their dominance is silent, but is stronger for it. Remember the killer fact: 40 per cent of your waking actions are habits. This is largely why time seems faster as you grow older, why days become unmemorable and why we are stupider than we like to think. An awful lot of stupid is down to daft routines.

If the strength of habits and routines is that they happen on autopilot, it is also their weakness; their inadequacies are not obvious and they are hard to budge. Once a sequence of ideas is laid down in our neural networks it lingers: hence you keep calling that man Patrick – or is it Peter? But life without habits would be hell. Imagine having to relearn how to brush your teeth on a daily basis. Days would jam up as we paused to evaluate, assess and debate what to do.

Your routine is the time machine that drives your life. Cast a cold eye over all the things you do without thinking. Tot up the squandered minutes. Multiply the lost time, the height-ened stress, by weeks, months, years. Is your routine due for an upgrade?

Do not overestimate the difficulty of making such a change. Unlike habits, routines are fairly easily disrupted: simply splice in a new habit. For proof, consider what brought print journalism to its knees; so many pleasant pastimes, such as walking to the newsagent's or completing the crossword, nullified by smartphones in no time at all. Habit extinction can be rapid. How else did Facebook colo-nize trillions of hours in less time than it takes to film a David Attenborough documentary?

1. Habits to form – or reform

Quit a habit and you create a vacancy, as James Goldsmith remarked of marrying his mistress. Ideally, you should replace a bad habit with a better one.

You might introduce a keystone habit. Neither rare nor particularly conspicuous, these small, everyday actions possess a knack of cascading change in seemingly unrelated areas. In *The Power of Habit*, Charles Duhigg observes that such habits create 'structures that help other habits to flourish'. Of course, any habit does this. Change triggers change. When I smoked, for instance, I also began other new things, like hanging out on dirty pavements. Likewise, stopping smoking brought new ways of occupying my hands, and I wrote more, concentrating for longer stretches. A wholesome keystone habit has similar knock-on effects.

But which habits to form? Flossing your teeth is a bell-wether for improved all-round efficiency, apparently. Perhaps the confrontation with your grinning face in the mirror is what does it (although I am mindful that serial killers are also supposed to care for their teeth). Exercise, good sleep and improved diet are also found to seed improvement elsewhere. Not so surprising really; grooming and wellbeing nourish the ego and, by extension, willpower. Regular family dinners tend to be a predictor of well-reared, confident children – although then again, a strong routine like that is symptomatic of a well-organized household. More instructive for me is that making your bed in the morning correlates with purposeful endeavour. Presumably this increases blood flow to the brain, getting the body going, but its chief asset is to strike a purposeful note at the start of the day. Engaging in an organizing action primes your mind into organizing thoughts about other things.

Patching an uplifting ritual into a routine – or relocating an old one to a more beneficial slot – can radically enhance your quality of life. As I learnt after having a baby, when, in my exhausted state, everything seemed a battle, and leaving home rarely took under an hour. In response I cut back on luxuries, like brushing my hair. And got slower. Days felt shapeless, and so was I.

So I adopted a new policy: try harder. I ditched trousers with elasticated waistbands and had my hair cut in a fringe. My hair does not sit in straight lines, but that was the point: bending it to my will forced me to face forgotten things like mirrors and shampoo. As I did, my routine pulled together. (Photographs testify that the fringe, now long gone, was vile, but only my mother minded.) Chucking this complication into my morning – a hard thing, tenacity expert Angela Duckworth would say – introduced a higher standard to aim at. I soon became better at organizing other things too, such as winkling my opinionated marshmallow of a baby into a snowsuit and out, heaven willing, to the sun.

New rituals nudge transformation by weaving good intentions into sequences of action. Try one. Leave your phone charging outside the bedroom (why pock your waking mind with that stressful first email or social media trawl?); put your jogging kit by the shower (it'll take you a stride nearer the park); move bath time to the evening (bye-bye, morning shower wars); turn off the radio so you can hear each other

– or yourself – think; take a micro-walk once an hour; go to bed twenty minutes earlier; take the long route home from the station, past those lovely houses, avoiding the fried chicken shop; find a window and look out of it to the furthest point your eye can see, ideally something interesting. Tomorrow, get up earlier and poke a moment of loveliness into your morning by sitting down to a proper breakfast (an option found by UNICEF and initiatives like Magic Breakfast to revolutionize children's behaviour and education, with similar benefits for adults: it is, hands down, the most important habit in my life). Not enough time? Make the choice and you will find there is.

Review the landscape of your routines and ask how well your habits serve you. Are they out of date? Still fit for purpose? Or are they traps? It would not be surprising if you found several of the latter.

Habits are often time capsules of ill-considered actions that assume biblical authority through repetition. Beware 'the power of the first decision,' warns behavioural economist Dan Ariely. Very often, we do something such as loading the dishwasher a certain way, haphazardly, not considering what might be the best approach. But having done it that way once, usually we do so again. A pattern calcifies into a habit. We do not pause to ask if there is a better way since this routine *feels* familiar, which lends it a spurious veneer of authority (this is an example of familiarity bias). Our agile brain then invents post-hoc justifications: bogus stories to convince us that this is indeed the finest of all methods for loading dishwashers. Since our mind is on autopilot when it performs habitual activities, time seems faster too, bolstering the illusion of efficiency. This is how, for several years, I drove a circuitous route to the M1, adding half an hour to a regular journey, until I invested a minute in a highly technical procedure: checking a map.

So take care how you tackle something the first time: you are writing the script for a habit. If you could do better, edit.

How to quit – or rewrite – a habit

Change takes sixty days to achieve. Does that seem a lot? The earliest days are hardest, requiring conscious prompts to perform a new set of actions. But the pain declines sharply thereafter, levelling off by day sixty, which should mark the last glimmer of awareness that you are exerting yourself to do something differently. Sixty days. Eight and a half weeks. 0.2 per cent of a 1,000-month life. Not so much.

Here is a method for changing habits adapted from Charles Duhigg (any mistakes are mine):

1. **Understand it.** Like a bad joke, a bad habit is a story in three parts. It consists of a *trigger*, a *routine* and a *reward*. First analyse the habit, identifying each stage: what sets you off (the trigger), what you do (the routine) and the reward. For instance, if each day you walk home past the chicken shop, the reward is not the bag of fries (this is the routine): the reward is what the fries give you – a moment to chat to the lady at the counter, to cheer yourself up, or a lift of energy, or perhaps that crunchy sound in your head.

2. **Smuggle in a new routine.** Now graft a new routine into the habit cycle – one without the negative effect but that delivers the same reward. Say the reward is an energy lift: why not stroll home by another route, armed with a nice crisp apple, and phone that friend you keep meaning to catch up with.

3. **Believe in change.** No resolution endures without faith, the science of habit formation finds. So believe in the new habit. Small ceremonies make even absurd pastimes feel sacred. My daughter's cello practice begins and ends with a bow, and she loves it. Reverence also worked for the painter Balthus, whose career, which began at the age of twelve, lasted into his eighties by cleaving to a routine of immense regularity. Each day commenced with a prayer, then 'exquisite moments of contemplation before a painting-in-progress, with a cigarette between my lips, helping me to advance into it'.

4. **Remember it is voluntary.** Habits are optional. Why be your own jailer?

2. A routine to speed where you want to go

Few of us consciously design our routine. We slide into it. To interrogate this daily pattern may strike you as another unwelcome chore. So ask yourself: if your day is shaped by unquestioned actions, what is their cumulative effect? How much of your irretrievable life leaks away on dross? Raising consciousness of what you do, when you do it and why, is liberating.

'Be regular and orderly in your life like a bourgeois,' advised the iconoclastic novelist Gustave Flaubert, 'that you may be violent and original in your work.' Let your routine free you to spend less time worrying about time in order to do something more interesting.

To make your routine ergonomic to your goals, it helps to identify your highest priority. As in, what is your overriding motivation? Is life about helping others? enrichment? family? creating? The more specific a priority, the more achievable it will be. At the secondary tier, what strategies, plans or goals will advance this motivation? Wine and head-scratching may help you fathom these dark waters. Emulate the ancient Persians, admired by the earliest travel writer, Herodotus, who took no major decision without first discussing it drunk, then again sober.

The hallmarks of a serviceable routine are:

1. **Priority:** events either necessary or pleasing lie at its heart.
2. **Simplicity:** it involves minimal transactions and distractions.
3. **Rhythm:** well-timed breaks.
4. **Momentum:** priming a sense of success in the morning is like strapping huskies to the sleigh of your day.
5. **Smooth transitions:** in-between moments are inconspicuous, but refining them reduces stress and timewasting.

Beyond that, there is no set menu to the ideal routine. Creative artists' regimens are particularly instructive on how motivation can be sustained, because with no salary or manager, the impetus to work has to come from within. For example, the subject matter of surrealist Louise Bourgeois was anxiety, so she arranged her day to cradle inner turmoil in routine's soothing embrace. After dressing she ironed a newspaper (to slay germs), then gulped marmalade from the jar for breakfast (on a sterile spoon) before hurtling in a taxi to her studio on 'a sugar high', said her assistant. Once there she worked first on sculpture, then 'something less physical', finding a 'second wind around 3.30 or 4.00 p.m.' for more sculpture. This wasp's diet and unswerving timetable kept her working like a fury until her death at ninety-eight.

Fellow artist Joan Miró built a routine like a citadel to fend off debilitating depression. His day began at 6 a.m. with ablutions and breakfast, then flat-out work from 7 a.m. to 12 p.m. and from 3 p.m. to 8 p.m., with lunch and an hour's boxing, skipping, swimming or running between. He died at ninety, his legacy a torrent of paintings, not long after his exhausted wife Pilar, thirty-six years his junior.

Such a pace might not have suited Carl Jung, founder of psychoanalysis, who was never happier than at his Bollingen Tower, a lakeside retreat free of creature comforts, far from his neurotic city patients. There he wrote, chopped wood, pumped water and felt 'most deeply myself ... These simple acts make man simple; and how difficult it is to be simple.'

If your day's framework is dictated by your office, international clients or school timetables, then the freedom to be simple may seem remote. But you have more discretion than you may think. Exercise it and you can eliminate the sense of chasing time that makes everything more complicated.

3. The Life Edit

To reshape your routine, first excavate its pattern. Keep a diary for a week or longer: any span that affords a representative slice of your current definition of normal life. Note what you do, when and why.

Now interrogate the pattern. Does the prospect scare you? What you are about to look at is your autobiography. Notice how you feel as you review it. These emotions indicate where to seek change: what to amplify or be rid of.

Find a green and a red pen and prepare to ask the hard questions. Your goal is threefold: to identify your prime tasks, prime times (for work, rest and play) and time pressures – the avoidable (red), unavoidable (green) and positively desirable (green).

Stage one: Task triage

1. **Quantify tasks:** draw up a list, from your largest tasks to your smallest, from regular to occasional. Now interrogate the underlying assumptions.
- Do these actions reflect your desires, needs or abilities? Mark those that do in green.
- Is the effort proportionate: do you spend too long on the wrong things, too little on what matters? Is this

the best approach, or have you acquired it through unquestioning habit? (As in, 'I always do this task in this way, because I always have done.') Mark in red anything you need to improve, brainstorming how you might do so.

2. **Review capacity:** are you doing too much or too little? If in doubt, your diary reveals what can be accomplished in a day. Reorganizing your routine could help you achieve more, but how much greater might be your attainments if you attempted less? Much misery comes of asking too much of ourselves, falling short and then (insanely, if correctly) feeling inadequate.

3. **Identify accelerants:** Which victories spur you on? Mark them in green. Is fun a priority? Is exercise? If not, why not?

4. **Redeploy:** Is this the best division of your workplace or household's labour? Mark in red any tasks you can defer, outsource or drop.

5. **Prioritize prime activities and tasks:** the activities and events that remain are those that bring joy, serve your purposes or cannot be avoided: your prime tasks. List them in order of importance. This is your chance to redefine what is necessary and urgent, according to what matters to you. Can you see more things to drop? Mark them in red.

6. **What are you missing?** Who or what should you see or do more of? Leisure and friendship tend to be the first gifts sacrificed to the god of spurious busyness. It is easy to keep in touch with people we care about

through digital media alone. Ask yourself: is this a substitute social life, or a decoy?

7. **Make time for admin:** Have you a dedicated weekly admin slot? How many cock-ups could you dodge if you did?
8. **Set a realistic daily tasks target:** For the big and small, plus the regular flummery that you cannot do without.

Stage two: Timing triage

This is about establishing how your day's tempo ebbs and flows, then improving it.

1. **Find and stretch your prime times:** Mark in green when you dig in and mine gold in your day. Are you utilizing these slots fully? Could you enlarge them?
2. **Identify time thieves.** What are your time pressures, procrastination triggers or brakes to momentum? Any routine, minor, soul-sapping disasters (lost keys/phone/socks)? Mark in red, then brainstorm solutions.
3. **Reappraise relationships' choreography:** When do you intersect with the people who matter to you? One night per week, sit down with your loved ones for a few minutes to compare diaries. Eliminate obstacles, extend the space you allow for pleasure, and many conflicts will dissolve instantly – the sort we often take for signs of discord, rather than anything so mundane as malcoordinated schedules.
4. **Experiment with sequence:** Timing can enhance momentum, such as the uplifting mini-task that buoys

you up for a challenge. Shuffle things about and problems can unravel. For years insomniac author Mark Twain relied on booze to nod off, at one point bedding down on his bathroom floor. Until he alighted on an outlandish notion: going to bed at ten o'clock. Sleeplessness never taxed him again.

5. **Focus on breaks, transitions and understudy moments:** Breaks place a frame around a time zone: instantly the time within it seems more urgent. To know your toil must end at 1 p.m. to walk the dog also focuses the mind, as well as extending a reward. So rifle through your diary for overlooked events that offer a change of pace. Perhaps it is murdering Aretha Franklin hits in the shower, a mid-morning vat of tea, a cigarette break, or that power pose you strike when nobody is looking. These punctuation points have a great if discreet influence on your tempo because they let you shift gear. But be clear: do they smooth your flow or ruck it up? Mark them in red or green accordingly. If transition points are hard to discern, perhaps you should introduce more punctuation marks: the extra contrast could sharpen your focus and make the day pacier. Why not refurbish a bad habit, or convert a time thief into a reward (e.g. a 2 p.m. email burst)?

6. **Slow times:** Down time is the essential foil to our ups. When does your pace slow? Most of us slump between 2 and 3 p.m. If a siesta is out of the question, make this your miscellaneous slot for boring tasks, be it answering non-urgent emails, or bumbling on Facebook while you idle in call-queue purgatory, deal

with the charmer in the IT department, or tackle the dog-eared, never-quite-reached end of your to-do list. If slow times go on too long, is there a physical cause – a shortage or surfeit of food, sleep or indulgence? Working in briefer bursts, adjusting your location, exercise or diet could pep you up. Flavonols aid alertness (this book was brought to you by liberal quantities of dark chocolate).

7. **Cudgel contingency slots:** Where is the spare time, ripe for a reward, rest, or to stand as a shock absorber? Carve regular buffer periods into the day, if for no better reason than to step outside the monomania of busyness. Every break frees your brain to rummage in its default system and unearth solutions to ticklish problems that resist direct attack.

8. **Prioritize peace:** Leave home fifteen minutes earlier and a daily crunch point can become a moment for reflection. A friend, one of my favourite time travellers, never fails to set aside ten minutes to be alone in the morning – somewhere she can be without having to be anything to anyone else. She uses it to walk, think, or sit and read before her working day begins. This calm well in time has a sustaining afterlife, easing the pressures that follow.

9. **Use tomorrow lists to get ahead and snap the reactive cycle:** Make a habit of task triage, establishing a nightly ritual of planning tasks for the next day. Crucially: *do not add any new goals* when the day itself arrives. Any unanticipated emergencies can be fitted into contingency slots.

Stage three: Draw the map

Find a large sheet of paper. Sketch out the bones of your ideal, pared-back daily and weekly routine. What do you want to do, when, at what tempo?

Review your notes to ascertain the key priorities or anchors for your routine. When scheduling, allocate the big tasks first, then the smaller ones (the latter can fit snugly into any left-over space). Be sure to use pace and contrast to lift the tempo, considering how the sequence of your day can harness the greatest momentum or comfortably ride the rise and fall of your biological timetable (see pages 170–3). Which time pressures could, with tweaks, be converted from stress bringers into tools to drive you on? Which time-enhancing habits are absent that could feed profitably into the mix?

However demanding your day may be, if it feels like your choice it becomes easier to play with the experiment of living – in your own good time.

1,000 MONTHS: YOUR TIME TRAVEL KIT

The triumph of any plan hinges on its timeframe. So how long have you got?

A thousand months, minus those you have already had, possibly more. If this seems too little for what you wish to do, you might consider that such an attitude turns life into work, and you into a producer of things called deeds. And then, all too easily, time can become a stick you beat yourself with – perhaps hoping to be rewarded one day for your virtuous endeavour with a happy life (an approach not dissimilar to that of Rumpelstiltskin, the fairy-tale villain who tirelessly spins straw into gold then demands to be paid with a baby).

We are swift to believe there is not enough time, and yet, as Leonardo da Vinci is said to have remarked, it waits long enough for anyone who uses it, anyone who treats it as their servant: as a tool that humanity invented to let our days count for more.

So set aside your to-do list. Here is a to-be list: ten guidelines to more rewarding time travel in this astounding, fast-forward world.

1. Change your attitude towards time

Whether you regard time as a bully or as your fondest pal, the results can be predicted, because your attitude towards time determines what you do with it. You could quake at what Shakespeare called 'Time's thievish progress to eternity'. Or practise denial, like poet Philip Larkin: 'I suppose everyone tries to ignore the passing of time

– some people by doing a lot, being in California one year and Japan the next. Or there's my way – making every day and every year exactly the same.' But well may life feel like a 'thievish' exercise in loss. There is more to commend a balanced time perspective, a stance psychologists find in sunny souls who experience time as a stream of well-connected moments, dancing from a past rich in joyful memories to a future ripe in hope. Some are born feeling like this, others need to re-engineer their outlook (see page 71).

2. Live simply – by your priorities

If our sole animating impulse is to service a lifestyle, existence can soon come to seem 'a quick succession of busy nothings', as Jane Austen lamented in *Mansfield Park*. Quality time hinges on three factors: ownership (you must feel time is yours), a focus and engagement. These honour the five planks of wellbeing: learning, noticing, giving, connecting and being active.

Humanity's first timekeeper was event time, and it remains the best. Prioritize higher goals and you gain perspective, purpose and depth of field, and are less likely to be governed by rush than if you micromanage time. So stitch your day together with actions, people and rituals that charge it with meaning. Only you know what is sacred. Barack Obama, while serving as US president, somehow managed to coach his daughters' school basketball teams. Benjamin Franklin rose early to 'sit in my chamber without any clothes' and write or read, claiming these 'air baths' summoned 'the most pleasing sleep that can be imagined'.

To draw dreams into your everyday existence, ask, 'What do I want to do today?' The next logical question is 'Why do anything else?' Maybe your heart's desire – say, to build treehouses – is inessential to your daily grind. Well, weave it in. It worked for Apple's Steve Jobs, who said in 2005: 'For the past 33 years, I have looked in the mirror every morning and asked myself: "If today were the last day of my life, would I want to do what I am about to do today?"' If he found himself answering no 'too many days in a row', he sought a new goal.

3. Let the regular happen better

Declutter your schedule to smooth the flow. Brittle routines buckle, so leave some free space. If minutes fall spare, they will fill. Why not revive that passion project that is languishing, velvet with dust, in your drawer? Or do nothing! Life is less than alive if you are too busy palpating a tablet or smartphone to notice it.

4. Redefine urgent and necessary

Adopt the mantra of Japanese tidiness guru Marie Kondo: unless something is essential to you or brings joy, let it go. Clarify your purpose each night with a tomorrow list outlining your top priorities for the coming day. Do not be defined by other people's definitions of urgent or fair, because such expectations are seldom consistent. Painter David Hockney spent 120 hours sitting for his portrait by Lucian Freud. 'He talked me into it,' he said. 'I was giving him all my precious mornings.' In return Freud permitted Hockney four hours to paint a double portrait of him and his assistant.

5. Value all of your time, teaching others not to undervalue it

Should you struggle to cherish your hours, try this mental exercise: price your time in a currency you value. For instance, that seven minutes you repeatedly squander hunting out shoes in a closet you never get around to tidying equates to an extra half-hour per week in bed, or a relaxed stroll to the train. A lunch hour sucked dry by Tinder could be spent talking to a pal.

To snaffle time thieves, think like Napoleon, who said, 'You can ask me for anything you like, except time.' Of course emperors rarely blanch at saying no. It is harder for lesser mortals, especially freelancers, whose job status is often interpreted as an open invitation to tea. But be firm – with yourself and others – about what each hour is for.

Some rhino-hided souls are blind to the possibility that their happy hours deny you yours. Send them a message. Composer Joseph Haydn was thrilled to be Nikolaus Esterházy's *Kapellmeister* until the prince refused to leave his summer palace, or to let his musicians visit their city homes. So he wrote a *Farewell Symphony*. At the end each player rose, score under his arm, and left. After the first performance, Esterházy relented and gave them all a holiday.

6. Let the irregular happen better: quarantine distractions

Picture the chump in the game show, trapped in a plastic bubble, trying to catch £10 notes flying around his head. That is you, scrambling to parry the blizzard of demands as they hit. Itty-bitty stuff devours disproportionate amounts of time and energy, not least because, however trivial an email or SMS, let it interrupt and countless minutes are lost to reconstituting your train of thought.

Instant is rarely either reasonable or sensible. Instead of taking a scattershot approach, bundle time thieves into a defined task in a set slot. And switch off. What would happen if you emulated film director Armando Iannucci and ignored computers and phones after 6 p.m.? Well, let it.

7. Sequence for success

Draw up your to-do list in order of importance, but bear in mind that this may not be the best order in which to execute it. Time actions to harness momentum and suit your body clock, allocating intellectually demanding work to mornings, when willpower is strong and distraction easier to baffle. This was the policy of Goethe, who wrote *Faust*, the iconic tale of a man selling his time too cheap, 'in the early hours of the day, when I am feeling revived and strengthened by sleep and not yet harassed by the absurd trivialities of everyday life'.

To boost your morale for less enthralling challenges, seek an easy win first. Write that thank you, do those push-ups. When serving as US Secretary of State Condoleezza Rice (once a child prodigy pianist and figure skater) would take to the treadmill at 5 a.m., kicking off her day in a mood of purpose. Swiss architect Le Corbusier also took his morale seriously. After morning exercise came several hours of painting, drawing and writing. His art had not a jot to do with his architectural practice – he only ever showed this work to his wife – yet to him these creative mornings were vital to his professional life, which began at 2 p.m., ending equally punctually when he left his office. At 5.30 p.m.

8. Use contrast to sharpen focus

There is never too little time to take time out. You cannot afford not to. If your work entails repetitive or drawn-out tasks, break it up, using light and shade to heighten interest. You could, like J. Alfred Prufrock in T.S. Eliot's eponymous 'love song', measure out life 'with coffee spoons'. Or in headstands, as Nobel laureate Saul Bellow did to revive his mind. You will benefit more if these punctuation marks are tethered to achievements (perhaps a five-minute Facebook trawl after every hour on those interminable contracts). And always have lunch, the kind you eat with both hands and cutlery.

Cultivate active pastimes. Notably successful creative figures, from Charles Dickens to Ludwig van Beethoven to Albert Einstein, swore by their daily constitutional, as did seventeenth-century philosopher Thomas Hobbes, who although he famously decried life as 'nasty, brutish, and short', was in reality no Gradgrind. He let ideas steal upon him during a long morning stroll, teasing them onto paper over the rest of the day, between naps, pipe-smoke and song.

9. Pick the right pace

Speed hinders us if as a result we become stressed or disorganized, lose focus or disengage. But any pace can serve if your focus remains true and you retain your capacity for slow, creative thought.

A fine example is that maestro of effervescent beats, Mozart. As a freelance man of music in eighteenth-century Vienna, his daily routine was a madcap 'rush and bustle', according to his startled father Leopold. Amid teaching, performing, buttering up patrons and skirmishing for a living, Mozart squeezed time to compose into the slender gap between breakfast and seeing pupils, with another jag at the end of the day before he collapsed into bed. This frenetic timetable had two advantages: it profited from the morning hours, when the mind is clearest, and also from our brain's default system; as he slept, melodies would have whirled on in his dreams.

Manipulate your mood to speed up or slow down. A sense of fun, novelty, ease or freedom complements creative tasks, as well as helping duller work to feel nearer to a hobby. Some decades ago an intuitive manager at a South American banana factory recognized this, recruiting a man to read aloud piquant snippets from the newspapers in order to make the workers chuckle. But this sort of mood is counterproductive to analytical tasks, when you need a vigilant head on, or if you need to create something tense. Patricia Highsmith abandoned the first draft of her bestseller, *The Talented Mr Ripley*, because she felt the prose was too relaxed, and resumed writing 'mentally as well as physically sitting on the edge of my chair, because that is the kind of young man Ripley is – a young man on the edge of his chair, if he is sitting down at all'. Perfectly nervy prose spilled forth.

In short, when ironing, tune the radio to pop, but switch it off before broaching your tax return.

10. Let your mind travel to the future you long for – then paint the picture

Two deeply impressive friends share a ritual. Every New Year, rather than form resolutions – what a baleful parade of jilted pleasures those are! – they draw up a wish list. Their wishes encompass four dimensions: work, relationships, body and spirit. They can hope for anything at all, providing it lies beyond what is immediately achievable. Then they write a plan with step-by-step targets, and show it to each other. Every few months they will take another look. At the end of the year they exchange lists again, champagne at the ready, and are often surprised at how close, slowly and steadily, they have come to those targets.

Visualizing the future can evoke a sense of inevitability that feels like destiny. As it proved for Olympic 400m hurdler Sally Gunnell, who pictured herself winning, bound by bound, up to seventy times a day before lacing up her shoes to take gold. Similarly, in his prime, footballer Wayne Rooney would visit the Manchester United kit man to check which strip the team would be wearing in the next day's match. Then he could picture himself playing – and scoring – as he drifted off to sleep the night before.

To seek a finer tomorrow is part and parcel of the ability possessed by prudent people – those able to forego short-term pleasure for long-haul gain – to entertain warm, friendly feelings for their future selves. (By contrast, brain scans find that short-termists can feel as unconnected to their future self as to a stranger.)

What powers a wish is hope. It alters our orientation in time: to progress and achievements, rather than to the dwindling returns of encroaching age. We find the life we seek when we commit to what we hope to become.

Acknowledgements

This book began in conversation, exhaustion and bewilderment. It would not exist without the support and contributions of many people.

First thanks must go to my brilliant agent, Eugenie Furniss, whose faith kept fizzing over some long years, and to the wonderful Rachel Mills, Rory Scarfe and Isha Karki at Furniss Lawton. I feel exceptionally lucky to have worked with Arabella Pike, wise and inspirational editor, who raised my game when I felt all played out, and the superb team at William Collins. I am particularly grateful to Iain Hunt, project editor, who wrangled the text into being with style and patience; designer Becky Morrison, who dreamt up a gorgeous, clever jacket; Alison Davies, tireless and uplifting publicist, and Tara Al Azzawi, marketing whizz, for their energy and insights; Marianne Tatepo, multi-talented publishing executive, and to my sharp-eyed copyeditor Steve Gove, proofreader Richard Collins and indexer Geraldine Beare.

Special thanks to Annie Auerbach, Nicola Barr, Margaret Behan, Jess Binns, Remy Blumenfeld, Jennifer Blyth, Caroline Bondy, Joshua Briggs, Helen Burdock, Kate de Carteret,

Zeina Chabarek, Soraya Chabarek, Maija Cirulis, Stacia Conlon, Courtney Corkhill, Jo Craven, Serena Davies, Anastasia Eliot, Theodora Fairley, Caroline Ffiske, Floriana, Annabel Freyberg, Harriet Gaillard, Richard Gaillard, Annie Gardner, Samantha Giles, Frances Gillam, Peter Gillam, Tanya Gold, Tami Goven, Clare Grafik, Germaine Greer, Louise Haines, Ben Hammersley, Andrew Hardwick, Shabnam Hariri, Melanie Harrington, Carolyn Hart, Paul Hartle, Hettie Harvey, Christine Hawkins, Henryk Hetflaisz, Po Ming Ho, Tim Humphrey, Virginia Ironside, Ashok Jansari, Michael Jenkins, Gillian Johnson, Alexandra Key, Sigrid Kirk, Irma Kurtz, Carolina Labadia, Sue Lascelles, Jean Lam, Michele Lavery, Faith Lawrence, Bernard Lewis, Ingrid Lewis, Leonard Lewis, James Lewisohn, Chun-Wei Lo, Francesca Maurice-Williams, Carmel McConnell, Paul McHugh, Joe Mole, Erin Moore, Thomas Moore, Heidi Morin, Paul Morin, Lucia Muerza, Deborah Nath, Gaurav Nath, Nina, Patricia Niven, Hylton Murray-Philipson, Francesca Oggioni, Emma Parry, Gerrie Pitt, Dominic Prince, Rose Prince, Alice Procopé, Robert Procopé, Sukeena Rao, Monica Rastogi, Miriam Rayman, Ana Del Rey, James Ribbans, Henrietta Rose, Kate Rowe, Kate Rupert, Tim Rupert, Laetitia Rutherford, Amit Sarkar, Rebecca Sarkar, Sophie Scott, Amanda Shakespeare, Christopher Shakespeare, Francesca Shakespeare, Nicholas Shakespeare, Vin de Silva, Helen Simpson, Sara Sjölund, James Skinner, Liane-Louise Smith, Vanessa Smith, Tim Sorrell, David Runciman, Susie Stanway, Selin Tamtekin, Anne Turner, Edward Venning, Sarah Venning, Nico Warr, Alexandra Warr, John Williams, Barbara Wilson, Bee Wilson, Jaime Yim and Toby Young.

Acknowledgements

Thanks also to the staff of the Electric Diner and the Tin Shed, for their kindness to the woman in need of an office.

My favourite time thieves, Saskia and Rafael, tolerated unaccustomed periods of absence as their mummy wrote about how to make better choices with time. Without my beloved parents, Stephen and Vivian Blyth, this circle could not have been squared. Heartfelt gratitude goes to Maureen Turner, Wen Yi Lo, Celia Stanbrook, Miss Amanda, Miss Sarah, Miss Beth, Miss Melinda, Miss Clark, Miss Hollingworth and Pippa Macmillan for making their precious early years so rich, and allowing me to feel less guilty. Greatest thanks of all are owed to my fellow time traveller, Sebastian Shakespeare.

Sources

Introduction: Piers Steel, 'The Nature of Procrastination: A Meta-Analytic and Theoretical Review of Quintessential Self-Regulatory Failure', *Psychological Bulletin*, 133, 1 (2007), pp. 65–94; Truman Capote, *Breakfast at Tiffany's* (London: Penguin, 2000); Philip Larkin, *Collected Poems* (London: Faber and Faber, 2003); Dante Alighieri, *Purgatorio*, translated by Allen Mandelbaum (New York: Bantam, 1984), III, pp.75–8; Pema Chödrön, *Start Where You Are* (Boston: Shambhala,1994); Marie Kondo, *The Life-Changing Magic of Tidying* (London: Vermilion, 2014).

THE TIME TEST: Teenie Matlock et al., 'On the Experiential Link Between Spatial and Temporal Language', *Cognitive Science*, 29 (2005); Lera Boroditsky, 'Metaphoric Structuring: Understanding Time through Spatial Metaphors', *Cognition*, 75 (2000).

Part One: How Time Went Crazy

1 Is the World Spinning Faster?: J. Oeppen et al., 'Broken Limits to Life Expectancy', *Science*, 296 (2002), pp.1029–

31; J. W. Vaupel, 'Biodemography of Human Ageing', *Nature*, 464 (2010), pp. 536–42; *Bhaddekaratta Sutta: An Auspicious Day*, translated by Thanissaro Bhikku, http://www.accesstoinsight.org/tipitaka/mn/mn.131.than.html; Henry David Thoreau, *Walden* (London: Penguin, 2016); Keith Richards, *Life* (London: Weidenfeld & Nicolson, 2010); Roger Bannister, *Twin Tracks* (London: Robson Press, 2015); H.G. Wells, *The Time Machine* (London: Penguin, 2005); https://www.bls.gov/tus/; https://www.ofcom.org.uk/; http://www.nielsen.com/us/en/insights/reports/2014/; Robert V. Levine and Ara Norenzayan, 'The Pace of Life in 31 Countries', *Journal of Cross-cultural Psychology*, 30, 2 (March 1999), pp.178–205; http://www.richardwiseman.com/quirkology/pace_home.htm; Robert Levine, *A Geography of Time* (London: Oneworld, 2006); https://hbr.org/2013/11/the-pace-of-technology-adoption-is-speeding-up; Liza Picard, *Restoration London* (London: Weidenfeld & Nicolson, 1997); J. Crofts, *Packhorse, Waggon and Post* (London: Routledge, 1967); Robert B. Handfield, *Re-engineering for Time-Based Competition* (London: Quorum, 1995); Arie W. Kruglanski et al., 'Experience of Time by People on the Go: A Theory of the Locomotion–Temporality Interface', *Personality and Social Psychology Review* (2015); Robert Levine, 'A Geography of Busyness', *Social Research*, 72, 2 (2005); Gloria Mark et al., 'The Cost of Interrupted Work: More Speed and Stress', in *CHI '08 Proceedings of the SIGCHI Conference on Human Factors in Computing Systems* (New York: ACM, 2008); Ambrose Bierce, *The Devil's Dictionary* (London: Bloomsbury, 2003); http://www.apa.org/research/action/

multitask.aspx; Richard Layard, *Happiness* (London: Penguin, 2005); Nadine M. Schöneck, 'Europeans' Work and Life – Out of Balance? An Empirical Test of Assumptions from the "Acceleration Debate"', *Time & Society* (2015); Paul Dolan, *Happiness By Design* (London: Penguin, 2014); S.E. DeVoe et al., 'Time is Tight: How Higher Economic Value of Time Increases Feelings of Time Pressure', *Journal of Applied Psychology*, 96 (2011); S.E. DeVoe et al., 'Time, Money, and Happiness: How Does Putting a Price on Time Affect Our Ability to Smell the Roses?', *Journal of Experimental Social Psychology*, 48 (2012); W.J. Friedman et al., 'Aging and the Speed of Time', *Acta Psychologica*, 134 (June 2010); Philip Zimbardo and John Boyd, *The Time Paradox* (London: Rider, 2010); David Halpern, *Inside the Nudge Unit* (London: W.H. Allen, 2015); Avner Offner, *The Challenge of Affluence* (Oxford: OUP, 2006); Daniel Klein, *Travels with Epicurus* (London: Oneworld, 2013); James Gleick, *Faster* (London: Abacus, 2000); Norman Juster, *The Phantom Tollbooth* (New York: Random House, 1961); https://harmon.ie/blog/i-cant-get-my-work-done-how-collaboration-social-tools-drain-productivity; https://kaiserfamilyfoundation.files.wordpress.com/2010/01/mh012010presentl.pdf; Tom Chatfield, *How to Thrive in the Digital Age* (London: Macmillan, 2012); Lisa Kennedy, 'Spielberg in the Twilight Zone', *Wired*, 1 June 2002; Amy Fleming, 'Screen Time v. Play Time', *Guardian*, 23 May 2015; http://www.oecd.org/publications/students-computers-and-learning-9789264239555-en.htm; https://lindastone.net/qa/continuous-partial-attention/; Andrew Sullivan, 'I Used to

Be a Human Being', *New York Magazine*, 18 September 2016; Sherry Turkle, *Reclaiming Conversation* (London: Penguin, 2015); Edward H. O'Brien et al., 'Time Crawls When You're Not Having Fun: Feeling Entitled Makes Dull Tasks Drag On', *Personality and Social Psychology* (2011); Judith Woods, 'Bill Loves Doing the Washing Up', *You* magazine, 26 April 2015.

BUSY: Lars Svendsen, *A Philosophy of Boredom* (London: Reaktion, 2005); Thomas Edison, *Ford Times*, 6 (1912), p. 136; https://www.brainpickings.org/2013/02/11/thomas-edison-on-sleep-and-success/; Margaret Visser, *The Rituals of Dinner* (London: Penguin, 2017).

Part Two: What is Time and Where Does it Go?

2 How Time Gives us the World: http://www.scottlondon. com/interviews/hillman.html; Henry Home, *Elements of Criticism*, 2 (Carmel: Liberty Fund Inc., 2005); Adam Frank, *About Time* (London: Oneworld, 1989); 'Oldest Lunar Calendar Identified', http://news.bbc.co.uk/1/hi/sci/ tech/975360.stm; Emile Durkheim, *The Elementary Forms of the Religious Life* (London: 1912); Adam Hart-Davis, *The Book of Time* (London: Mitchell Beazley, 2011); James Shapiro, *1599* (London: Faber and Faber, 2006); Tang Kaijian, *Setting off from Macau* (Leiden: Brill, 2015); Dava Sobel, *Longitude* (London: 4th Estate, 1996); Norman Lewis, *The Happy Ant Heap* (London: Picador, 1999); Charlene W. Billings, *Grace Hopper: Navy Admiral and Computer Pioneer* (New York: Enslow, 1990); Saint

Augustine, *Confessions* (London: Penguin, 2002); Steven Strogatz, *Sync* (London: Hachette, 2004); James Broadway et al. (eds), *The Long and Short of Mental Time Travel – Self-Projection Over Time-Scales Large and Small* (Lausanne: Frontiers Media, 2015); Jay Griffiths, *Pip Pip* (London: Flamingo, 2000); Lera Boroditsky, 'How Languages Construct Time' in *Space, Time and Number in the Brain* (Cambridge: Academic Press, 2013); Asifa Majid et al., 'Time in Terms of Space', *Frontiers in Psychology*, 4 (2013); Seneca, *Moral Letters to Lucilius*, Letter 12; Helen Forman, 'Events and Children's Sense of Time: A Perspective on the Origins of Everyday Time-Keeping', *Frontiers in Psychology*, 6 (2015); Karen Armstrong, *The Spiral Staircase* (London: Harper Perennial, 2005); Aleksander Janca et al., 'The Aboriginal Concept of Time and its Mental Health Implications', *Australasian Psychiatry*, 11 (2003); Claudia Hammond, *Time Warped* (Edinburgh: Canongate, 2013); Edmund Burke, *Reflections on the Revolution in France* (London: 1790); Zimbardo, op. cit.; Sir Walter Ralegh, *Selected Writings* (Manchester: Carcanet, 1984); Richard Wiseman, *59 Seconds: Think a Little, Change a Lot* (London: Pan, 2009); R.A. Emmons et al., 'Counting Blessings Versus Burdens', *Journal of Personality and Social Psychology*, 84 (2003); L.A. King, 'The Health Benefits of Writing about Life Goals', *Personality and Social Psychology Bulletin*, 27 (2001); C.M. Burton et al., 'The Health Benefits of Writing about Intensely Positive Experiences', *Journal of Research in Personality*, 38 (2004).

On Time

MENTAL TIME TRAVEL: F. Scott Fitzgerald, *The Great Gatsby* (London: Penguin, 2005); Günter Grass, *Peeling the Onion* (London: Harvill Secker, 2007); Walter Benjamin, *Illuminations* (London: Bodley Head, 2015); *Machiavelli and His Friends: Their Personal Correspondence* (DeKalb: Northern Illinois University Press, 1996); Sarah Bakewell, *How to Live: A Life of Montaigne* (London: Vintage, 2011); Emma John, 'GB Women Win Historic Hockey Gold', *Guardian*, 19 August 2016; David Alliance and Ivan Fallon, *A Bazaar Life* (London: Robson Press, 2015).

3 Slaves to the Beat: Joe Mole, interview with author; http://www.gutenberg.us/articles/dyschronometria; William James, *Principles of Psychology* (New York: 1890); Donald J. Wilcox, *The Measure of Times Past* (Chicago: University of Chicago Press, 1989); A.M. Johnston, 'Time as a Psalm in St Augustine', *Animus*, 1 (1996); Jamie Sayen, *Einstein in America* (New York: Crown, 1985); François Truffaut, *Hitchcock* (London: Simon & Schuster, 1986); Robert Burton, *Anatomy of Melancholy* (New York: NYRB, 2001); Richard Gross, *Being Human* (London: Routledge, 2012); Nelson Mandela, *Long Walk to Freedom* (London: Abacus, 1995); Ralf Buckley, 'Slow Time Perception Can Be Learned', *Frontiers in Psychology*, 5 (2014); David Hart Dyke, *Four Weeks in May* (London: Atlantic Books, 2007); Chess Stetson et al., 'Does Time Really Slow Down during a Frightening Event?', *PLoS One*, 2 (2007); Sylvie Droit-Volet et al., 'Perception of the Duration of Emotional Events', *Cognition and Emotion*, 18 (2004); R.J. Maddock et al., 'Reduced Memory for the Spatial and Temporal

Context of Unpleasant Words', *Cognition and Emotion*, 23 (2009); Jennifer M. Talarico et al., 'Positive Emotions Enhance Recall of Peripheral Details', *Cognition and Emotion*, 23 (2009); Stephen Grosz, *The Examined Life* (London: Vintage, 2014); Sophie Scott, interview with author; Strogatz, op. cit.; J. H. Wearden et al., 'What Speeds Up the Internal Clock? Effects of Clicks and Flicker on Duration Judgements and Reaction Time', *Quarterly Journal of Experimental Psychology*, 70 (2017); Luke A. Jones et al., 'Click Trains and the Rate of Information Processing: Does "Speeding Up" Subjective Time Make Other Psychological Processes Faster?', *Quarterly Journal of Experimental Psychology*, 64 (2011); Edna O'Brien, *Desert Island Discs*, 19 January 2007; D. Draaisma, *Why Life Speeds Up As You Get Older* (Cambridge: CUP, 2006); Michelangelo Buonarroti, *Selected Poems and Letters* (London: Penguin, 2007); T. McCormack et al, 'Developmental Changes in Time Estimation', *Developmental Psychology*, 35 (1999); John Duncan et al. (eds), *Measuring the Mind* (New York: OUP, 2009); Ashok Jansari, interview with author; Tara Kelly, 'Jamie Ogg, Baby Pronounced Dead Then Revived by Mother's Touch, Celebrates Second Birthday', *Huffington Post*, 3 September 2012; Sofia Dahl et al., 'Preferred Dance Tempo: Does Sex or Body Morphology Influence How We Groove?', *Journal of New Music Research*, 43, 2 (2014); Barbara Ehrenreich, *Dancing in the Streets* (London: Granta, 2007); Adharanand Finn, 'Does Music Help You to Run Faster?', *Guardian*, 22 April 2012; Dan Peterson, 'Music Benefits Exercise, Studies Show', LiveScience.com, 21 October

2009; K. Brooks et al., 'Enhancing Sports Performance through the Use of Music', *Journal of Exercise Physiology*, 13 (2010); J. Edworthy et al., 'The Effects of Music Tempo and Loudness Level on Treadmill Exercise', *Ergonomics*, 49 (2006); Victoria Williamson, *You Are the Music* (London: Icon Books, 2014); R. Yalch et al., 'Effects of Store Music on Shopping Behaviour', *Journal of Consumer Marketing*, 4 (1990); Irena Vida et al., 'The Effects of Background Music on Consumer Responses in a High-End Supermarket', *The International Review of Retail, Distribution and Consumer Research*, 17 (2007); J. Duncan Herrington, 'Effects of Music in Service Environments: A Field Study', *Journal of Services Marketing*, 10 (1996); Ronald E. Milliman, 'The Influence of Background Music on the Behavior of Restaurant Patrons', *Journal of Consumer Research*, 13 (1986); L.W. Turley et al., 'Atmospheric Effects on Shopping Behaviour: A Review of the Experimental Evidence', *Journal of Business Research*, 2 (2000); Bethan Alexander et al., 'Multi-Sensory Fashion Retail Experiences', *Handbook of Research on Global Fashion Management and Merchandising* (London: IGI Global, 2016); Mike Wooldridge, 'Mandela Death: How He Survived 27 Years in Prison', BBC News, 11 December 2013; D. Klein, op. cit.; William Styron, *Darkness Visible* (London: Vintage, 2001); http://www-groups.dcs.st-and.ac.uk/history/Biographies/Renyi.html; Nicholas Humphrey, *Seeing Red* (Cambridge: Harvard University Press, 2008); Yair Bar-Haim et al., 'When Time Slows Down', *Cognition and Emotion*, 24 (2010).

WHAT NOW? A FLEETING BIOGRAPHY OF THE PRESENT:
Robert Browning, *Complete Works* (East Sussex: Delphi
Classics, 2012); Ashok Jansari, interview with author;
Gross, op. cit.; Benjamin Libet, 'Unconscious Cerebral
Initiative and the Role of Conscious Will in Voluntary
Action', *The Behavioural and Brain Sciences*, 8 (1985);
Ernst Pöppel et al., 'Temporal Windows as a Bridge from
Objective to Subjective Time', in Valtteri Arstila and Dan
Lloyd (eds) *Subjective Time* (Cambridge: MIT Press, 2014);
Irmgard Feldhütter et al., 'Moving in the Beat of Seconds:
Analysis of the Time Structure of Human Action', *Ethology
and Sociobiology*, 11 (1990); Marc Wittman, 'Time
Perception and Temporal Processing Levels of the Brain',
Journal of Biological and Medical Rhythm Research, 16
(1999).

4 It's Not Working: http://www.ons.gov.uk/ons/
dcp171766_310300.pdf; http://www.mentalhealth.org.uk/
publications/living-with-anxiety; Justin McCurry, 'Head of
Japanese Ad Firm to Quit after New Recruit's Death from
Overwork', *Guardian*, 29 December 2016; 'Teacher Killed
Herself "Over Work Stress"', *The Times*, 18 November
2016; Tina Nguyen, 'Goldman Sachs to Interns: Fine, You
Can Leave the Offices Before Midnight', vanityfair.com, 17
June 2015; Joshi Hermann, 'A Year on from Intern Moritz
Erhardt's Death, Has Banking Industry Changed its Ways?',
Independent, 9 August 2014; Tina (not her real name),
interviewed by author; interview with senior employment
lawyer; Dolan, op. cit.; Denis Campbell, 'Serious Mistakes
in NHS Patient Care Are on the Rise, Figures Reveal',

Observer, 1 January 2017; Oscar Williams-Grut, 'Mark Carney: "Every Technological Revolution Mercilessly Destroys Jobs Well before the New Ones Emerge"', uk. businessinsider.com, 6 December 2016; http://www. oxfordmartin.ox.ac.uk/downloads/reports/Citi_GPS_ Technology_Work_2.pdf; Michael Chui et al., *The Social Economy* (McKinsey Global Institute, July 2012), http:// www.mckinsey.com/industries/high-tech/our-insights/ the-social-economy; https://www.glassdoor.co.uk/blog/ uk-employees-losing-quarter-annual-leave-glassdoor-uk- annual-leave-survey-2014-2/; Lauren Davidson, 'Email Deluges and Huge Workloads Are Ruining Holidays', *Daily Telegraph*, 23 June 2015; http://www.gfi.com/company/ press/2013/05/survey-checking-email-at-night-on- weekends-and-holidays-is-the-new-norm-for-the-uks- workforce; 'Workers' After-Hours Emails Cancel Out Entire Annual Leave Allowance', *Daily Telegraph*, 12 January 2016; https://techtalk.gfi.com/survey-81-of-u-s- employees-check-their-work-mail-outside-work-hours/; Kathryn Dill, 'You're Probably Checking Your Work Email On Vacation – But You Shouldn't Be, Study Shows', forbes. com, 17 June 2014; http://www.careerbuilder.ca/ blog/2015/06/18/3-in-10-workers-check-work-email-while- on-holiday/; https://www.shrm.org/resourcesandtools/ hr-topics/employee-relations/pages/unused-vacation-.aspx; P. Verduyn et al., 'Predicting the Duration of Emotional Experience: Two Experience Sampling Studies, *Emotion*, 9 (2009); Jocelyn K. Glei (ed.), *Manage Your Day-to-Day: Build Your Routine, Find Your Focus, and Sharpen Your Creative Mind* (Amazon Publishing: 2013); Sendhil

Mullainathan and Eldar Shafir, *Scarcity: Why Having Too Little Means So Much* (London: Allen Lane, 2013); Martin Gardner, *The Annotated Alice* (London: Random House, 1998); J.M. Darley et al., '"From Jerusalem to Jericho": A Study of Situational and Dispositional Variables in Helping Behaviour', *Journal of Personality and Social Psychology*, 27 (1973); Walter Mischel, *The Marshmallow Test* (London: Little, Brown, 2014); Edward M. Hallowell, *Driven to Distraction at Work* (Brighton: Harvard Business Review Press, 2015); Carson Tate, *Work Simply* (London: Portfolio Penguin, 2015); Daniel Kahneman, *Thinking, Fast and Slow* (London: Penguin, 2012); Clive Thompson, 'Meet the Life Hackers', *New York Times* magazine, 16 October 2005; Jonathan B. Spira et al., *The Cost of Not Paying Attention*, http://iorgforum.org/wp-content/uploads/2011/06/CostOfNotPayingAttention.BasexReport1.pdf; https://www.fastcoexist.com/1682538/stream-these-coffee-shop-sounds-to-boost-your-creativity; http://psych.cf.ac.uk/contactsandpeople/jonesdm.php; Shai Danziger et al., 'Extraneous Factors in Judicial Decisions', *PNAS*, 108 (2011); J. Monterosso et al., 'Behavioral Economic of Will in Recovery from Addiction', *Drug Alcohol Dependence*, 90, Suppl. 1 (2007); George Ainslie, *Picoeconomics* (Cambridge: CUP, 1992).

WORK-LIFE BALANCE: Arlie Hochschild, *The Time Bind* (New York: Metropolitan Books, 1997); Arlie Hochschild et al., *The Second Shift* (New York: Avon Books, 1990); Ehrenreich, op. cit.; Griffiths, op. cit.; Keith Thomas, *Religion and the Decline of Magic* (London: Penguin,

2003); Christopher Rosen, 'Sia Wrote Rihanna's "Diamonds" in 14 Minutes', *Huffington Post*, 21 April 2014; Aida Edemariam, 'The New Monroe Doctrine', *Guardian*, 4 September 2004.

5 The Good, the Bad and the Ugly of Procrastination:
Leonardo da Vinci, *The Notebooks*, http://www.gutenberg. org/cache/epub/5000/pg5000-images.html; Giorgio Vasari, *The Lives of the Artists* (Oxford: OUP, 2008); Steel, op. cit.; Robert Boice, 'Quick Starters: New Faculty Who Succeed', *New Directions for Teaching and Learning*, 48 (1991); Chrisoula Andreou et al. (eds), *The Thief of Time*, (Oxford: OUP, 2010); *Delphi Complete Works of Thucydides* (East Sussex: Delphi Classics, 2013); Ben Zimmer, 'How We Got a Word for "Putting Things Off"', Slate.com, 14 May 2008; Ann Wroe, *Pilate* (London: Vintage, 2000); Samuel Johnson, *Essays from the Rambler, Adventurer and Idler* (New Haven: Yale University Press, 1968); Randal Keynes, *Annie's Box: Charles Darwin, His Daughter and Human Evolution* (London: 4th Estate, 2001); Frank Partnoy, *Wait* (London: Profile, 2012); John Guy, *Elizabeth: The Forgotten Years* (London: Viking, 2016); Mary Budd Rowe, 'Wait-Time and Rewards As Instructional Variables, Their Influence On Language, Logic, and Fate Control: Part One – Wait-Time', *Journal of Research in Science Teaching*, 11 (1974); Andreou, op. cit.; Robert Cialdini, *Influence* (London: Harper Business, 2007); Stuart Jeffries, 'Hilary Mantel: "If I Am Suffering I Can Make that Pay"', *Guardian*, 17 October 2012; Mason Currey, *Daily Rituals* (London: Picador, 2013); Dame

Kathleen Ollerenshaw, interview with author; John Perry, *The Art of Procrastination* (New York: Workman, 2012); Dan Ariely, *Predictably Irrational* (London: HarperCollins, 2009); Andreou, op. cit.

CLOCKWATCHING: Norman Lewis, *Naples '44* (London: Eland, 2002); Sebastian Shakespeare, interview with author; William Faulkner, *The Sound and the Fury* (London: Vintage, 1995); Floriana, interview with author.

Part Three: How to Get it Back

6 Body Clocks: Jorge Luis Borges, *Collected Fictions* (London: Allen Lane, 1999); Patti Smith, *M Train* (London: Bloomsbury, 2016); Marco Hafner and Wendy M. Troxel, 'Americans Don't Sleep Enough, and It's Costing Us $411 Billion', *Washington Post*, 30 November 2016; Gross, op. cit.; Craig Callender and Ralph Edney, *Introducing Time* (London: Icon, 2010); Hart-Davis, op. cit.; Ashok Jansari, interview with author; Joshua Foer, 'Caveman: An Interview with Michel Siffre', *Cabinet*, 30 (2008); Stefan Klein, *Time: A User's Guide* (London: Penguin, 2008); Till Roenneberg, *Internal Time* (Cambridge: Harvard University Press, 2012); Leonardo, op. cit.; Strogatz, op. cit.; Dervla Murphy, *On a Shoestring to Coorg* (London: Flamingo, 1995); Apa Pant, *A Moment in Time* (London: Hodder & Stoughton, 1974); M.A. Carskadon et al., 'Regulation of Adolescent Sleep: Implications for Behavior', *Annals of the New York Academy of Sciences*, 1021 (2004); F. Danner et al., 'Adolescent Sleep, School Start Times, and

Teen Motor Vehicle Crashes', *Journal of Clinical Sleep Medicine*, 4 (2008); C. Randler et al., 'Correlation Between Morningness, Eveningness and Final School Leaving Exams, *Biological Rhythm Research*, 37 (2006); James Badcock, 'The End of the Spanish Siesta?', http://www.bbc.co.uk/news/magazine-35995972; Buckminster Fuller, *Nine Chains to the Moon* (Philadelphia: Lippincott, 1938); Currey, op. cit.; Jean-Claude Marquié et al., 'Chronic Effects of Shift Work on Cognition: Findings from the VISA Longitudinal Study', *Occupational & Environmental Medicine*, 72 (2014); Cody Ramin et al., 'Night Shift Work at Specific Age Ranges and Chronic Disease Risk Factors', *Occupational & Environmental Medicine*, 72 (2014); Zachary M. Weil et al., 'Sleep Deprivation Attenuates Inflammatory Responses and Ischemic Cell Death', *Experimental Neurology*, 218 (2009); Mika Kivimäki et al., 'Long Working Hours and Risk of Coronary Heart Disease and Stroke: A Systematic Review and Meta-Analysis of Published and Unpublished Data for 603,838 Individuals', *The Lancet*, 386, 31 October 2015; Henry Marsh, *Do No Harm* (London: Phoenix, 2014); http://www.salk.edu/news-release/more-than-3000-epigenetic-switches-control-daily-liver-cycles/; Gross, op. cit.; http://researchnews.osu.edu/archive/dimlightham.htm; Laura K. Fonken et al., 'Influence of Light at Night on Murine Anxiety- and Depressive-Like Responses', *Behavioural Brain Research*, 205 (2009); Michael Price, 'The Risks of Night Work', *Monitor on Psychology*, 42 (2011); http://www.journalsleep.org/Articles/250312.pdf; Helen J. Burgess, 'Evening Ambient Light Exposure Can Reduce Circadian Phase Advances to

Morning Light Independent of Sleep Deprivation', *Journal of Sleep Research*, 22 (2013); S. Klein, op. cit.

HOW TO BECOME A LARK (OR AN OWL) AND BEAT JET LAG: C.N. Douglas (comp.), *Forty Thousand Quotations: Prose and Poetical* (New York: Halcyon House, 1917); Victoria Woodhall, 'Machine-Washable Cashmere Is Coming Our Way, Thanks to Designer Shannon Wilson', *You* magazine, 11 October 2015; Currey, op. cit.; Charmane I. Eastman et al., 'How to Travel the World Without Jet lag', *Sleep Medicine Clinics*, 4 (2009); http://www.med.upenn.edu/cbti/assets/user-content/documents/Burgess_UsingBrightLightandMelatonintoAdjusttoNightWork-BTSD.pdf.

7 Time Rich: Dolan, op. cit.; S.E. DeVoe et al. (2012) op. cit.; Levine (2006), op. cit.; Lao Tzu, *Tao Te Ching* (London: Penguin, 1964); S. Klein, op. cit.; Breffni M. Noone et al., 'Perceived Service Encounter Pace and Customer Satisfaction: An Empirical Study of Restaurant Experiences', *Journal of Service Management*, 20 (2009); Breffni M. Noone et al., 'The Effect of Meal Pace on Customer Satisfaction', *Cornell Hospitality Quarterly* (2007); Breffni M. Noone et al., 'The Effect of Perceived Control on Consumer Responses to Service Encounter Pace: A Revenue Management Perspective', *Cornell Hospitality Quarterly* (2012); Robert Louis Stevenson, *Travels with a Donkey in the Cevennes* (Oxford: Oxford Paperbacks, 1992); Chen-Bo Zhong et al., 'You Are How You Eat: Fast Food and Impatience', *Psychological Science*, 21 (2010); Robert J. Sternberg, 'The Theory of Successful

Intelligence', *Interamerican Journal of Psychology*, 39 (2005); Bernard Lewis, interview with author; Partnoy, op. cit.; Currey, op. cit.; Jordan Ellenberg, *How Not to Be Wrong* (London: Penguin, 2015); Tessa Jowell, speech to BBC executives; Piper Kerman, *Orange Is the New Black* (London: Abacus, 2013); Nora Ephron, *I Feel Bad About My Neck* (London: Black Swan, 2006); Mihaly Csikszentmihalyi, *Finding Flow* (New York: Basic Books, 1997); https://www.gov.uk/government/uploads/system/uploads/attachment_data/file/292453/mental-capital-wellbeing-summary.pdf; Matthew A. Killingsworth et al., 'A Wandering Mind Is an Unhappy Mind', *Science*, 330 (2010); https://www.trackyourhappiness.org; Alexis Petridis, 'Prince: "Transcendence. That's What You Want"', *Guardian*, 12 November 2015; Kahneman, op. cit.; Daniel Pink, *Drive* (Edinburgh: Canongate, 2011); Halpern, op. cit.; Richard Sennett, *The Craftsman* (London: Penguin, 2009); Charles Duhigg, *Smarter, Faster, Better* (London: William Heinemann, 2016); Currey, op. cit.; Marsh, op. cit.; Robert Macfarlane, *Landmarks* (London: Penguin, 2016); Judith Thurman, *Secrets of the Flesh: A Life of Colette* (London: Bloomsbury, 1999); https://www.nationaltrust.org.uk/documents/read-our-natural-childhood-report.pdf; Sei Shonagon, *The Pillow Book* (London: Penguin, 2006); Richard Mabey, *Turned Out Nice Again* (London: Profile, 2013); Smith, op. cit.; Mark Williams and Danny Penman, *Mindfulness* (London: Piatkus, 2011); Ashok Jansari, interview with author.

8 Time Thieves: https://www.benhammersley.com/
worknotes/2015/1/19/socialfacilitationandbots; Norman
Triplett, 'The Dynamogenic Factors in Pacemaking and
Competition', *American Journal of Psychology*, 9 (1898);
Currey, op. cit.; Kees Keizer et al., 'The Spreading of
Disorder', *Science*, 322 (2008); Allen Johnson, 'In Search of
the Affluent Society', *Human Nature*, 1 (1978); Sue
Bowden and Avner Offer, 'Household Appliances and the
Use of Time: The United States and Britain since the 1920s',
Economic History Review, 47 (1994); Cialdini, op. cit.;
Andreou, op. cit.; Mischel, op. cit.; Tate, op. cit.; Dan,
interview with author; interview with author; Finn Scott-
Delany, 'Mobile Phone Signals Blocked from New Hove
Gin Bar', *The Argus*, 22 July 2016; Jessica Salter, 'Digital
Detox: Could this Jewellery Give You Your Life Back',
Daily Telegraph, 15 November 2015.

CARPE DIEM: https://www.poets.org/poetsorg/poem/virgins-
make-much-time; Horace, *The Complete Odes and Epodes*
(Oxford: OUP, 2008); Marcus Aurelius, *Meditations*
(London: Sacred Texts, 2006); Thich Nhat Hanh, *The Path
of Emancipation* (Berkeley: Parallax, 2000).

9 Timing: Francis Bacon, *The Essays* (London: Penguin,
1985); Anthony Bourdain, *The Nasty Bits* (London:
Bloomsbury, 2006); Yorck Von Wartenburg, *Napoleon as a
General* (London: Kegan Paul, 1902); Nancy Newhall,
Ansel Adams: The Eloquent Light (New York: Aperture,
1980); 'Ansel Adams: The Last Interview', http://www.
maryellenmark.com/text/magazines/art%20

news/905N-000-001.html; Henri Cartier-Bresson, *The Mind's Eye* (New York: Aperture, 2004); Bertrand Russell, *Has Man a Future?* (London: Penguin, 1961); Cialdini, op. cit.; Malcolm Gladwell, *Outliers* (London: Penguin, 2009); https://en.wikipedia.org/wiki/Relative_age_effect; http://voxeu.org/article/relative-age-effect-over-long-term; Kelly Bedard et al., 'The Persistence of Early Childhood Maturity: International Evidence of Long-Run Age Effects', *Quarterly Journal of Economics*, 121 (2006); Rasmus Landersø et al., 'School Starting Age and the Crime-Age Profile', *Economic Journal* (2016); Hesiod, *Theogony and Works and Days* (Oxford: OUP, 2008); Miyamoto Musashi, *The Book of Five Rings* (Boston: Shambhala, 2012); Andrew Gimson, *Gimson's Kings and Queens* (London: Square Peg, 2015); Richard Williams, *The Death of Ayrton Senna* (London: Penguin, 2010); Michael Goldfarb, *The Essay: Trip Sheets*, http://www.bbc.co.uk/programmes/b04k744m; 'Squeezing In', *Economist*, 23 May 2015; 'Breathtaking', *Economist*, 30 July 2016; http://www.ancient.eu/Battle_of_the_Granicus/; Eric Charles White, *Kaironomia: On the Will-to-Invent* (Ithaca: Cornell UP, 1987); Lauren Indvik, 'Anna Wintour Insists She's Not a Micromanager', *Fashionista*, 29 October 2013; Kathleen M. Eisenhardt, 'Making Fast Strategic Decisions in High-Velocity Environments', *Academy of Management Journal*, 32 (1989).

ON TIME: Chris Weller, 'Jim Dunbar Diagnosed with Chronic Lateness', Medicaldaily.com, 27 August 2013; Levine (2006), op. cit.; Harris poll for careerbuilder.com,

2009; Harry Mount, 'Better Always to Be Late than Selectively So', *Spectator*, 24 October 2007; Erin Meyer, *The Culture Map* (New York: Public Affairs, 2014).

10 Sticking at it: Alfred North Whitehead, *An Introduction to Mathematics* (Aberdeen: Watchmaker Publishing, 2011); Robert Holden, *Authentic Success* (London: Hay House, 2013); Currey, op. cit.; Hammond, op. cit.; Andreou, op. cit.; Mary Cross, *Madonna* (Santa Barbara: Greenwood, 2007); http://www.billboard.com/articles/events/women-in-music/7617021/madonna-billboard-women-in-music-2016-speech; Angela Duckworth, *Grit* (London: Vermilion, 2016); https://www.britannica.com/topic/broken-windows-theory; Charles Duhigg, *The Power of Habit* (London: William Heinemann, 2012); Twyla Tharp, *The Creative Habit* (London: Simon & Schuster, 2007); Leo Tolstoy, *War and Peace* (London: Vintage, 2009); Pink, op. cit.; Edemariam, op. cit.; Philip French, 'I Figured I'd Retire Gradually, Just Ride Off into the Sunset …', *Observer*, 25 February 2007; Matthew Syed, *Black Box Thinking* (London: John Murray, 2016); Martin Johnson, 'What I've Learnt', *The Times*, 26 September 2015; Currey, op. cit.; Don A. Moore et al., 'Time Pressure, Performance, and Productivity', in Volume 15, *Looking Back, Moving Forward: A Review of Group and Team-Based Research* (Bingley: Emerald Group Publishing Limited, 2012); Gleick, op. cit.; Olivia Sharpe, 'Tom Aikens: In Good Taste', *Notting Hill & Holland Park* magazine, November 2016; Duhigg (2016), op. cit.; Syed, op. cit.; Chrisoula Andreou, 'Coping with Procrastination', in Andreou, op. cit.; Jessica

Salter, 'Professor Iain Hutchison: "Stitching Up People's Faces in Casualty Excited Me"', *Daily Telegraph*, 8 May 2015; Oliver Burkeman, 'Goals to Achieve? Will Telling Others Help?' *Guardian*, 27 June 2009.

MOMENTUM: https://reelrundown.com/film-industry/ The-History-Of-Home-Movie-Entertainment; https://en. wikipedia.org/wiki/VX_(videocassette_format); http:// www.city-data.com/forum/history/1595490-history-home-video-technologies.html; http://copyright.laws.com/time-shifting; Jack Schofield, 'Why VHS Was Better than Betamax', *Guardian*, 25 January 2017; Hitesh Bhasin, 'Sony Betamax Brand Failure', www.marketing91.com, 17 January 2010; Greg Satell, 'A Look Back at Why Blockbuster Really Failed and Why It Didn't Have To', forbes.com, 5 September 2014; Patrick J. Kenney et al., 'The Psychology of Political Momentum', *Political Research Quarterly*, 47 (1994); P.G. Weyand et al., 'Faster Top Running Speeds Are Achieved with Greater Ground Forces Not More Rapid Leg Movements', *Journal of Applied Physiology*, 89 (2000).

11 The Life Edit: Sigmund Freud, *Civilization and its Discontents* (New York: W. W. Norton, 2010); Ray Pillai, interview with author; Kahneman, op. cit.; Bianca Bosker, 'Facebook Now Takes Up About As Much of Our Time as Grooming or Chores', *Huffington Post*, 23 July 2014; Duhigg (2012), op. cit.; Ariely, op. cit.; Gustave Flaubert, letter to Gertrude Tennant, 25 December 1876; Duckworth, op. cit.; Katy Diamond Hamer, 'Assistant for 30 Years: Life with Louise Bourgeois', vulture.com, 18 December 2014; Currey, op. cit.

1,000 MONTHS: William Shakespeare, 'Sonnet 77'; Currey, op. cit.; Zimbardo, op. cit.; '"You've Got to Find What You Love," Jobs Says', news.stanford.edu, 12 June 2005; Fiachra Gibbons, 'First View of Freud's Portrait of Hockney', *Guardian*, 16 January 2003; J. Christopher Herold, *The Mind of Napoleon* (New York: Columbia University Press, 1955); David Nelson, 'Haydn, Symphony No. 45, "Farewell"', inmozartsfootsteps.com, 27 October 2010; Currey, op. cit.; Patricia Highsmith, *Plotting and Writing Suspense Fiction* (New York: St Martin's Press, 2001); http://www.brookeweston.org/News/NewsItem.aspx?id=281.

Index

On Time

Index

Dolan, Paul, *Happiness by Design* 41
Dole, Bob 266
downtime 280–1
dreams 159–60
Duckworth, Angela 251–2
Duhigg, Charles 273; *The Power of Habit* 270
Dunbar, John 242
Durkheim, Émile 53
Dyke, Captain David Hart 83–4, 112
dyschronometria 77–9
Dyson, James 254

Eastwood, Clint 253–4
Economist 235
Edison, Thomas 44–5, 167, 254
ego-depletion 120
Egypt 52
Ehrenreich, Barbara, *Dancing in the Streets* 123
Einstein, Albert 55, 81
Eliot, T.S. 288
Elizabeth I 54, 56, 69, 136, 225
Elizabeth II 243
Ellenberg, Jordan 185; *How Not to be Wrong* 186
email 216–19; abolish cc and bcc 220; be concise to focus attention 219; chunk it 220; consider alternatives 219; declutter 220; demand less 219; go on a text fast 220; never reply instantly 219; respond at a time that suits you 220; scan 220
Enlightenment 24, 51
entrainment 89–90
Ephron, Nora 188, 191; *Heartburn* 188; *When Harry Met Sally* 188
Epicurus 28
Erdős, Paul 97
Erhardt, Moritz 104
Esterházy, Nikolaus 286
European Social Survey (2011) 28–9
European Union (EU) 164, 238
Evanston University, Illinois 156
event expectancy 190
event time 62–4
Exxon Valdez 166

Facebook 32, 34, 67, 117
Falklands 83
faraway blur 249
fast pace 180–4
fatalism, fatalist 69, 134
Faulkner, William 149
festina lente (hurry slowly) 130, 184

Fitzgerald, F. Scott, *The Great Gatsby* 73
Flaubert, Gustave 275
flexitime 15, 105, 245
Focus clothing collection 222
Ford Motor Company 40
Foresight Project on Mental Capital and Wellbeing 189, 195
France 25
Franklin, Benjamin 284
Franzen, Jonathan, *The Corrections* 207
Frazer, Captain 148
Freud, Lucian 285
Freud, Sigmund 268
Fuller, Richard Buckminster 164

Gates, Bill 41
Gates, Melinda 41
generational time 80; biological clock 87; look after your brain 88; memories 88; and old age 87–8; relativity 87; resist glide into autopilot 88
Germany 155, 244–5
The Gin Tub, Hove (Sussex) 221
Gladwell, Malcolm, *Outliers* 230
Gleick, James, *Faster* 30
Goethe, J.W. von, *Faust* 287
Goldfarb, Michael 234–5
Goldman Sachs 104
Goldsmith, James 270
Google 38, 40
Grand Theft Auto 80
Grass, Günter 73
Grosz, Stephen 84
Gunnell, Sally 290

habits 248–9, 268–9; believe in change 274; form/reform 270–3; quit/rewrite 273–4; smuggle in new routine 274; understand it 273
Hall, Jerry 161
Hallowell, Edward 115, 242
Halpern, David 30
Hammersley, Ben 206
hangover effect 197–8
happiness: appearance of 39; boosting 189–90; engagement as hallmark of 190–1; pursuit of 49; short-term 27–8; and time 29
Harald Hardrada 233
Hardy, Thomas, *Tess of the D'Urbevilles* 55
Harrison, John 54–5
Harvard University 190
Haydn, Joseph 286

319

Index

Index